SHEPHERD OF MANKIND

SHEPHERD OF MANKIND

A Biography of
Pope Paul VI

WILLIAM E. BARRETT

Garden City, New York

DOUBLEDAY & COMPANY, INC.

1964

Nihil obstat: Very Rev. John J. Danagher, C.M., J.C.D.
Imprimatur: ✠ Urban J. Vehr, D.D., Archbishop of Denver
                Denver, Colorado, November 22, 1963

Acknowledgment

The biography of a pope cannot be written until his reign is completed, his last earthly commitment made; years must pass before a definitive biography may even be attempted. This volume follows the career of a living man from childhood to the papal throne and locates him in relation to historical events, many of them precedent to his birth. The facts on which I have had to rely were obtained from a great many interviews in Rome, Milan, Brescia, and Concesio; from Italian periodicals and books, including three by Giovanni Battista Montini; from material generously supplied by journalists and by individuals close to the people and to the events described. I have incurred many debts.

I wish to express my gratitude to John J. Delaney who suggested that I fly to Rome and write this story; to His Excellency, the Most Reverend Urban J. Vehr, Archbishop of Denver and the Most Reverend David M. Maloney, Auxiliary Bishop of Denver, who generously paved my way with letters of introduction; to Very Reverend Terence J. O'Driscoll, Procurator General, Collegio San Columbano, Rome, in whose house I lived and to Reverend Donal O'Mahony who introduced me to him; to His Excellency, the Most Reverend Martin J. O'Connor of the North American College on the hill and to Right Reverend Monsignori John J. Fleming and Joseph L. Zryd of Humility

Street to whom my debt is particularly deep and to whom I owe my wonderful point of vantage at the Mass of the Holy Ghost and the Coronation; to Dr. Luciano Casimiri, Chief of the Vatican Press Office, for wise and generous counsel and for calling so many people on the phone; to His Excellency Raimondo Manzini, Director of Osservatore Romano who spared time for me when there were many other demands; to Reverend Charles Burns of the Vatican Archives; to Reverend Ralph M. Wiltgen, S.V.D., expert on the Council; to Reverend Joseph W. Higgins, M.S., authority on St. Peter's and a tireless guide to Rome offstage; to Frank Hall, Director-emeritus of N.C.W.C. News Service in Washington, D.C., who wrote letters and shared anecdotes, and to Monsignor James I. Tucek and James C. O'Neill of the Rome staff who opened many channels of information to me, to Floyd C. Anderson, Director of N.C.W.C. News Service upon whose knowledge and good nature I have drawn many times; to Robert B. Kaiser, Vatican correspondent of *Time* who shared generously his wide knowledge of history and affairs; to Padre Giuseppe Persico, S.J., for a most valuable interview and for his blessing; to Padre Giovanni Dossi, S.J.; to Palumbo Carmelo.

It is not possible to measure the aid given to me by my Italian publishers, Pietro and Lia Berretta, Edizioni Librarie Italiane of Milan. I owe much, too, in that city to Padre Silvio Springhetti, S.J.; to Don Ottorino Marcolini; to Dr. Franco Sirletti, a most companionable interpreter and guide; to Erich Linder, whose command of information nearly equals his command of languages; to my fellow novelist, Dino Campini, and to Nilde Cavo Marabotti; to Monsignor Carlo Marcora, Dottore Dell'Ambrosiano di Milano; to the erudite Piero Gnecchi Ruscone; to Monsignor Giuseppe Cavalleri of Collegio Cesare Arici in Brescia for access to the Montini school records and for anecdotes; to Don Carlo Montini for a interesting visit and many facts; to Don Giuseppe Tomasini, pastor of the church of San Antonino in Concesio where Giovanni Battista

Montini was baptized; with his name, incidentally, spelled "Giovan" in the baptismal record.

Listing all of the friends, relatives, acquaintances, and associates interviewed is an impossible task, but I wish to express my thanks to those whom I have mentioned in the book or upon whose memories I have drawn: Don Giulio Bevilacqua, Count Aristide di Viarigi, Ezechiele Malizia, Teresa Alghisi, Anna Mariannini, Dr. Ugo Piazza, Ernesto Pasini, Luigi Bolognini, Dr. Appollonio Zerba, Primo Savoldi, and Don Luigi Benassi.

A special note of thanks is due to Dr. Ciro Scotti of Providence, Rhode Island, who was one of the famous FUCI warriors of Don Battista; to Mark Gnerro, of Alexandria, Virginia, who was my authority in Italian, the translator of innumerable documents including the *discorsi* of Archbishop Montini; to Mrs. Charles Day who typed all of these words, some of them many times; to my son, Bill, whose pen name is Edmund Barrett, for skillful and immeasureably valuable aid in the research and the writing.

It would be ungrateful not to mention the libraries of the Catholic University, Georgetown University, and the Pan American Union in Washington, D.C., and the Italian periodicals upon which I drew: the magazines, *L'Europeo, Incom, Missioni, Oggi,* and *Orizonti;* the newspapers, *L'Italia, Il Messagero, Paese Sera, Il Tempo,* and the indispensable *L'Osservatore Romano.* An extra note of thanks to the staffs of *La Voce di Popolo* and *Giornale di Brescia* who produced material from their files for me.

These debts are mine, and many more, particularly to those who, for good reasons of their own, requested anonymity. Responsibility for the book is also mine; the facts, the interpretation, the delineation of character. Time may reveal deeper facts beneath the facts which I found, or errors in my point of view, or mistakes in the accounts of events which I accepted as they were related to me. These are the hazards of writing about a living man against a contemporary background. I liked the

7

man I found. There is little possibility that Time will change that.

WILLIAM E. BARRETT

Washington, D.C.
November 4, 1963

Contents

9

CONTENTS

Illustrations

Prologue

CRIMSON light flooded St. Peter's Square, painting the colonnades of Bernini. The entire sky was bright. Beneath the window of the pope's apartment an altar had been erected and an outdoor Mass was being celebrated. The worshipers knelt in prayer, following the Mass but lifting anxious eyes to the window. The awareness of what was happening in that room muffled the voices which responded to the prayer of the priest.

In the Vatican press office, to the right of St. Anne's Gate, an announcement was flashed. It was 7:50 P.M. on Monday, June 3, 1963. Three minutes later the message reached Piazza San Pietro. The Mass had ended when the voice of Vatican Radio spoke:

"With a soul profoundly moved, we give this following sad announcement: The Supreme Pontiff, John XXIII, is dead."

The bells of St. Peter's started to toll and within minutes the yellow and white Vatican flags were unfurled at half-mast. The flags of Italy on all of the government buildings of Rome joined the flags of Vatican City in the salute of mourning.

A papal reign was ended, a reign that had lasted for four years, seven months, and six days. The ending climaxed an extraordinary week in the history of Rome, a week that had witnessed an unprecedented number of men and women in a death watch for a pope, people of all degrees, wealthy and poor, Catholic and non-Catholic, priests, nuns, children. They had endured the heavy rains of Sunday and for four days in the space before St. Peter's, within sight of the pope's bedroom, they had waited, settling into night-long vigils; not because they had any hope of drama, excitement, or spiritual reward, a procession or a blessing from a balcony, but because they could do nothing else for a man whom they had learned to love.

In a sense, they were seated at his bedside, all of these people, and they waited the night through, the several nights, while other people on other continents who had never seen him personally, people of his faith and not of it, waited beside radios or television sets, bought late editions of the newspapers as they appeared on the streets, and discussed the dying man with friends as they would discuss one of their own circle.

Now it was over. Pope John XXIII was dead. He had returned the authority by which he had ruled 560 million Catholics to the source from which he had obtained it; a pope having no succession of blood, of intellectual choice, of affection.

The world, Catholic and non-Catholic, waited on the choosing of a successor, in hope that John XXIII would outlive the years allotted to him through the expansion of his policies, in fear that a successor might turn men back from the steps which they had taken toward one another. The press, not unreasonably, discussed the papabili, the most likely candidates, in the political terms of left and right, liberal and conservative, but the classifications were only an attempt to translate for the public mind the untranslatable. Political terms lose their meanings when brought in contact with the supernatural. While the press speculated, the cardinals on whom the choice of a pope rested, were engaged in a novena of Masses called the Novendiali.

The Novendiali for Pope John XXIII ended with the Solemn Mass of June 17, 1963, the last of the period of mourning, the actual boundary line probably between two pontificates. The Mass was a State occasion calling for the attendance of the diplomatic corps, representatives of the arts, sciences, and professions, sons and daughters of noble Italian families.

A catafalque draped in the crimson of papal mourning rested between the Altar of the Confessione and the Altar of the Chair. The body of Pope John XXIII lay in the crypt beneath St. Peter's, near to the tomb of Pius XII, facing the tomb of Pius XI, but his earthly remains were symbolically in the coffin between the two altars. The cardinals, each preceded by an attendant, filed slowly in, past the Altar of the Confessione at which only a pope may say Mass. The Bernini baldachin above the altar was as marvelous to behold this morning as on that other June day in 1633 when Pope Urban VIII first unveiled it. The four supporting columns were of bronze from the pagan pantheon, twisted into solid smoke which curled upward forever from the place of sacrifice to the light-filled dome of the basilica 394 feet above. A few yards beyond, a bronze St. Peter sat on his marble throne, older than the ghost of Bernini or any of Bernini's works by at least ten centuries. The cardinals walked solemnly past him, past the tribune of St. Longinus where a temporary stand had been erected for invited guests. Those without invitations had crowded in where they could. Two nuns were standing on the base of the statue of St. Elena.

The cardinals took their seats in two facing lines on either side of the catafalque. The Mass was celebrated by tall, bearded Eugene Cardinal Tisserant at the Altar of the Chair beneath the gilt throne which four gigantic Fathers of the Church supported. Somewhere in those two violet-clad lines, or at the altar assisting the Dean of the Sacred College of Cardinals, was the future pope; or, if one encouraged the thought inevitable in this atmosphere, the pope in actuality, his identity hidden in the hearts and minds of his fellow cardinals, each of whom held secret his own small share of that identity. These were the Princes of the Church, made noble in their own time through achievement; out of no dynasty and establishing none, diverse in origin and attainment, but united in prayer. Their prayers

17

rose for the man they had known as Angelo Cardinal Roncalli and as Pope John XXIII, the third of a poor farmer's thirteen children, who had commanded the tears of a world in his dying.

The choir, standing with the papal altar behind it, added imploring voices to that of the priest: "Out of the depths have I cried to Thee, O Lord. Lord, hear my prayer!" This man had been Vicar of Jesus Christ on Earth and Bishop of Rome, the Supreme Pontiff of the Universal Church, proclaimed a saint by countless mourners who kept a vigil for him; but the Church approves presumption no more than it approves despair. The Church prayed for a sinner.

This had been, in his simplicity and complexity, a great pope, a pope who had sought for the commonality of men rather than stand on the ground which divides them. The papacy had demanded of him only the years when most men rest but, with the years that were left to him after his seventy-seventh birthday, he had "opened a window and let fresh air into the Church." The virtue of fresh air had to be balanced, of course, against the evil of drafts. It would be the task of the next pope to establish that balance.

Hush descended upon St. Peter's Basilica at the moment of consecration when bread and wine became the Body and Blood of Christ, the moment which makes the greatest demand upon faith, which creates in churches great or small this interval of almost unbearable silence, quiet in which minds with a single focus of worship create thought forms more elaborate than sound patterns, more eloquent than color and light; a quiet into which Jesus Christ came as He had come into a locked room in Jerusalem long ago.

This was the mystical. This was the Mass; the perfect expression of the sorrow of the Church as it was the perfect expression of its joy. The celebrant moved back and forth at the altar, so many steps this way, so many steps that. He wore vestments which were a combination of many garments. He intoned words, Latin words. He extended his hands in an invitation to pray and again in blessing. It was at once elaborate and incomprehensible, simple and reducible to the understanding of a child. The steps were symbolical steps, representing the many steps which Christians took in memory of the Master when they walked where He had walked until the persecutors made the walking too hazardous. The garments were the many garments in which the life of the Saviour was re-enacted commemoratively during the months and years after His death; symbolically, the garments of judge and soldier, shepherd and rabbi. The Latin was one language rather than many as proof against the errors of translation, the words of the witnesses to the events out of which Christianity emerged. Men who could no longer enter Jerusalem as an act of faith, and leave it again to climb the hill of crucifixion, were making that solemn journey every day in churches wherever they might be, re-enacting the drama of redemption, offering the sacrifice of the cross. Seventy-six cardinals in purple garments, the liturgical color of mourning, participated today, as did thousands of laymen crowding St. Peter's, in this Mass for the soul of John XXIII.

At the end of it, the solemn words spoken in Latin by a cardinal praying before the catafalque were the words that the humblest Catholic knows and has spoken: "May his soul and the souls of all the faithful departed rest in peace." Nothing more profound than that.

On the gospel side of the Piazza outside, in the shadow of the Truscan colonnades, people were waiting patiently in a long queue for their turns at the window of the Vatican post office. This period between the death of one pope and the election of the next was, among many other things, a philatelic interval. The interregnum was marked by a special issue of stamps inscribed "Sede Vacante."

Invisible to the people in the square, beyond the atmosphere and the gravitational pull of earth, a man and a woman circled like moths. The man, Valery Bykovsky, had been blasted into orbit on the fourteenth of June, and the woman, Valentina Chereshkova, had joined him on the first Sunday after Trinity, June 16. He and his astronaut companion knew as little about

19

Trinity Sunday and the Novendiali as they knew about Masses for the dead, but they knew the meaning of orbital velocity, of perihelion and ophelion, of perigee and apogee. As other men and women did, who served supernatural concepts, these two people were risking their lives and dedicating their careers to their own concept of Reality. On the nineteenth, when they re-entered the atmosphere of earth and made their landings safely, there was another Mass in St. Peter's.

This was a joyous Mass, the Mass of the Holy Ghost. The cardinals sat once more between the papal altar and the Altar of the Chair but they had laid aside the somber hues of mourning and had donned their ceremonial scarlet. Women of the Italian nobility and guests wore the traditional black dresses decreed by Vatican custom but the men of the various semi-military orders were attired in crimson and black, gold and dark wine, with white ruffs and short breeches. The window of the dove above the high altar was bright with the sunlight behind it. The voice of the celebrant rose in entreaty to the Holy Spirit that the cardinals who would vote shortly for a pope would be guided surely in their choice, that they would name the man who would best serve the Church and the world.

The great imponderable lay in this, the immeasurable force and influence in the election of a pope; the fact that these men who would vote were priests, that they prayed at this Mass and at the altars of their own private Masses for aid and inspiration as they approached their great task of decision. They were men, too, certainly, with human weaknesses, prejudices, political leanings, ideas of their own about the world and the Church and their fellow men, cardinals whose responsibilities of rank called for executive ability mixed with at least a reasonable amount of guile. Each man of them would be drawn to a candidate for the papal crown whose ideas most nearly matched his own, each man would have relevancies and irrelevancies in his mind which would color or influence his judgment; but they were men who believed in the mystery of One God and Three Divine Persons, who had lived long lives in that belief and who, remembering Pentecost, believed in the guidance and influence of the Holy Spirit in the Church. When that guidance became manifest, when a new pope emerged from their deliberations, there would be no party of opposition, loyal or otherwise; there would be only the pledge of fealty.

That evening the cardinals followed the papal crucifix into the Sistine Chapel while the choir sang "Veni, Creator Spiritus." The door was sealed behind them and they were cut off from communication with the people of earth more completely than was an astronaut in space. They could neither be seen nor heard.

Men and women of all faiths, and of none, watched then a slender pipe on the roof of the Sistine Chapel for the smoke signal which would announce the election of a new pope. They watched in their massed thousands from Piazza San Pietro and in countless numbers before television sets. They watched with their ears through standard radios and transistor sets.

The smoke of Thursday, June 20, was black at noon and black again in the evening. Black was the color of inconclusiveness, of voting without verdict. The crowds streaming away from the piazza were noisy with discussion. It would be difficult to select a pope because the Curia feared reform, they said, and because there was strong feeling between those who favored a continuation of Pope John's Council and those who did not. Never before had there been so many cardinals voting nor cardinals who knew one another so well; all of which increased the chances of discord. Heads wagged and hands gestured and every man was an expert while the smoke was black.

The conviction built overnight, spreading more or less silently through the city of Rome that there would be no decision for several days, that the deliberation would be long. The Piazza San Pietro crowd of midday on Friday, June 21, was less than either crowd of the day before. The heat was murderous and people clung to any patch of shadow. Priests and laymen wore handkerchiefs over their heads and over the backs of their necks, Arab fashion. Many of them fashioned hats of newspapers, as did women, even the nuns whose heads were already covered.

Some male tourists wore the hats of their women without self-consciousness and the women wrapped scarves or handkerchiefs around their heads. Soda-pop salesmen could not keep up with the demand.

At 11:19, before anyone expected it, there was a puff of smoke from the pipe, two puffs. They appeared to be black and the alerted crowd groaned. The groans turned to cheers as the smoke turned white, definitely white. The smoke plume waved and dipped.

The descent upon the piazza before St. Peter's was like the coming of a high wind or the invasion of locusts on the land. The multitudes left their television sets and radios, swarming to the heart of action, of significance, of event. The traffic of a great city came to a halt, hopelessly blocked, locked, and snarled. Drivers, having gone as far as they could, abandoned their vehicles and raced to the center of Christendom.

There were 100,000 people in the square some estimates said, and others said 300,000. There was no room to move in the piazza itself or the length of Via della Conciliazione. At 11:59 the Nobile Guards marched out of St. Peter's. At 12:12 Alfredo Cardinal Ottaviani, senior Cardinal Deacon of the Sacred College, appeared on the balcony and in a hoarse, unsteady voice, proclaimed:

"*Annuntio vobis gaudium magnum; habemus papam.*" ("I announce to you tidings of great joy; we have a pope.")

His voice came under control and he pronounced the name: "His Eminence, the Most Reverend Lord Cardinal Giovanni Battista . . ."

The assembled people finished the announcement with a mass shout: "Montini!"

There was a tall crucifix coming onto the balcony behind Cardinal Ottaviani and the cardinals were occupying the side balconies. The pope, garbed in scarlet and white, appeared in the center to raise his hand in blessing: *urbi et orbi* . . . to the city and to the world.

Another reign was in its beginning. The 262nd Pope had an

identity and a name. Men could inquire about him and seek in his origins and in his career for an augury of the future. He was Paul VI and he had been Giovanni Battista Montini, a small boy once in the town of Concesio on the outskirts of Brescia in the Valley of the Po, in northern Italy.

The boy did not walk onto a bare stage. The scenery was in place and a drama in progress. The drama had been written by other men and he had to find his place in it. It was the story of the papacy and of the birth of Italy. Italy had not found a bare stage either, when it came newborn into the family of nations. Italy is only twenty-seven years older than Paul VI. They must be considered together and the story of the elder comes first.

BOOK I

The Throne and the Altar

1

THE PAST IS ALWAYS PRELUDE

THE papal throne is the oldest continuously occupied throne on earth, the most ancient authority. The papal government, seemingly rigid, shaped to an elaborate framework of tradition, is so only on the surface; in its depths it is realistically fluid. Realism, in papal terms, consists of the recognition that all other governments, being man-conceived, man-inspired, and man-made, must fall and be supplanted by variants of themselves. It follows that papal diplomacy is the art of avoiding engulfment in the fall of nations.

Sometimes, however, even papal definitions become obscure and papal diplomacy, being only a stepchild of the Holy Ghost, is susceptible to error. A modern pope is heir to the glory of reigns preceding his, to accumulated beauty, wisdom, and grace, to the definition of terms and the clarification of doctrines: he is also heir to mistakes and their consequences. He must be studied in himself, in what he has been and in what he is, and he must be considered in terms of his inheritance. Italian history provides the background of the Vatican State in which the papacy lives and works in our time. That history, for a nation established on such ancient soil, is amazingly short.

Modern Italy was born of revolution during the middle decades of the nineteenth century, which was a century of revolt, of rising, of struggle. Italy, fighting what was probably the most

gallant and colorful of all the mid-century wars, met world disapproval and coldness in its quest for internal unity and for
identity as a nation. Italy wrote history under a dark cloud
which dulled the bright colors of its heroism. The revolution
was called the Risorgimento.

The Italian people, in the decade of the 1840s had wearied
of the arrogant carving of Italian territory by Austria and
France. In their revolt, they had the leadership of a veteran
revolutionist, a fiery agitator, Giuseppe Mazzini; and of a pic-
turesque soldier of fortune, a daring field commander, Giuseppe
Garibaldi. They had a monarchial symbol of Union in the person of Prince Charles Albert of Sardinia. They had little money
for arms and few resources to support an army in the field, but
they had men willing to fight. Their weakness was Charles Albert. They needed a more vital symbol, one around whom the
people of the many states would rally with faith and devotion.
Prince Klemens Wenzel von Metternich, the Austrian Chancelor, watched their efforts with cynical amusement.

"Italy," he said, "is only a geographical expression."

In 1846, Pope Gregory XVI died. He had been a stern, withdrawn man, a friend of Prince Metternich. The people of the
many small states were incredulous, then widely enthused, when
the news spread that the cardinals in conclave had elected as his
successor the Cardinal Bishop of Imola, Giovanni Maria Mastai
Ferretti, who would reign as Pius IX. Mastai Ferretti was a
liberal. At Spoleto and at Imola, he had been known for his
piety, his generosity, his concern for the poor, and his sympathy
with the aspirations of those who talked of representative government, freedom of the press, of speech, and of assembly.

The hard-bitten realists who were leading the revolution, anticlerical by habit, training, and instinct, responded as the people
did to the hope which the new pope inspired. Giuseppe Mazzini
wrote to him, offering him the leading role in the creation of a
united Italy. He was not a Catholic and he did not think in
Catholic terms, but he incorporated in his letter a statement no

less sincere because it was conciliatory: "The spirit of God descends upon many gathered together in His name."

Austrians and friends of Austria in Rome were alarmed at the enthusiasm for the new pope and one of them visited Metternich in Vienna. "You should have prevented the election of this man," he said bluntly. "You could have vetoed him in the Council. A liberal in the Vatican is a danger to us."

Metternich walked across the room to a wall map. He ran the tip of his forefinger around the Papal States which stretched from one coast to another, cutting the projected Italy in two. Within the line he traced were seacoast towns and cities on the Adriatic and the Tyrrhenian Seas, important cities such as Perugia, Spoleto, Frascati, and Tivoli, mountain country beloved of the nobles, jeweled with bright lakes and adorned with castles, palaces, and magnificent villas.

"A liberal pope is an impossibility," he said.

Pius IX walked, however, in the glow of public approval. An epileptic in his youth, he had never been strong nor forceful but he possessed charm and a fine voice, which was one of his vanities. He was an amiable, friendly man. He met individuals well and he met crowds well. As one of the first acts of his reign, he granted an amnesty to all political prisoners in the prisons of the Papal States and to all in exile from it, more than fifteen hundred people in total. There were torchlight processions to the Quirinal Palace, in honor of Pius IX and in approval of the amnesty. He liked the applause, the tokens of public affection, the approval, the excitement of surging crowds, the fond way in which "Pio Nono" was intoned.

Pius IX was going to build railroads in the papal territory, a project which his predecessor had refused to consider. He was going to have gas street lights installed in Rome. He was going to have a scientific congress under his personal sponsorship. Under a law which he had had enacted on March 15, 1847, he established a free press, but also a board of censors. He announced a liberalization of the Papal States by appointing an advisory board of laymen who would meet with Giacomo Cardinal Antonelli and discuss problems. It was all quite sincere, liberal almost to the point of daring by his standards, and quite inadequate to the demands of the time. He was, of necessity, taking first steps in a day that called for striding.

By March 13, 1848, the spirit of revolution had caught up with Metternich and he was forced to flee from Vienna into exile. Louis Philippe was also in flight from France and in five days of fierce fighting the people of Milan (March 18–23) drove the Austrians from their city. Charles Albert declared war on Austria and his troops marched.

It was logical that the war for complete severance from Austria should start in the north where Milan was the principal city. Austria had invaded, raided, occupied, and tyrannized the cities and states of the north for generations, taking advantage of their political separation from one another. In union the Italians were prepared to strike back and the other Italian states, physically removed from the frontier but affected by anything which happened there, sent troops as a token of solidarity. Pius IX permitted his general, Giovanni Durando, to lead the papal army out of Rome for the north but he stated later that he consented to their use only in defensive action.

As in every war in history, the definition of defensive action and the definition of aggressor depended in 1848 upon the mind, sentiments, and attachments of the definer. General Durando committed the troops he commanded to the Italian cause. Austria protested the use of papal troops in the north and Pius IX issued his famous allocution of April 29, 1848, in which he not only disavowed either leadership or participation in the war against Austria but all sympathy with the cause of union and of national liberation.

The people who had cheered the pope and staged his torch-light processions did not understand. Troops from all the Italian provinces, including the Papal States, were engaged in battle and it seemed that the Holy Father was casting them out of his heart, withholding his blessing from them. To Pius—all other considerations aside—his position was clear and logical and beyond any need for discussion. He could not, as ruler over the Papal States, make war against the Austrians who were his children and who were, to him as Pontiff of the Universal Church, a charge and a responsibility.

On that issue, his Prime Minister, Count Mamiani, resigned. It was obvious, he declared, that supreme spiritual and temporal powers could no longer be combined in one man. They were not reconcilable into any consistent policy. Pius, who possessed those powers, had to try to reconcile them.

Count Pellegrino Rossi became papal Prime Minister. A professed free-thinker, Rossi was a promoter of sorts, a speculator and a political opportunist who had adventured behind many scenes in Switzerland and France. His first act was an unpopular one, the placing of a French commander over the papal troops. He addressed himself then to the task of overhauling the Vatican financial structure and entered into correspondence with the Rothschilds.

The army of Charles Albert met the Austrians at Custozza, near Brescia, on July 25 and suffered a shocking defeat. There were bittter echoes in Rome where the people gathered outside the Quirinal Palace shouting abuse at their erstwhile idol.

As Metternich had stated confidently, a liberal pope was an impossibility; impossible in revolutionary terms. Pius IX faced that now. Revolution in Italy, as elsewhere, meant the passing of a gracious and a charming way of life. It was a way of life that provided grace and charm, beauty and ease, for a few, of course, and far too little of anything for the many.

Pius, in the nature of things, had to identify with tradition, with the Princes of the Papal States and their ladies, with the owners of the palaces and the villas, the adorners of churches, the civilized men and women who had been the patrons and the patronesses of painters and sculptors, composers and writers, the sponsors and the preservers of their work, the custodians, if not the creators, of so much that was beautiful, so much that was appreciated and valued and linked to the native genius by visitors from abroad. Some of the revolutionary packs had looted and defaced and vandalized villas and churches in their path and their conduct made the entire movement suspect to Pius IX, and indicted the leaders who permitted it to happen.

On November 15, 1848, Count Pellegrino Rossi was assassinated. The Pope linked Rossi's death to the violent demonstrations outside the Quirinal and he feared for his own life. He and his newly appointed successor to Rossi, Giacomo Cardinal Antonelli, fled in disguise to Gaeta where Pius IX accepted the protection of the King of Naples and quarters in the royal palace. He left a triumvirate of cardinals in Rome, charged with responsibility for Vatican affairs.

The Italian government in the field, when its leaders had recovered from their surprise and dismay at the news from Rome, sent a deputation to the pope-in-exile requesting his return to Rome and promising him protection. Pius IX refused to receive them. The government acted then to set up a Junta and a Constitutional Assembly was called for December 29.

Pius IX made a fateful decision, one that was to breed consequences for generations. He condemned the assembly in advance, issued an absolute prohibition against the participation of Catholics, and threatened with excommunication those who did not obey him.

With that letter, Pius IX drew for the first time a line which Catholics in Italy could not cross, a line that would divide generations unborn. Public affairs were, in the most solemn terms, defined as not the concern of a Catholic, as closed to him by edict. Pius drew his line and wrote his prohibition in the palace of a king whose kingdom had only a short existence left to it. He opened his epistle with the phrase: "Within this peaceful retreat whither it has pleased Divine Providence to lead us . . ."

Catholics were bewildered and the revolutionary leaders proceeded with their plans. As Pius had made inevitable, the Constitutional Assembly, with no Catholics participating in its deliberations, was hostile to the Church. It voted the end of the temporal power of the pope and the establishment of a "pure democracy" to be called the Republic of Rome.

Pius IX immediately started a letter-writing campaign to every government in Europe, even to England, asking for armed aid. The only one who saw advantage to himself in involvement was Napoleon III. His troops, in July 1849, moved on Rome, defeated the Italian army and established a provisional government. There was harsh work to be done in bringing the Papal States under subjection and Pius did not return to Rome until that work was completed. He rode into Rome triumphantly in April 1850, escorted by French troops.

The pope and the Italian government, which was struggling to come into being, were hopelessly estranged now and many Catholics had to make the hard choice between the struggle which enlisted their sympathies and the pope who commanded a French enclave in the heart of Italy. Prince Charles Albert sustained another defeat at Novara in the north and abdicated in favor of his son, Victor Emmanuel.

Victor Emmanuel and his wife were devout Catholics. The new Prince tried to establish relations with the pope and failed; but all other forces in Italy were rallying to him. Giuseppe Garibaldi, after his conquest of Naples was a powerful dictator with rich lands that he had taken in battle and with men who flocked to his standards. A republican, as anti-Monarchist as he was anti-Catholic, Garibaldi tossed his army and his lands and the Kingdom of Naples into the hands of Victor Emmanuel with an offhand phrase: *"Si Faccia l'Italie!"* ("Let Italy come into being!") He retired then, without recompense, and went to live on an island.

Pius IX did not know the best men of the revolution. He was alienated by the scoundrels, the looters, the iconoclasts, the savages who are a part of every revolution, used by the revolution and eventually eliminated. In the Prince who constitutionally became King, Pius had a Catholic voice and influence in the camp of his enemies and he excommunicated that King.

Italy came into being without Pius IX. Prussia defeated lordly

33

Austria in seven weeks, then crushed Napoleon III and the French. The French troops were withdrawn from the Papal States and Pius IX was confronted with his own countrymen. Victor Emmanuel made one last appeal for a meeting to establish some basis for agreement with the Pope, offering his own spiritual submission, but Pius IX, denying that the government of Italy had legal existence, refused to treat with it. The army of Victor Emmanuel, victorious over all its enemies on all of its borders, entered Rome on September 20, 1870.

"The Roman Question" was created with the events of September 20. Pius IX, self-imprisoned, described himself as the "Prisoner of the Vatican." It was a telling phrase and not entirely inaccurate. Pius could not, consistently, surrender one foot of papal land or consent to its transfer. He considered the Papal States the property of the See of Peter beyond his power of disposal. By refusing to step on papal land which had been taken by force, he was serving dramatic notice of the fact that he had granted no consent, tacit or otherwise, to the usurpation.

The "Prisoner of the Vatican" phrase was destined to live long. Only dimly comprehended, it prejudiced the people of the world against the Italian government and Italians, cast in the role of cruel and unjust jailors; a prejudice which was to outlive the issue and to dim the bright colors of Italian heroism in the fight for independence.

King Victor Emmanuel occupied the Quirinal as a royal palace and his government drew up the Law of Guarantees which recognized the Pope as a sovereign, his person sacred and inviolable, his diplomatic relations with other countries protected. He was granted his personal guard, his own postal and telegraph services and exclusive use of the Vatican, St. John Lateran, and Castel Gandolfo. The government of Italy was to provide him with 3,225,000 lire annually.

Pope and King lived many years within the City of Rome without contact, diplomatic or otherwise. In 1878, they died, a few weeks apart, a few miles apart.

Victor Emmanuel was called the "father of his country" and

legends grew around him but he had never been brilliant either as a military leader or as a statesman. He had many frivolous tastes and much instability of character, but he chose good ministers and advisers and he did not assert his will in fields where his knowledge was weak. He was sincerely disturbed over the rift with the pope which he tried many times to mend and he received the last rites of the Roman Catholic Church before he died.

Pope Pius IX had had the longest reign since Peter, thirty-two years, and in many respects it had been a notable reign. He had declared the doctrine of the Immaculate Conception, he had defined the infallibility of the pope and he had re-established the Roman Church in England. In the closing days of his life, the number of diplomatic representatives at his court had shrunk to four and he was no longer a wielder of influence in the secular world, but the tragedy of his reign, as he saw it, was his loss of the Papal States. In the perspective of time, the ending of temporal power and its corollary, temporal responsibility, was a blessing, a great blessing upon all future popes who were freed from the burdens of problems in two spheres forever irreconcilable.

The real tragedy of Pius IX is not that he lost land but that he lost people, so many sincere Catholics caught up in the swift social, economic, and political currents of those times and swept away from the Church. Those people of the Church, but outside of it, were his heritage to his successors, a problem in one form or another to every pope of the twentieth century and still unresolved.

The restating of the problem belongs in the story of Pope Paul VI because it surrounded the years of his growing.

2

THE MONTINIS

PANDOLFO NASSINO, historian of Brescia, wrote in the sixteenth century of the Montinis: "They are not an old house of Brescia but they are gallant and well-behaved men."

The earliest records indicate that the Montinis came down from the mountains to the Lombardian plains early in the fifteenth century. By arriving so late they missed many stirring events; by arriving as early as they did, they participated in many. Frederick Barbarossa was defeated there in 1238 after laying siege to the city, and Ezzelino sacked it in 1258. In the wars for, and against, Venice there were Montinis. They were Brescians when the Chevalier Bayard, knight *sans peur et sans reproche* was wounded during an attack on the town and nursed back to health by one of the Brescian families. All of which is comparatively modern history. Brescia and the other towns and cities of Lombardy are old.

There were Gauls in the Valley of the Po three centuries before Christ and Etruscans before the Gauls. Milan was Mediolanum in the Roman era and Brescia was Brixia. Hannibal and his troops and his elephants came over the Alps to the Valley and, many centuries later, Leo the Great met Attila on the shores of Lake Garda near Brescia and turned him back from Rome.

Today one drives fifty-eight miles over the Autostrada from

Milan (pop. 1,269,000) to Brescia (pop. 141,800). Caraveggio, the birthplace of Michelangelo, is off the highway at the twenty-five-mile mark and five miles farther is the exit for Bergamo, always an important city but remembered forever now because Pope John XXIII was born at Sotto il Monte, one of its suburbs. The next exit to Bergamo is Brescia. Verona is beyond that, then Venice, but Brescia is to Pope Paul VI as Bergamo was to John.

There was no Autostrada in 1897 when the future pope was born and there were no automobiles. The railroad trip from Milan (pop. 425,800) to Brescia (pop. 61,000), with a change of trains at Bergamo, consumed four hours. Travel in the area was by horse-drawn vehicles and could be quite pleasant as the following description of Edward Hutton's *The Cities of Lombardy* indicates:

"There is no more delightful and consoling road in all north Italy, south of the mountains, than that which leads at last from Bergamo to Brescia . . . for the way is by no means a monotony of flatness, but is broken by low hills and downs, and little passes and valleys about the feet of the mountains, and there, on the hilltops or beside the rivers, stands many a fair town worthy of remembrance, to say nothing of the castles, shrines and churches which are often worthy of Tuscany, and of Tuscany at its best."

Giorgio Montini, the father of the future pope, was born at Brescia, June 30, 1860. This was one year after the close of the decade of resistance, *"decennio della resistenza,"* a period of harsh Austrian occupation, during which Italians pledged themselves to have no unnecessary commerce with Austrians, not even speech. It had opened with the attack of the Austrian General, Baron Julius von Haynau, on Brescia. He had slaughtered the defenders, burned houses and public buildings and whipped the survivors as a measure of discipline. The men of the Italian revolution became heroes during this decade and Victor Emmanuel the symbol of freedom from oppression. Neighbors found themselves in disagreement, sometimes violent, over the conflict between Church and State.

Giorgio Montini was born into this conflict and he grew up in it. He was ten years old when the infallibility of the pope was declared and the *Non Expedit* that same year, a Papal Bull formalizing previously declared strictures upon Catholics, forbidding them to vote or to hold any office, elective or appointive, in the government of Italy. He had completed his Lyceum studies at Padua and was enrolled in the Law School of the University of Padua when Pius IX died on February 7, 1878. Some of the young men whom he knew were hopeful that a new pope might find a way of living in harmony with the government, permitting Catholics to vote and participate in politics, but Montini held no such hopes. He was of the new breed of radical, a Catholic who practiced his faith, and accepted the penalties exacted of a professed Catholic. The penalties were many.

Since Catholics did not vote, the parties were made up of free-thinkers, members of secret societies, atheists, a very few Jews, fewer Protestants. Law makers and law interpreters, legislators and judges, came from the party ranks. Among young law students it was considered the utmost in folly to retain religious ties, to be associated with religion and still hope to earn a living in the law. There was nowhere to go, no road to preferment for a Catholic in public life and so much of business and commerce was linked to the political world in one way or another. Young men whose families had retained the faith through the difficult revolutionary years, who had been raised in the faith, found the burden too great in their own adult years.

There existed in this peculiar, out-of-reality world of Catholics forbidden to vote in a traditionally Catholic country another group which included priests, laymen, and even a few bishops; a pro-loyalist group resigned to the loss of the Papal States and seemingly without any problems of conscience on the score of the Pius IX prohibitions, the uncompromising *Non Expedit* and the later, even more chilling *Non Licet*. There were men living in the area who had been whipped by Haynau, "the hyena of Brescia," when Austria held control and men who had fought at Custozza when Charles Albert was defeated in his attempt to drive the Austrians out. There were families who had lost fathers, sons, husbands in the war for independence and who could not be expected, reasonably, to renounce the cause to which they had given blood. In all of these groups there were Catholics who had remained in the Church or returned after being away, anti-Catholics, and those wistful individuals who remained home for material advantage while their families went to Mass, resolved to come back on their deathbeds to the Church. It was difficult in the discord and the confusion for a young man to orient himself.

At this critical period, Giorgio Montini came under the influence of Giuseppe Tovini, one of the first organizers of Catholic Action, and joined the Society of Sts. Faustino and Giovita, a group of young people who met regularly under the leadership of Dom Angelo Angelini and Dom Pietro Capretti. The youths of this society had learned through an exchange of experience and ideas how to handle the taunts of people who ridiculed Catholics as having been outside the battle which freed Italy. They had learned how to overcome the feeling that they were despised and to seek for opportunities to serve the community even if such service worked to the advantage of their enemies. Rhetoric could not answer the challenge "How can one be an Italian and a Catholic?" Action was the only adequate reply to it.

"Community service is the political arena," they were told. "We can serve our country and make our influence felt without voting or seeking office."

The program of Catholic Action seemed visionary and idealistic and far out of the world of the practical and the possible but Giuseppe Tovini was exhorting older men, and women within a limited sphere, along similar lines and the young men had guides while they were developing their own leaders; many of them men with shrewd and clever minds, born politicians deprived of the normal outlets for their talents. They had idealistic priests, too, who had heavy odds in their own field with which to contend and who emphasized that the intellectual, the social, the humanitarian designs of the group would fall apart if they tried to act without God. Prayer and the Sacraments held the young people together.

Giorgio Montini's gift was the written word. He was less effective on his feet than he was with his pen, but in the work of the Society he developed eloquence.

"We Catholics must free ourselves from the Circle of Solitude which excludes us from the Nation," he wrote.

The process of escaping from that circle, for a young man, consisted of joining any community organization for which he was eligible and of making his presence and his opinion felt, even if the organization he joined was dominated by anti-Catholic elements. It meant joining labor unions and it meant attending public meetings, prepared to ask questions and to challenge speakers who were reckless with facts. It meant the study of one's faith and the position of the Church on controversial subjects. It meant violence or the acceptance of humiliation and of ridicule but the young men who participated had the reward of comradeship when they had nothing else; occasionally there were triumphs.

"You will discover moderate elements in the ranks of those who oppose us," Giuseppe Tovini said, "because it is more in the nature of man to be moderate than to be an extremist. If you, too, are moderate and remember that a man may oppose your beliefs and still be honest, you can find a meeting ground on which you may exchange ideas."

It proved to be a sound principle. Work done conscientiously for the community, ideas well expressed and arguments fairly presented won respect and in some cases friendship for the young Catholics from the liberal groups with which they had had no contact heretofore except for passages at arms. More important, the Catholic young men abandoned their apologetic and defensive attitudes and in thrusting into the life of the community many of them found careers. All of which, of course, took time, patience, organization discipline, and the will to accept frequent failures. In other communities similar groups were in operation and there were exchanges of experience and of ideas. A Catholic press was essential to the work of Catholic Action and the press came into being.

In 1881, before he had finished his law studies, Giorgio Montini was invited to become the director of *Il Cittadino di Brescia*, a Catholic newspaper which needed a strong editorial policy if it were to survive.

There was much in Italy to engage the mind and pen of a crusading journalist; currency crises, railroad construction scandals, public works scandals, low wages, high taxes, unemployment. Giorgio Montini became a student of his own time and a revolutionary of a sort: not of the sword and gun but of the heart and mind. Although a landowner himself, with tenant farmers, he advocated more generous contracts with farm workers. He favored the "new idea" of holding an employer liable for accidents to workers in his employ. As a Catholic journalist he could not, however, become absorbed in secular affairs. His position was defined roughly by one of the many Catholic Action slogans: "Point the way! Do not pause to argue differences!" It was his task to chronicle the deeds of Catholics, individually and en masse, to hearten his confreres with public recognition and to keep Catholics aware of their growing influence in the nation and the world.

Leo XIII who succeeded Pius IX as Supreme Pontiff in 1878 had been crowned in one of the dark hours of the Church. Newspapers in London, Paris, New York, and Rome declared editorially on the death of Pius IX that he was taking the Church of Rome into the grave with him. Leo XIII was in correspondence on the day of his election with the nations which had withdrawn Vatican envoys, not waiting to be crowned. He started his astonishing series of encyclicals within six weeks of his coronation, inaugurating a teaching program and an interpretative program on the mind and will of the Church which electrified

Catholics and which commanded the attention of the world. Mindful, perhaps, of the controversy aroused by the decree of papal infallibility, Leo never spoke ex-cathedra but he declared emphatically that the teachings of the encyclicals must be followed and obeyed by Catholics.

It was Giorgio Montini's great regret that his own newspaper appointment did not come two years earlier when Leo XIII received in audience a thousand newspapermen representing over 1300 periodicals. A "press conference" in the Vatican was a daring innovation but Leo handled it in masterly fashion. He invited the questions and the interest of the secular press and laid himself open to interviews. Not all newspapers and magazines were good, he said; some were definitely evil in principle and methods. It should be the task of Catholic journalists to "equal or excel" the evil journalists rather than contenting themselves with criticism, acting with moderation and with "avoidance of intemperate bitterness."

Leo XIII was, in himself and in his writing, the prime source of inspiration for the Catholic journalist of his time. He did not, however, grant Catholics permission to vote or to hold office. Pius IX had placed a double lock on his prohibition which made it difficult for a successor to move in that field without repudiating him. Leo shared, too, the distrust which had made Pius fear that Catholic participation in a government hostile to the papacy might result in making the pope a subject of the Italian monarch. Events early in his reign did nothing to convince Leo that revolutionists in power were cats of a different color from the revolutionists whom he had known as Archbishop of Perugia where some of the most brutal and ruthless events of the revolt occurred.

In the year 1879, the Italian government confiscated 3037 monasteries and 1907 convents. In the same year the government forbade the teaching of religion in the schools. Any religious instruction must be outside of regular school time, reducing religion to a lesser position than any other subject; as an intelligent child would, of course, recognize. It was a bold move for control of youthful minds.

"Give us the vote and we will create a political party which will reverse this trend of godlessness and confiscation," one cardinal archbishop said that year, speaking for a group of bishops who had met to discuss the school edict.

Leo shook his head. "Patience!" he said.

He was to hold out against similar appeals in 1886 and in 1888, a virtual demand in 1900. He was changing the position of the papacy in the world by following his own precept of surpassing the enemy in brilliance and in logic, in precision of mind and clarity of expression. He did not deign to notice Italian statesmen but he was aware with amusement that the world compared them to him and to their disadvantage. He never referred to the King of Italy. Humbert who had succeeded his father, Victor Emmanuel, on the throne was "the Duke of Savoy" to Leo XIII; never more than that. He did not, however, release the power of Catholicism at the ballot box nor permit Catholics to send their own champions into the political arena. The dead hand of Pius IX restrained him and his own sense of timing which said, not yet.

Giorgio Montini grew to maturity in the world of Leo XIII. He became a man of standing and of influence in the community. In the early '90s he is described by a contemporary as "a man of calm self-possession with a precise and elegant manner which did not detract from the audacity of his undertakings and his daring political ability." He was in his middle thirties when he married Giuditta Alghisi in 1895.

Giuditta was a bright-eyed vivacious girl, a native of Verolavecchia which had once been known as Verola Alghisi. The Alghisis were of the minor nobility, an older family than the Montinis, with a large villa which was known locally as "the palace." Giuditta was a cousin of Geralamo Rovetta, author of the drama *Romanticism*, and of many novels, the best known of which was *Mater Dolorosa*. He was active in Catholic writing groups and a friend of Giorgio, delighted that his friend and his cousin were attracted to each other. The romance of the two young people was a genuine love match and remained one; so much so that Giorgio Montini could say when youth had left him:

"The great blessing of my life is my family, with my wife a saintly, affectionate creature who has shared with me every joy, concern, and sorrow of the years."

From the outset they were dedicated, as individuals and as a couple, to the same ends, sharing a deep attachment to the Church, a profound love of ritual, ceremony and quiet prayer, a career and life involvement in Catholic youth and Catholic journalism. Giuditta is described, in that first year of her married life, as "a petite woman who wore black mantillas and small high boots with little buttons from the ankle up." She was proud of her husband. She did not understand his work too well nor the issues which he discussed so fluently but she was an accomplished hostess in the Montini house on Via San Maria delle Grazie in Brescia and, as his career advanced, entertained many distinguished guests there.

The first son of the Montinis was born in 1896 and they named him Ludovico. The second son, born a year later, nearly cost his mother her life.

3

BATTISTA

THE second son of Giorgio and Giuditta Montini was born on September 26, 1897. He entered the world diffidently, pausing at the door, uncertain. The midwife bent over his mother and the other women in the room watched anxiously.

"He came too soon after the first," they said.

That was true, as it was often true with a woman and her second child, or her third. The women in the room were of the country, astonished by neither birth nor death yet awed by both, the commonplaces forever touched with wonder.

Giorgio Montini met this crisis in his life as he met all crises, with prayer. He prayed desperately while his wife hung suspended between being and nonbeing, while his son clung to the thin line of breath which sustained him. When they were out of danger, Giorgio walked to the Church of San Antonino, a short distance down the lane, to offer his prayer of gratitude. Four days later, September 30, he took his infant son to the church. Don Gio. Fiorini baptized him, with Enrico Manzoni, a Brescian attorney and friend of Giorgio's, in the role of godfather.

The infant's name was: Giovan Battista Enrico Antonio Maria Montini.

The font at which the water of baptism flowed over him was in the rear of the church on the gospel side. The great and the humble had been baptized there and Concesio was particularly

45

proud of the two bishops who had received the first sacrament in San Antonino's: members of the Ladrone family, Francesco in 1600 and Sebastiano in 1643. Concesio was proud, too, that the son of the distinguished Dr. Giorgio Montini had been born within the town. Normally, the family would spend only the early months of summer in Concesio, the latter half of August and most of September in Verolavecchia where Giuditta's family lived.

Giuditta was still very weak and another problem had to be met, a not uncommon one of the period. Clorinda Peretti, wife of Ponziano Peretti, was engaged as the infant's "wet nurse." She took him to her home at Sacca Di Nave and cared for him. Giuditta's recovery was slow and the child remained for months in his foster family. There were three Peretti children: Giovanni, Pietro, and Margherita. They became so attached to the baby that after his father took him to Brescia, Giovanni and Pietro walked eight miles to see him again. They were Giovan Battista Montini's first friends and they shortened his name to "Battista," the name by which he was to be known to intimates through all of his life.

Many observers of the Italian scene at the turn of the century have commented upon the gravity of Italian children, solemn little creatures who seemed to be walking perpetually among great and towering thoughts. Battista Montini was one of the grave children; serious, studious, with intent eyes that were startlingly like his mother's. In his early years, he seems to have been born to listen rather than to speak; but he was a boy and any legend which overspiritualizes him is an exaggeration.

"He was not a saint, I can tell you that," Anna Mariannini, the one-time Montini housekeeper, says today. "He was as mischievous as any boy his age."

The first teacher of young Battista, the man who taught him to read and write, is Ezechiele Malizia of Brescia. He remembers him as frail, restless, but never lacking in vitality. "Sometimes I had to spank him," he says.

Spanking was no novelty to children of the era. In Italy,

they were not abused but they were disciplined and discipline was considered the foundation of dignity in poor homes or wealthy ones. Children in north Italy were accustomed to keeping the hours their parents kept, to staying up late and listening to adult conversation, fascinated even when it was incomprehensible. There were no amusements provided, no equivalents of the motion picture, radio, and television of later generations, so a child found entertainment in whatever occurred, or whatever was available, in his own environment; either that or he was not entertained, with no one greatly concerned. Children were noticed, and knew that they were. They were treated with affection, praised and admired within reason but reduced in importance when other adults were present, a condition which they understood and respected. It is possible to speak in generalities because there were conventions, universal customs, more generally observed than violated. In addition to the community codes there were household rules which varied from family to family and which children learned as they advanced out of infancy. The Montini family was considered exceptionally religious and their way of life regarded as more complicated than comfortable.

The greater part of the Montini year was spent in Brescia, which had always been noted as a weapon and armament center: the place where for centuries Brescia blades were forged and tempered, where guns were later made and cannon. It had been a greater town than Milan once but too many wars had rolled over it and it had been flattened too often. It was a center of journalistic feud, of controversy, in which Giorgio Montini played a leading role.

Battista and his brother, Ludovico, accompanied their mother each morning to Mass at Santa Maria delle Grazie. The church, erected in 1522, was only a few yards from their home. Battista grew to an appreciation of art in his parish church ultimately but his interest was kindled earlier in the equestrian statue which dominated the view from church or home. The mounted, arrogant figure was Giuseppe Garibaldi.

The heroes of the Risorgimento and the saints of the church were neighbors in many sections of Brescia and the boy knew most of them before he knew who they were, or what they had been, before he had any understanding of the chasm of circumstance which separated one set of heroes from the other.

Life in the city was, in great part, rather formal and precise. Battista wore velvet suits, usually blue, when he was five or six years old. He was not encouraged to engage in sports or any strenuous activity during the Brescia intervals. The Montinis took their responsibilities as parents seriously and they accepted as wisdom the custom of their time which decreed that boys should learn masculine strength, firmness, courage and fortitude from fathers; gentleness, sympathy, and the soft virtues from mothers. Giorgio Montini, a tenacious fighter for causes, was courageous and unswerving, a man of stern qualities, who reserved the soft side of his nature for his wife. He was never brutal to his sons but he chastised them with strokes of a ruler or a belt end across their outstretched palms when they broke rules or became unruly; and he held them to strict accountability for their conduct. On the other hand he was a sentimental man whose voice would break when he spoke of his family.

Battista was always in awe of his father, intensely devoted to his mother.

The great realities in the life of Giuditta Montini were spiritual. She participated in the activities of women's groups and she visited the ill and the poor, alleviating suffering where she could and not sparing herself; but she retained her bright imagination and a certain childlike quality which made her religion a happy part of her life, her church a place which she visited with a certain eagerness. Her sons were to remember those visits because they shared so many of them.

There was a day in Santa Maria delle Grazie when Battista was very young. He accompanied his mother who sat in a pew, knitting. He sat quietly beside her as he had been taught to do, but he had reached the age of asking questions.

"Don't you pray?" he asked. "Don't you say the Hail Mary?"

His mother shook her head. "Not today," she said. "I came only to keep the Blessed Mother company."

Each of her sons shared such quiet times in church without prayer and they learned that it is not necessary to storm heaven constantly, that there is quiet and beauty and companionship in the mere placing of oneself in the presence of the Blessed Mother and the saints under the eye of God. They learned, too, a quiet certainty in those simple visits, an unquestioning faith in a world beyond the senses, a world in which friends dwelt, sharing the friendship of God.

This was one gift of Giuditta to her children and it was no slight gift.

The family went to Concesio in the Easter season and in the early summer. Life was relaxed for adults in the country. Giorgio wore old clothes and visited with the tenant farmers and people of the town. He was less concentrated, less tense. Giuditta, too, dressed simply and shared the small talk of the women, the talk of preserves and recipes, of dressmaking and needlepoint. There were usually people with trouble of one kind or another who commanded her interest and concern. It was more difficult for children to find the human values in the country and the adults did not understand that or even think about it.

Ludovico and Battista, and later Francesco, who was three years younger than Battista, were strange to the boys of Concesio who were together all year long. Boys were more aware of social differences than their parents. Giorgio could find much in common with the men who worked his land and the men accepted him as their sons could not accept his sons. Speaking of Battista many years later one of those boys referred to him as "the little master." The caste line was there and it was difficult for boys to cross it. Over the years there were a few solid friendships in the country for the Montini boys, but comparatively few. They were good companions for one another.

Battista loved the house in which he was born, a huge house by village standards with the living, visiting, cooking, and dining rooms on the ground floor, five bedrooms on the second and four more on the third. Rambler roses climbed the walls and the Alps came tumbling down toward the garden, almost into it, foothills that seemed high because they were so close. There were three large flower beds which changed color and design according to the month. Orchards stretched away from the garden area, rich with blossom in one season, with fruit in another.

Primo Savoldi, one of the boys who knew him well, says that Battista, although thin and never strong, was extremely agile and could climb a tall tree faster than any of the local boys.

Tree climbing was part of a boy's life but Battista genuinely liked churches, not only because he had the habit of prayer but because he found friendliness in them and beauty and a sense of wonder. He visited the Church of San Antonino frequently and knew it well. He was linked to it through the baptismal font. It bore the name of an early saint, a saint of Roman times, and the boy knew Roman ruins as he knew treetops. Vespasian had left temples, forums, and circuses behind him in this country of Brescia and Concesio for boys to explore. The Church of San Antonino was not comparable to the churches of Brescia in an art gallery sense but there were paintings of the Virgin, an Immaculate Conception, and a Queen of Heaven, facing each other across the church; and two fine old paintings, St. Thomas Aquinas on the epistle side and St. Charles Borromeo on the gospel side.

Battista Montini had a particular devotion to St. Charles. It was easy for a boy of Lombardy to develop an admiration, even an affection, for the great Saint of Milan. A boy named Angelo Roncalli in Sotto il Monte, thirty-six miles from Concesio, was devoted to him and that boy was destined to become Pope John XXIII. Battista Montini, who knew nothing about the other boy, liked the dark old mysterious painting in the Concesio church. It was recessed above a side altar between the mid-church pulpit and the high altar. He prayed there often, losing track of time.

St. Charles Borromeo had created most of his legends in places familiar to a boy of North Italy; his heroic mountain climbing, his fighting of the plague, the Black Death, and the nursing of its victims, his conversions of brigands. A prince of one of the great noble families, accepting poverty for Christ, there was an appeal to boys in Carlo Borromeo such as few saints had. His story was told and retold in the classrooms and one anecdote always separated a class, any class, into two groups. It concerned the Saint's encounter with a beggar on a cold night. Having no money, Carlo Borromeo took off his cloak and gave it to the man. The man looked at the cloak, saw how shabby it was and scornfully hurled it back.

At this point, even in a class of solemn small Italian boys, half of the class laughed or smiled; the other half looked startled or shocked.

There is no record of how young Battista Montini first received that story but a poll of a half-dozen people who knew him at various times in his life resulted in a unanimous verdict: he was not one of those who laughed.

There was a second change of scene for the Montini boys in midsummer. Having spent the early summer in their father's town, they moved next to the home of the Alghisis, their mother's family. The move was always exciting because they traveled by steam tramway, which was noisy, smoky, and terrifyingly fast. The trip from Brescia to Concesio was tame by comparison, a jaunt behind two sturdy horses.

Verolavecchia was still known as Verola Alghisi to the older residents but there were few of the Alghisi family left. The arrival of Giuditta, her husband, and her family was always the event of the summer. After the traditional first calls to the church and to the pastor there was open house for old friends and neighbors; Benassis, Pasinis, Benaninos, Ziliolis, and many others. The boys played tag or played catch with a ball, but in the memories which have survived "they always seemed like city boys even when they were dressed like country boys and doing the same things that country boys do."

An awesome fact still remembered of the Alghisi Villa and the Montini visits was the bell. It tolled solemnly at three o'clock, the hour that Christ died, and at the first sound the Montini boys stopped whatever they had been doing, stood straight like soldiers at attention and prayed.

There were cherry orchards in the region of Verolavecchia. Boys, naturally, ate cherries to excess. Battista, because he had been ill, was limited by his mother to ten cherries a day. He was told that he could eat ten and no more.

"You know how boys are," a cousin of his said. "As soon as we learned that he could only eat ten, we tried to tempt him to eat more, or bully him into doing it. He never did. Sometimes he would carry a cherry in his jacket until the end of the day so that he would have one to eat if he was tempted too much; but it was one of his ten."

It is difficult to unravel memories and lay them straight. A boy's memories of a community or of its people and the community's memory of the boy have this in common: they criss-cross the years, making a web of them. The events of one year are attached to those of two or three years later, or earlier. Always, however, there are memories which stand tall and alone, apart from all others, occupying their own certain and unalterable place in time. Such was Battista's memory of the death of Leo XIII.

Battista Montini was in his sixth year, not to be six years old until September, when Leo died on July 20, 1903. The Montini family was in Concesio. The rambler roses were in bloom and there was fragrance everywhere, a fresh flow of air from the mountains in the evening after the heat of the day. There were neighbors visiting, men and women, vague later in memory as adults are always vague in the memory of a child. The women sat in a half-circle, talking, their heads moving up and down. The men sat some distance away, their pipes brightening in flame and dimming in ash like mechanical fireflies. One remembered it in that way, the tranquillity of it, knowing that it must have often been like that since the picture came back so faithfully, recalled by all of the senses; the seen, the inhaled, the heard, the touched, and the tasted.

The other picture—the night they heard of the pope's death
—was the same picture momentarily, then frightening in its
breaking up, in the raising of voices, the swift movement of
bodies, the adult preoccupation in something adult which completely shut out a child's sudden fear, a child's questions. After
those first few minutes, fear was dispelled by the reassuring gentle presence of God. Men, women, and children were on their
knees, their voices rising and falling as they intoned the Rosary.

One remembered the prayers and, later, the solemn Masses in
San Antonino's because in them there was one's first awareness
of death, hazy and ill-defined, felt as an absence rather than as a
presence. There was in them, too, a first awareness of a pope as
other than a word, of a pope as a person who lived and died;
an awareness, too, that was of loss rather than of gain. There
was a pope and his name was Leo XIII and he was dead. He
was in all of the conversation that one heard in those solemn
days and one remembered.

A boy did not, of course, remember what was said of a man
nor make any coherent pattern of thought out of the opinions
of adults. He could only remember the event and let the years
gather facts and speculation around it.

Leo XIII was ninety-three years old when he died. He was
within days of his sixty-eighth birthday when the conclave which
followed the death of Pius IX elected him pope. He was Gio-
acchino Cardinal Pecci entering that conclave and he entreated
the cardinals to pass him over when his election on one more
ballot seemed indicated.

"I am too old," he said, "and too feeble in health. I shall die
soon under this responsibility if you insist that I accept it; then
you will have your work to do again."

Father Calenzio, secretary to another cardinal, visited the
troubled Cardinal Pecci in his room. "Eminence," he said, "the
present position of the Church has come about through no
fault of ours. God willed that it should reach such a state, or
permitted it. It is the wish of God, not of men that Your

Eminence should be pope. They cannot vote contrary to His will."

"It is beyond my strength. They vote me death."

"It shall be in the will of God, not your will or theirs, if you die and they choose again," the priest said. "It shall be in the will of God if you serve long and if you justify the votes of those who serve His will in electing you. Dare you to refuse, Eminence?"

Cardinal Pecci did not refuse and he did not die prematurely under the awful responsibility which he assumed. The Church when he began his quarter-century pontificate was at the lowest point in world influence and in internal morale that it had touched since the Reformation. As Leo XIII he faced the world revolution and the dislocations of a civilization becoming industrialized. He faced changing government patterns and philosophies of government hostile to all religion. He faced the ebb of faith as science flooded the world with new terms and new promises, holding out to mankind the laboratory-made apples which would make men wiser than God.

"There is nothing more useful than to look at the world as it really is," he said, "and, at the same time, to look elsewhere for a remedy to its troubles."

He looked at his world and he presented its troubles with astonishing clarity in a series of encyclicals which have become a part of world literature. He stated problems and he answered them with the wisdom of the Church, looking so far beyond his time that generations after his own would study him, finding his reasoning fresh and new. He set forth the nature of man and the nature of the State, the relationship of Church and State, the sanctity of marriage, the responsibility of parenthood, the dignity of family. He defended Holy Scripture against the challenges of the myth-builders who would dismiss it as folklore and he wrote with moving eloquence on the love of God. He called Thomas Aquinas out of the neglected, dusty shelves of libraries and restored philosophy to the Church.

The Socialists and Communists were eloquent and making

converts amid injustice and cruel economic unbalance. Leo looked at the same evils which their prophets saw but dismissed their remedies as illusory, false, as productive of human misery as the evil they proposed to correct. In 1891, he wrote the encyclical *Rerum Novarum (Of New Things)*, one of the world's great social documents, a high point of Christian thinking on the condition of the laboring classes and on the relationship between employer and employed. Leo did not offer men straw out of which to make bread; he wrote a charter for capital and labor and set forth an economic philosophy based upon Christian principles which offered protection to property, assured capital of its right to earn and to profit, demanded for labor a just wage, the right to organize and the dignity due to a partner in enterprise. *Rerum Novarum* commanded the attention and respect of men and nations. Study clubs were organized around that one encyclical which reproduced itself many times in the paraphrasing of politicians, labor leaders, educators, and journalists. It crossed all lines to universality.

When Leo died, a glowering young journalist named Benito Mussolini expressed well the dilemma of the anticlerical, anti-Catholic, many-partied radical Italian who liked and admired Leo XIII, however grudgingly:

"We Socialists, without disdain but with indifference, pass before the corpse."

4

THE SLINGSHOT

THE summer when Leo XIII died, Giovan Battista Montini was moving out of childhood. He was starting school in the fall and for an Italian boy that was, as it was to Shakespeare, the passing from one of the ages of man into another.

The school was Collegio Cesare Arici and it stood on Via Trieste, Number 17, in Brescia. It had been a palace of the Conti Martinengo Cesaresco and it was still more palace than school; the long, high-ceilinged, richly decorated corridors, the reception rooms and parlors of the professors hung with tapestry, walls covered with satin, panels intricately carved. The main buildings dated from the second half of the fifteenth century, with one "modern" wing built in the seventeenth. The boys of Cesare Arici attended school in a museum, instructed by the walls which enclosed them. It was a long and subtle instruction. Boys entered, as Giovan Battista Montini did, in the first grade and finished the equivalent of an American high school before leaving it. It was a Catholic school under the direction of the Jesuits and its existence was a monument to Giuseppe Tovini and to his protégé, Giorgio Montini.

Giuseppe Zanardelli, one of the figures of the Risorgimento, represented Brescia in the legislature and exerted tremendous influence in municipal affairs through his political position and the editorship of *La Provincia di Brescia*, the dominant newspaper of the region. Zanardelli, a free-thinker and an anticlerical, was one of the sponsors of the bill which eliminated all references to God or to religion, and all prayers, from the classrooms of the public schools. He was the rock of opposition in the path of any Catholic-sponsored project.

Giuseppe Tovini had opposed unsuccessfully God's banishment from the classroom. As he outlined his belief for Montini, the evil of this policy was apparent, the consequences inevitable. Children could be taught at home, as they were, that meaning and purpose in life rest upon a belief in God, faith in His wisdom, His mercy, His justice, but if the school, the fountain of knowledge, considered God of such small significance that He was not even mentioned in connection with the wonders of creation, a child would find difficult the preservation of faith. There had to be a major school in the community in which God was acknowledged, worshiped, and studied. Tovini traveled tirelessly, talking to individuals and to groups on the need for a new Catholic school. He gained support for the idea and he raised money.

Giorgio Montini wrote editorials, crossing rhetorical swords with the veteran Zanardelli. He spoke to his fellow members of the Society of Sts. Faustino and Giovita, and he wrote speeches for others to deliver. It was his first major campaign and he won his spurs in it.

In 1882, the Cesaresco palace was obtained and that fall the Jesuits moved in.

An incensed Zanardelli intensified his campaign, seeking to have the school closed and the Jesuits forbidden to teach in Brescia. He was a fiery fighter, a brilliant writer, and *La Provincia* carried his thunder. Giorgio Montini matched him in eloquence and exceeded him in logic, to the surprise of his fellow citizens. At the end of four years, Collegio Cesare Arici was firmly established, Zanardelli and his followers defeated and the right of parents to direct the education of their own children established.

Giorgio Montini and Giuseppe Zanardelli were uncompromising foes. Montini outlived his rival and, in his later years, walked along Corso Zanardelli whenever he visited the cathedral.

Monsignor Angelo Zammarchi, Brescian historian, writing of Collegio Arici's battle for survival, speculates on the possible influence on the Montini boys of attendance at the school which was such a shining symbol in their father's life. He quotes, figuratively rather than literally, perhaps, a statement of Giorgio Montini, speaking to his three sons about Giuseppe Tovini:

"Sons, I, at the *Cittadino*, was always close by his side, close to my great friend, supporting him with writing and with prayer during the bitter quarrels of our time and in many exhausting enterprises."

Twenty-one years after his conflict with Zanardelli, Giorgio Montini walked with his small son through the doors of Collegio Cesare Arici and enrolled him as a pupil.

The grandeur of the school overwhelmed Battista and he was slow in making friends with it. He was slow, too, in making friends with contemporaries at the school. In his first few years, he seemingly created no lasting memories with either his contemporaries or his teachers. After three years, when he was nine years old, his personality was more fully developed.

"I saw Battista get into a fight, a fist fight, only once," his classmate Luigi Bolognini says. "A boy named Luisin tied an old pan to the tail of a cat. The animal was terrified. Everyone laughed except Battista who sprang angrily in front of Luisin and commanded him to free the cat. Luisin refused to do so and they started fighting. I do not remember which of them won. Neither, I imagine. Someone separated them. It was the only time I ever saw Battista lose his stirrups."

Other companions and classmates of the period remember young Montini as a brilliant student but quiet and seldom a participant in student activities. One contemporary described him as "studious, pious, a mild character, reserved but cordial." To many people the three Montini brothers seemed self-sufficient, playing together and doing many things together, not needing other children. Three people state that Battista was often in church and had a habit of visiting churches, and one of the three adds the interesting comment: "He liked to look at the paintings."

The man, Giovanni Battista Montini, became later a collector of paintings, particularly interested in the Brescian school. That interest obviously developed early when he left the beauty of his school for the streets of Brescia and took refuge from ugly industrialism in the churches. The churches are still there and the paintings of Moretto, Romanino, Ferramala, Moroni, and Cristoforo Foppa of the native school; giants such as Tintoretto from afar. Sometimes, perhaps, a small boy saw only the Madonnas and the saints, praying to them, and at other times saw a painting and admired the painter. If so, he had many illustrious and saintly predecessors of similar mind and habit.

On December 4, 1906, the year that Battista reached his ninth birthday, Giorgio Montini celebrated the completion of twenty-five years as a journalist. He and his family were invited to the hall adjoining the Church of Saints Faustino and Giovita in which Giorgio had started his long career in Catholic Action. They listened while Nicolo Rezzara, secretary of the Economic Social Union, delivered a discourse to a large audience. The speaker reviewed Giorgio Montini's career; his work for Catholic youth, his close collaboration with Giuseppe Tovini, his many battles in behalf of Catholic education, his unflinching courage in the long struggle against radical political parties dedicated to the destruction of Catholicism.

"This is his virtue and that of few others," the speaker said. "He spoke as much as was necessary when it was prudent to speak. He never hesitated to intervene in an argument, or respond to an opponent, when he was armed with reason, with facts, with proofs. He was then formidable, but always honest and always fair, reaching his objectives without dishonoring or humiliating anyone."

The family was surrounded when the discourse was finished and Giorgio Montini was the center of congratulation, of admiration, of affection. He did not give way to his feelings until he was out of the public eye. In his own home, away from friends, neighbors and well-wishers, he embraced his wife silently, then walked around the room, tears in his eyes. He embraced his boys and patted them on the shoulders but he did not speak to them.

That night, or soon thereafter, Battista resolved to be a journalist. The desire to write had been in him as far back as his memory reached. He excelled in all of his studies at Collegio Cesare Arici but his interest focused on reading, on expression in words, on history, and on languages. He was devout in chapel, more apt to solitary prayer than the average boy but he did not speak of becoming a priest and his contemporaries did not, as they did of others, think of him as a future priest.

On June 6, 1907, he received his First Communion and on July 21, 1907, he was confirmed by His Excellency Giacomo Pellegrini in the chapel at Collegio Arici. Pius X was the reigning Pope and the ages for receiving First Communion and for Confirmation were to be lowered during his pontificate but not until August 8, 1910.

There was a strong spiritual tide moving in Italy while Pius X occupied the throne of Peter. The enemies of the Church did not relax and the situation in France became grave, but in Italy there was a noticeable movement back to the Church and greater stability among Catholics. Pius X expressed his accord with the principles enunciated by Leo XIII. The encyclicals of Leo were already part of the mind of the Universal Church; one accepted them as the statement of great truth. Leo had defined the rights of man on earth and the concern of the Church in the establishment of those rights; Pius was to address himself to man's spiritual need, to the hunger of the soul.

Battista Montini lived through his formative years during the pontificate of Pius X. He crossed an invisible boundary with his teens; and he was growing tall. Dr. Appollonio Zerla, who knew him then, recalls him as remarkably thin, "speaking as though he had memorized the entire dictionary." He had, of course, the vocabulary of a boy who read and who wrote, who spent much of his life alone and with words. Never robust, always susceptible to colds, Battista was often forced to miss classes in the years when the classes were of greatest interest to him.

He was editor of the school paper, *Eco Vita Collegiale*, and he was its principal contributor. His pen touched many subjects: the artists of Brescia and the art treasures, the superb Winged Victory of gilded bronze which was excavated in 1826 from the ruins of an ancient Corinthian temple outside the city; the crypt under the Duomo Vecchio in which St. Filastio was martyred in the eighth century; the Dante manuscript in the Biblioteca Quirana and the Petrarch manuscript, the ninth-century Book of Gospels. He was interested in Pliny's statement that the Mincio River flows through the Lake of Garda without permitting its waters to mingle with those of the lake. He was equally fascinated with the other legend, that where the Mincio issues from the lake at Peschiera, Pope Leo the Great faced Attila the Hun in 452.

Battista Montini was interested in anything and everything as he grew, but he did not like writing for rhetoric's sake and he did not like static subjects. The love of controversy was in his soul and he yearned to be "the lion" as his father was, to have people refer to him as a "Lombard fighter." When he was sixteen he joined the group with which his father had started his apostolate, the Society of Saints Faustino and Giovita. He launched a magazine, with the aid of other young crusaders, designed to forward the aims of the Society, to combat current evils and to serve the cause of Christian democracy. Despite the high-sounding and ambitious program, he was humble with self-knowledge and he did not deceive himself that he was ready for big game or that he would fire any shots heard round the world. He called his magazine *La Fionda* (*The Slingshot*).

In 1912, when Battista was fifteen, his father retired from *Il Cittadino di Brescia*. The young amateur with his slingshot was the only Montini left in the field of journalism and he had only the time for it which could be spared from a heavy study program. His energy at fifteen flowed powerfully into anything which he undertook and his will-to-do was always urgent but he drew heavily upon his source of energy and doctors warned him that he was headed for trouble.

His impatient answer to warnings was a quotation from St. Charles Borromeo: "Of what use is health to me if I do no work?"

Giorgio Montini, too, had always ignored the physical signals of warning when he felt that he was needed, so when he offered the state of his health as his reason for retiring from the newspaper there were lifted eyebrows. He was, his contemporaries said, not sufficiently challenged in the reign of Pius X. There were conflicts still, many of them, errors to be challenged and evils to be corrected, but they were, in his estimation, best met in the idiom of younger men.

Giorgio was seeing as a possibility now the ideal for which he had worked: Catholic participation in politics, Catholics voting and Catholics holding public office, Catholics supplying balance against the excesses of radical groups. Men had learned politics, pledged to community betterment without votes to implement their efforts, and Giorgio Montini wanted to concentrate on those activities now without the burden and the responsibility of editing a newspaper.

The Roman Question was dying. It was the way of Pius X to not kill but to let die. Early in his reign he let it be known through subtle means used by all popes that any miraculous restoration of the Papal States and temporal power would horrify him. He received the Duke of Genoa and his family in audience, the first time since 1870 that any member of the House of Savoy had been received at the Vatican. The Duke of Genoa was the brother of the Queen of Italy. Finally, on June 11, 1905, he assured the final settlement of the supposedly insoluble problem by a device as simple as it was wise. He wrote an encyclical, *Il Fermo Proposito*, granting the bishops power to permit or forbid Catholics in their own individual dioceses to vote.

The answer of Pius X to the problem was neither a repudiation of Pius IX nor a repeal of *Non Expedit* and *Non Licet*; nor was it a release of withheld Catholic voting power against a hostile government. Pius merely eased a restriction, made possible the lawful breaking of a lock, leaving the rest to time and to the tempers of men.

In 1909, four years after the Roman Question was referred to the Bishops by the papacy, twenty-four Catholics were elected to the Chamber of Deputies. They were too few to accomplish reform, to materially change existing legislation, and they had come more than a half century late to the halls of legislation, to the business of government, but they were a vanguard.

Battista Montini was in tune with the thinking of his time, politically and philosophically, through his active role in the discussion groups of Brescia, older than his years intellectually and younger, perhaps, emotionally. A priest of Brescia asked him to write sermons for him when he was only sixteen and he wrote sermons for at least a year, the first of his many ghost-writing experiences.

The year 1913 was an eventful one in his life but before school opened in the fall, before his sixteenth birthday on September 26, the prophecies of doctors were fulfilled. Battista drew too heavily on his vitality and the well did not refill. He was confined to bed and, when he was convalescing, he was told that he could not return to school; school had to come to him.

The nature of young Montini's illness, at this distance, is obscure. It seems to have been a respiratory ailment, recurring frequently but from which he had long periods of relief; an allergic condition, possibly, or conceivably asthmatic. Whatever it was, it subjected him to fits of coughing which left him exhausted and it contributed to his dangerous underweight.

The school came to him. Padre Giuseppe Persico, S.J., made daily visits to the house on Via Santa Maria della Grazie to tutor him in mathematics and history; a gentle man who had learned much guile and counterguile in a decade of teaching and who put his young charge to many severe tests. Looking proudly back, now, Padre Persico says:

"Never once did I trap him. Never once did I discover him unprepared. And I knew how, I tell you! He had a fine mind and he always prepared his assignments. Always!"

Battista asked the opinion of Padre Persico on some of his independent writing and the Jesuit read his manuscripts. "I did not teach literature; my field was primarily mathematics, but it seemed to me that he was a fine writer for his age, or beyond his age. He was a simple young man, earnest about his work but not conceited or calling attention to himself."

Count Aristide Biglione Viarigi, who *was* Battista's tutor in literature and language, believed so ardently in his future as a writer that he saved the pens and tablets which his student used and still possesses them.

Despite the fact that he maintained his scholastic rating during his year of absence from school, Battista Montini lost ground in so many other areas that he was besieged by depression. He could no longer attend meetings and participate in public discussion and he missed the classroom contacts which were his closest approach to contemporary friendships. His brothers spent time with him but they had their own groups and were developing interests far removed from his. He could not physically compete in an active world so he retreated from it. He spent much time in prayer and he studied the life of St. Charles Borromeo. The great Saint of Milan had made many trips to Brescia and had officiated at the funerals of two Brescian bishops: Dominico Bollini in 1579 and Giovanni Delfino in 1584.

It interested Battista that Bishop Delfino had died only sixteen years before Bishop Francesco Ladrone was baptized in Concesio in 1600; in the same font as that in which he, himself, had been baptized. The event was commemorated on a plaque beside the font. The circumstances dramatized the continuing, unchanging spirit of the Church, using the same materials over and over, accommodating itself to evolving cultures and governments, burying its bishops and baptizing babies who are bishops-to-be, using its saints in the service of those who are not saints and then recalling them.

Nothing that Battista wrote during that year satisfied him. His health was improved when the summer of 1914 came and he traveled to Concesio but even there he was out of touch with his contemporaries. Sixteen is a bad age at which to get out of step. His vitality was low, too, and the distances around Concesio, normally a stimulating challenge, were beyond his strength. He spent his time within a tight circle of space and that circle ultimately enclosed a sympathy and a compassion for others in distress which he retained for a lifetime.

"You may guess what you like about him and predict what you believe he will do," said a distinguished contemporary of many years later, "and you may be right or wrong. He is difficult to forecast. You may be certain of this, however: he will always understand people who are alone and ill and poor. His heart will be open to them."

A man could spend a year of his life in learning less than that.

5

ET INTROIBO AD ALTARE DEI

BATTISTA MONTINI attained his full height, a half inch over five foot, ten, during the summer of 1914. It was a dangerous period in which to attain manhood, or the semblance of it. The sullen thunder of war was over the rim of the world and it was only a question of when the storm would break. The anticipation of it dominated every conversation, provided an "if" for every future plan. Austria declared war on Serbia, July 28, and the lightning chain reaction of violence which involved nearly all of Europe, left Italy in a quiet pocket. The Italian government declared for neutrality, despite a treaty of alliance with Austria. The Austrians had slighted Italy as an ally in not consulting with her and the alliance did not pledge Italy to an aggressive policy.

It was less than fifty years since the unification of the Papal States into the Italian nation. The revolution which had expelled Austria and France, which had enthroned a King and established a parliament had written an incredible chapter of history but when it was over, Massimo d'Azeglio, the first Secretary of State, could say: "We have made Italy, now we must make Italians."

For Battista Montini, the student and the reader, that summer of 1914 opened a door to the world. Despite his wide reading, his study groups, his intellectual curiosity, he had been a

Brescian, or in a slightly larger sense, an Italian, no more than that, until the nations moved out of the leather-bound volumes into blazing conflict that was alive, immediate, present. The troops marched and the guns moved up, not in the cold fog of narration which wrapped the past but in the hot reality of action unfinished and unpredictable which did not wait upon narrators. A young man who lived and breathed was part of it despite whatever prejudices he might hold personally, whatever action the nation might take, or take not.

On August 20, Pius X died. Those close to him considered this the ultimate disaster of the month which brought war to Europe. The holiness of the personal life of Pius X had been extraordinary, even in a milieu where personal holiness is taken for granted, but Pius had not withdrawn from the world. He had been alert to the practical necessities of the Church and among his many accomplishments, the revision of the Code of Canon Law ranks high. He reorganized the Roman Curia and he raised the United States from its status as a missionary country to full ecclesiastical rank, naming two new American cardinals: William H. O'Connell, Archbishop of Boston, and John M. Farley, Archbishop of New York. The mark of the pontificate, however, was the emphasis placed upon the mystical side of Catholicism, the calling of people to Christ in the Holy Eucharist.

The finest troops of Great Britain and France were being driven back before the powerful German war machine and the drama of death in Flanders dwarfed the death of a gentle man in Rome. The cardinals gathered in conclave to select his successor, men of the Church from the countries at war, cardinal archbishops of dioceses whose young men were in the field, killing or being killed by the young men of cardinal archbishops across the table. Out of this strained meeting of minds, souls, and consciences came the new pope, Giacomo Cardinal della Chiesa, Archbishop of Bologna, who chose to reign under the name of Benedict XV.

No one had predicted this outcome of the voting. The greats

among the cardinals, the favorites in speculation, had been passed over to achieve it, to elect a thin, pale, undersized aristocrat with a twist in his spine, one of the least prepossessing of popes and, in many ways one of the most extraordinary.

The general public did not know Giacomo della Chiesa nor recognize his name, but he had been a Vatican favorite during the reign of Leo XIII, recognized as one of the most ingenious minds in the Secretariat. Della Chiesa had been secretary then to the towering Mariano Cardinal Rampolla. When Rafael Cardinal Merry del Val became the youngest Secretary of State in modern papal history, Della Chiesa was sent to Bologna, a see which called for a red hat which Della Chiesa did not get. The removal to Bologna was, supposedly, a promotion but no one inside the Vatican was deceived.

This was an old process with a title: *Promoveatur ut Amoveatur* (Let him be promoted so that he can be removed).

It took seven years at Bologna, in a cardinalitial see, for Giacomo della Chiesa to ascend to the red: then only because Pius X became aware of the situation and acted over the head of his Secretary of State.

Battista Montini, not quite seventeen that year, read of the election of the new pope, but he knew nothing of backgrounds nor of the drama behind the scenes. He had never been inside the Vatican and he had never seen Benedict XV nor Rafael Cardinal Merry del Val. It would be an absurdity to imagine that he, himself, would ever be in a position where men would look back and say: "Remember how Della Chiesa went down to Bologna?"

Within a few weeks, criticism of Benedict XV poured in from all of the warring countries. They blamed him because he did not denounce, did not bless, did not rebuke, did not favor, as each embroiled nation believed, certainly, that he should.

"I should regret it if any of my clergy should take sides in this conflict," he said. "It is desirable that we pray for the cessation of war without dictating to Almighty God in what way it should end."

Later, expressing his concern for people caught up in the war, Benedict XV said that we "must consider not the special interests that divide them but the common bond of faith which makes them brothers."

Italy declared war on Austria on May 24, 1915.

Battista had passed, intellectually, through the various phases of the Italian shift from reluctance to belligerence, almost without realizing it. Back in school, with occasional absent periods, he had tried to resume his old interests. The young intellectuals he had known in the Catholic societies of Brescia, older than he for the most part, had been no longer discussing such subjects as Modernism which had once engaged their intense interest; the subjects in favor were war provocation claims, the moral obligations involved in treaties, the airplane as a new and possibly ultimate weapon of war. When Italy entered the war, these young men disappeared one by one as they volunteered or were called to the colors. Battista Montini attended the farewell parties for several of them.

His call came early in 1916 after he finished a course of studies at Licio Arnaldo of Brescia. These supplemented the home and class study at Cesare Arici. His certificate was comparable to a high school graduate's diploma in the United States. He reported for his Army physical examination with Primo Savoldi whom he had known since childhood. Savoldi was accepted but Battista was rejected as physically unfit for service in the armed forces of Italy.

The Army verdict was not unexpected but once again Battista had been denied an opportunity of establishing a share for himself in the common experience of his time, of becoming a true contemporary with those in his own age group. After the first temporary depression had passed he faced the verdict as all of the training and discipline of his life had taught him to face verdicts: on his knees before the altar.

He had been rejected as a candidate for warfare. There had to be another role for which God had reserved him. He offered himself to that role.

One of Battista's firm friends in Verolavecchia was Luigi Benassi, a boy of his own age whom he had seen nearly every summer of his life. Luigi's maternal grandmother lived with the family. Her name was Maddalena Tagliani, who, at ninety-two, commanded this description from him:

"A grand, beautiful old lady, quite loquacious despite her age."

Maddalena liked boys. Battista had always been one of her favorites and he felt relaxed with her. That summer of 1916 he had dinner with the Benassi family a few days after he arrived in Verolavecchia. They were seated at a table under the trees. Although the daily war news was dreadful, the war itself seemed far away from this table.

"Battista, my Bigi wants to study to be a priest," Maddalena Tagliani said. "I am certain that he has told you of this but what is to be done for him? How can we manage? We cannot. I am beside myself."

Battista smiled at her. "Aren't you forgetting God, Grandmother Maddalena?" he said.

He walked later in the garden with Luigi. "You will be leaving soon for Brescia," he said. "Depend on it. We shall be classmates. I, too, am going to be a priest. Do not tell anyone. It is still a secret."

That night Battista walked with his father as he had walked with Luigi, two men in a fragrant garden with a half-moon above the shadowy Alps. Before the week had ended, Luigi Benassi had a letter from the Scholarship Fund, informing him that he had been chosen, all expenses paid, to study for the priesthood at the Seminary of Brescia.

Luigi Benassi, who is now the parish priest of Farfengo, did not learn until several years later that Giorgio Montini was president of the Fund which granted his scholarship.

Battista went quietly into the seminary that fall. The summer had been good to him. He had gained a little weight and he seemed to be in good health. He brought tremendous concentration to bear upon study, however, and his body would not support his will. He had to be dispensed from classroom work and permitted to cover the required studies at home with tutors, as he had done during part of his time at Cesare Arici. With the exception of a comparatively few months his entire seminary career was an invalid's study course, lacking in the companionship which most candidates for the priesthood find essential to their vocation.

During one of his active periods when he did attend classes, he served Mass for visiting priests. One morning he served Monsignor Andrea Morandini, chaplain of the 77th Italian Infantry, who horrified him by asking him to sing responses.

"I can't," he said. "I'm tone-deaf. I can't sing a note."

The Army chaplain laughed at him. "You'll have to learn. What will you do when you are a bishop?"

"I'll never be a bishop," Battista Montini said.

Once his attention had been directed to a lack in himself of which he had always been aware and which he had taken for granted, the young seminarian studied music. He was tone-deaf and nothing could be done about that but he could approach music intellectually, discover what it was and what it did and why people found inspiration and meaning and joy in it. He became, eventually, a lover of fine music, with his favorite composers, knowing that there were people who heard in it what he would never hear but happy in what it brought to him. That achievement, however, was not of a month or a year; it was a slow-growing.

To Giorgio Montini, the year 1917 brought his greatest honor. Benedict XV invited him to Rome and requested him to assume the presidency of the newly formed Electoral Union of Italian Catholics.

The post was both a culmination and a prelude. In accepting it, Giorgio Montini felt himself rewarded for many years of effort, much unpublicized drudgery, and particularly for his work since his retirement from editing in 1912; in accepting it, he knew, too, that the pope was planning to eliminate forever the *Non Expedit* which had driven Catholics to subterfuge and to awkward expedients in their efforts to be worthy citizens of their own country.

Giorgio Montini was one of the followers of Don Luigi Sturzo, a Sicilian priest of ancient and noble family. Devout, obedient to the Church but a realist, Father Sturzo had organized in 1912, with the help of the elder Montini and other politically minded Catholics, the Christian Democratic Party. It had been little better than a shadow party since too few bishops had taken advantage of the Pius X relaxation of voting prohibitions, but it had served to train leaders. The end of the war would see great changes in politics and it was time for Catholics to carry their share in the work to be done.

In preparation for the political tomorrow, Don Luigi Sturzo had organized Azione Cattolica, a central clearing house for Catholic organizations. When Giorgio Montini became president of the Electoral Union of Italian Catholics, Sturzo knew that the hour for which he had been waiting and working was about to strike, the hour when Italian Catholics would walk freely to the polls with the blessing of their Church. Thus would an anomaly be erased. In no other nation did the Church interfere with the voting or nonvoting of Catholics.

Benedict XV, having taken time for a purely Italian problem, moved on to the larger affairs of his pontificate. He had offered several peace feelers to the warring powers and he felt sanguine of success when, on April 23, 1917, he appointed one of his brilliant young diplomats, Eugenio Pacelli, Nuncio to Bavaria, entrusting him with a personal letter to Kaiser Wilhelm II of Germany. The mission failed but only because of an unfortunate combination of circumstances and not because of any short-coming on the part of the future Pius XII.

The following year when Russia collapsed and Poland tasted freedom for the first time in over a century, Benedict sent the librarian of the Vatican, Achille Ratti, a man without diplomatic experience, as Apostolic Visitor to Poland on March 1, 1918, and the future Pius XI acquitted himself with distinction.

Battista Montini, unknown even to most of his classmates,

studied the subjects which represent the soul, the mind, the body of the Church, and the ritual which is its raiment. The war ended and he knew that ending in terms of the disappointment and disillusionment in all conversations. One of the victorious Allies, Italy had fared badly in the opinion of Italians and there was little profit, less glory in the peace. Before the year was over, Benedict had signed the *Non Expedit* of Pius IX out of existence and Don Luigi Sturzo was ready. Partito Populare Italiano (the People's Party), known as "Populari" to the press, came into existence and Giorgio Montini was one of its founders. Battista who had grown up with his father's dream, hearing long hours of discussion on the Roman problem, celebrated this triumph with his family but he was already detached from what it represented.

On May 29, 1920, Giovanni Battista Montini was ordained by the Most Reverend Giocinto Gaggia in the Cathedral of Brescia. When he said his first Mass in Santa Maria della Grazie he wore a chasuble made from his mother's wedding dress. He brought the consecrated Host to her and to his father at the communion rail and he faced the familiar church, the friends, and the neighbors with his first blessing:

"May the Blessing of God Almighty, the Father, the Son and the Holy Ghost, descend upon you and remain with you forever."

6

AS THE ROMANS DO

D on Battista Montini entered the Lombard Seminary in
Rome on November 10, 1920. He registered for courses
at Gregorian University and at the University of Rome. The
career which lay open to him was not the one that he had
planned. In his dreams of ordination and a priestly career, he
had assumed that he would be assigned to a parish, but the
Bishop of Brescia, Monsignor Giacinto Gaggia decided that his
obvious talents, his high rating in seminary studies, and the
scholarly inclination of his mind were all signposts pointing in
the direction of Rome. He assigned his protégé to Monsignor
Ettore Barangini, rector of the Seminario Lombardo, with his
blessing.

The status of Don Battista was odd, as was that of other
student-priests in Rome. Priests they were, with priestly duties
and responsibilities, but they were students, too, under student
disciplines while they worked for various advanced degrees.
There were many houses which were classified according to nation or province. They were called colleges, universities, or seminaries, but were used actually as living quarters; the North
American College, the Irish College, the English College, the
Greek College, and scores of others. Religious orders and
societies, too, had their own houses, Jesuit, Dominican, Francis-
can, in which their men lived while assigned to studies. Priests,

and some unordained seminarians, met in classes at the Gregorian, the Propaganda, or any of a great number of colleges or academies with impressive names; as the College of Consistorial Advocates. It was a community apart within the great city of Rome but Battista Montini first saw Rome.

He saw it as a great wheel around the hub of St. Peter's. The basilica came first and he adjusted slowly to the perfect proportioning which makes the massive seem normal and right and in due relation to all else. The imagination and the eyes and the hands of genius had adorned these altars, these tombs, these aisles and crypts, the Vatican stairs and corridors. When Don Battista walked in St. Peter's or crossed the piazza to the streets of Rome, he was not a mere body in motion; he was mind and memory carrying uncounted books. He found the Romans in the ruins of their temples, their forums, their baths, and their circuses; the Middle Ages in churches and monasteries and convents, in stone and marble, in mosaic; the Renaissance in palazzo and piazza, in canvas and stone, fountains and the names of places. He walked Rome and there were no strangers anywhere. History lived for him and literature and Holy Faith. He encountered them around any corner he turned, down any street he walked.

Physically, Don Battista was more fit than he had been in years, walking long miles without tiring, sleeping deeply without the awakening cough. He fulfilled a priest's dream, standing humbly before an altar in the crypt, saying a Mass in St. Peter's.

His parents accompanied him to Rome and he had several days with them before he entered the Lombard Seminary. Giorgio Montini would be spending part of the year in Rome while the legislature was in session and it had not been decided whether Giuditta would take residence with him or remain in Brescia. The party which Giorgio Montini had helped to build on paper and then in reality over long voteless years, Partito Populare Italiano had done very well in the last election. Going to the polls for the first time after the lifting of *Non Expedit*, the Catholic Party had elected 101 deputies to 156 Socialists, and thirty War Veterans. Giorgio Montini had been one of those elected.

"We do not want to be the Catholic Party," he said. "We are what we have named ourselves. Catholics are free to join any party and we hope others will join us."

Don Luigi Sturzo was preaching the same doctrine. Catholics should bring their ideals to politics, but eschew exclusiveness. Pope Benedict XV having made it possible for Catholics to vote, had ignored the election. Giorgio Montini was hopeful of a new day in Italian politics, more equitable laws, a balance in legislation, greater victories for the Populari as the reward of service to their country.

"We must conduct ourselves well," he said. "We will be watched."

When his parents left, Don Battista settled into the task of learning a new way of life, of meeting and knowing Rome, of serving his priesthood. The Lombard Seminary in which he lived had been founded by St. Charles Borromeo who seemed to enter his life in hours of decision and of commitment. He found the favorite church of St. Charles, Santa Prassede, after walking the long street, Via Merulana which leads from St. John Lateran to Santa Maria Maggiore. It was built in 822 and there was much grumbling when the great Carlo Borromeo restored it in 1582. "A man of great piety and little taste," the critics said.

Priest-seminarians did not have much time for sight-seeing although they were encouraged to visit the different sections of the city. There were duties and devotions in their own houses and the study load was heavy. All subjects studied at the Gregorian, for example, were discussed with fellow students and with professors in Latin. Don Battista had, of course, studied Greek. He had also studied French and German. Spanish and English were still ahead of him. He had classes in philosophy and canon law at the Gregorian, and literature and languages at the University of Rome which had been founded by Boniface VIII in 1303 and which was housed in the Palazzo della Sapienza.

Students traveled in pairs and they wore long black cassocks. The wearing of the cassock was compulsory for priests and seminarians who never appeared in public unless so attired. For street wear, a soprano was added to the costume, a cape of heavy cloth. The hat was black, low of crown, and broad of brim. Seminarians of various degrees, during their first patrols in Rome, were interested in the distinctive variations of the common clerical garb which distinguished the different houses. The English wore three-cornered hats; Spaniards, cassocks of black and deep sky blue; Scots, purple cassocks and dark red sashes; Germans, flaming red cassocks; Americans, black cassocks with sky-blue piping. The most exotic "plumage," in clerical language, was worn by the Greeks: ultramarine cassocks with orange sashes.

The junior cleric's special vocabulary, the vernacular or slang of his calling, was colorful, shaded by humor, often shocking to the uninitiated in its play upon the semi-sacred and the half-holy. The Americans were the most artful in the creation of new words and terms in this borderline language, the Italians the least; in the making of Latin puns and the writing of limericks in Latin, the Italians were most gifted and the Americans the least. Eventually, the most interesting word play of any house circulated to the others, with the classrooms as centers of exchange. The clerics lived in a tight community behind invisible walls. The opera, the concert, the motion picture, all public entertainment, was strictly out of bounds for clergy of any rank in Rome, but their experience was unique in this world and each man contributed something which would make it forever memorable to others.

Don Battista brought no special gift to the community of clerics save his gift of listening. He gave rapt attention to anyone who had anything to say, his eyes intent, alive with interest. As a newcomer, little else was expected of him; certainly nothing original. The first Roman quality developed by anyone who had not been born a bore was the sponge quality of absorbing.

Benedict XV received the students from the Gregoriana in

audience. Don Battista Montini entered the papal quarters of the Vatican for the first time, met his first pope, kissed the ring of the fisherman.

The pope was sixty-six, not an advanced age for the successor of Leo XIII who lived to be ninety-three and Pius X who reached seventy-nine. But Benedict looked older in his frailty. The war years had not been kind to him and his postwar concerns were many. Despite all that had been said and written about Benedict XV, few people were prepared for his physical insignificance, the small bent body, the twisted spine. Don Battista and all other seminarians had heard the little anecdote from the conclave that elected Benedict and, seeing him, it was easy to credit.

In compliance with tradition, the Vatican tailor made three sets of vestments for the conclave which followed the death of Pius X. He was prepared to vest temporarily a large, small, or medium-sized pope, a heavy man or a thin one. The conclave elected Giacomo Cardinal della Chiesa and the tailor was aghast. He had nothing that would fit. The newly elected pope shook a thin finger at him.

"Carlo, Carlo," he said. "You forgot me."

That seemingly inadequate body had carried the indomitable will of Benedict through the horror of the First World War. Twice he had come close to achieving a peace short of the ultimate anarchy and, failing that, he had established the machinery for easing the lot of war prisoners on both sides, establishing communications with their families and arranging for the exchange of ill and badly wounded prisoners. He had impoverished the Vatican and given away all of his personal funds in caring for refugees and for the orphans of war, the children who were its saddest victims.

The peace treaty disturbed him greatly. He had been excluded from the making of it, although he had sought a just peace through all the years of conflict. The grave disorder at that gathering together of men for the avowed purpose of achieving peace and justice in the world was the absence of God. God had not been invited to the peace table, either, nor invoked. It did not surprise Benedict that the treaties were written in a spirit of continuing hatred and revenge, promising to the future only an increase in evil, not its abatement.

Facing Don Battista Montini and his companions, the Holy Father spoke of the missions, which were the great concern of his late years. The great powers, he told them, had taken the natives from mission countries and had made soldiers of them, sending them into action to kill Europeans whose faith they had accepted in the name of a gentle, forgiving Jesus. It was difficult to reach those native people again, difficult to explain the madness of war and the greater need for Christian compassion in the wake of it.

"You are learned young men," the pope said. "If God has not called you to the missions, be at one with those whom he has called. The missionary is a priest of more than ordinary learning. He is in his field without access to libraries and without access to the learned. He must carry a library in his head."

Whether Benedict was responsible or not, Don Battista became a stanch friend of the missions and of missionaries who, strangely, are not always sure of friends in high places. A short time before his talk to seminarians, Benedict had had two Irish priests in audience; Father Edward J. Galvin and Father John Blowick, who were seeking approval for the formation of an Irish missionary society to make converts in China (ultimately the Society of St. Columban). They were offering to tap the great reservoir of Irish vocations in behalf of the missions and Benedict XV was greatly interested in them, not only as missionaries but as symbols of unrest in the young clergy, a desire for difficult apostolic labor.

Don Battista, meeting his first pope, was standing in a low place and looking to the heights but he had one quality in common with the Holy Father. When Benedict XV had been merely Giacomo della Chiesa, he had aspired, too, to authorship and he had ventured into creative fields. When he was a student at the University of Genoa, he had written plays.

The hand of Benedict no longer wrote plays but it still wrote drama. In 1921, in line with his concern for the missions, he decided to reorganize the Sacred Congregation for the Propagation of the Faith and he brought to Rome from Bergamo a brilliant young monsignor named Angelo Roncalli.

In the secret knowledge of God, then, and not his own, the next four popes stood visibly in line under Benedict XV who had appointed them to their posts, or, in the case of Don Battista, approved the appointment. Pius XI (Achille Ratti) was Cardinal Archbiship of Milan. Pius XII (Eugenio Pacelli) was Papal Nuncio to Germany. John XXIII (Angelo Roncalli) was papal appointee to the Sacred Congregation. Paul VI (Giovanni Battista Montini) was a lowly cleric at the Lombard Seminary.

7

POLAND

THE years 1921 and 1922 were the great rich years of
Don Battista Montini's life. The study load at both the
Gregorian and the University of Rome was heavy but his health
seemed to improve as he carried it and he was able to assert
the rights of his priesthood while accepting his responsibilities
as a student. He said his daily Mass, alone at first, then for
the nuns or brothers of some religious house. He heard confessions in a parish church where a priest was ill or absent and
took over a meeting or a devotion occasionally as a substitute.

It wasn't enough. For Don Battista, it wasn't enough. He had
the flaming zeal of a young, newly ordained priest and no parish
of his own in which to exercise it. In his earnest belief, all of
the problems of the world, all the problems of Church and
State, had their beginnings in a single parish, any parish, wherever people were gathered together. He wanted to meet the
problems of the world on that level. He did not want sheltered
people; he wanted to minister to those whom life had wounded,
the bitter people, the passed-over people, the unfit.

He volunteered for service on his own time in the poor sections where priests might need help. "In those sections, they
always need help," he was told.

Don Battista went among the migrant workers who lived in
tents or huts on the city's edge and he went to the section that

had always been poor, the Trastevere. He helped the workers of St. Vincent de Paul in the wretched squalor of Porta Metronia. He was inexperienced, he had missed even ordinary seminary give-and-take through illness but he did not flinch in the face of insult and of hostility that verged on hatred. He walked into tough and brutal neighborhoods, neighborhoods which he had been told were heavily Communist, and he talked to men who called him vile names. He did not admonish them nor tell them that they should be in church; he asked them why they were Communists. He exerted a special effort to reach the young.

It shocked the young priest that there were young boys in their teens, Romans, born virtually in the shadow of St. Peter's, who had never entered the world's most famous basilica. He talked to them about their heritage and he planned a series of tours to St. Peter's, leading groups of boys from the poor and underprivileged areas.

On his first tour, his boys were out of control and many of them out of sight before he was fairly launched on his carefully prepared lecture. Two of them were arrested for annoying one of the Swiss guards and Don Battista discovered the depths of his own unimportance, and his own lack of influence, when he tried to have the boys released. It took him all of a day to accomplish it and two severe admonishments from superiors.

The defeats and the inadequacies, the confessions of the faithful and the complaints of those who had no faith were an education beyond the books, beyond the farthest library wall. Don Battista matured physically and emotionally, making a slight gain in weight despite a heavy loss of sleep. He was on easier man-to-man terms with his father who spent much of his time now in Rome. When they could find time to spend together, Battista enjoyed discussing problems and politics with him.

Giorgio Montini had won re-election as deputy to the legislature from Brescia but he was worried. The Populari although still strong had lost ground and there was a new party in contention, known as Partito Nazionale Fascista, soon to be known merely as "Fascist."

"They claim to be the opposite pole from the Communists," the elder Montini said, "but they resemble them more than they differ from them. It is meaningless to be opposed to Communists. One must have a different faith, different methods."

On January 22, 1922, Benedict XV, the oddly made, irascible, quick-tempered, strangely lovable pope, died.

Don Battista became part of the ceremonial majesty of the Church in mourning, a humble, inconsequential cleric for whom no place of honor or distinction had been reserved, but one of the inheritors, through Holy Orders, of the ritual; whether for the living or the dead. He walked past the bier of the Holy Father whom he had met in audience and he watched Princes of the Church file slowly into the great basilica. The bishops and the lesser clergy followed the cardinals, and the noble families and men in the uniforms of vanished centuries. There was solemnity, but to a young man there was electric excitement, too.

There was speculation on the identity of the new pope. The newspapers of Rome carried learned analyses and the young clerics dismissed them airily in favor of their own profound and deeply reasoned guesswork. Pietro Cardinal Gasparri was the heavily backed favorite with Peter Cardinal La Fontaine granted a chance, but the sentimental favorite was Rafael Cardinal Merry del Val, who, reputedly, had come within a few votes of election in 1914.

The Lombard house had its own cardinal in residence but he was new to the College of Cardinals and not considered among the papabili. Achille Cardinal Ratti had, however, a three-way link to the Lombardians. He had been born in Desio, a suburb of Milan. He was an alumnus of the house. He was Archbishop of Milan. He came in quietly after the death of Benedict XV and he lived at the house during the period of mourning; a stocky, athletic man who wore thick-lensed eyeglasses, a grave, courteous, reserved man with a slow smile. He took the students for granted, as the proper people in their proper place, and they accepted this from him as the proper attitude; familiarity to or from a cardinal would be uncomfortable.

There was a reception for Cardinal Ratti at the house on the night before the sealing-in for the conclave. He was invited to dinner with friends after the reception and the friends presented him with a white bouquet, symbolic of their hope that, by some miracle, he would be chosen pope. Cardinal Ratti brought the bouquet back with him to the Lombard house and placed it on the altar of the Blessed Virgin.

When Don Battista saw him again, Achille Cardinal Ratti was Pius XI and he was bestowing his blessing from the outer balcony of St. Peter's; *urbi et orbi* (to the city and to the world).

That benediction was a historical event. No pope had faced outward with a blessing in more than fifty years. In blessing the city in which the Italian government dwelt, Pius XI had cut with that upraised hand a dark and dingy curtain of hatred and distrust. He signified in that blessing his devout wish that the curtains which divide men would come down. He was still, by inheritance, "Prisoner of the Vatican" and the Roman Question was still unanswered, but Benedict XV had erased *Non Expedit*; Pius XI was willing to take one more step.

Life in Rome picked up as it seemed always to do when there was a new pope. People painted houses and invested in new wardrobes. Times were hard in Italy with widespread unemployment but there was a feeling of expectancy in press and politics, a feeling of a new beginning. Much of the feeling of a change for the better was unjustified, a mere psychological lift, but the forces of change moved decisively for Don Battista. After reports on student work for the year were posted in June, he received a summons from Monsignor Giuseppe Pizzardo.

"You belong in diplomacy," Monsignor Pizzardo said bluntly. "You have the mind for it. I am recommending you to the Accademia dei Nobili Ecclesiastici."

The Noble Ecclesiastics represented a high point in the clerical circles of Rome, a school of diplomacy restricted to carefully chosen men and to many of the clerics it was a remote point in which they had no interest. Don Battista was not convinced that he wanted what it represented, a career in Vatican diplomacy, a career in the Curia. He offered the objection that he had not finished his studies in literature at the University of Rome, nor in Canon Law at the Greg. Monsignor Pizzardo waved the objection away.

"A degree or two! What difference do they make, degrees? Let them go! The Church needs certain qualities in certain places. God provides those qualities in certain people. You have the mind of a diplomat."

There was no more to be said after that. Don Battista Montini entered the Academy of the Noble Ecclesiastics in the fall of 1922. When he did so, he fell into step behind a procession that was over two and one-half centuries long.

Other men were on the march, too, that year, men who knew nothing of subtle diplomacy, whose methods were direct, violent, and crudely effective. The Fascists became a political party and, almost immediately afterward, an armed mob, breaking the general strike of August 1922. In October they marched on Rome and Benito Mussolini became premier. In November, he assumed full powers and put Italy under a dictatorship.

It was difficult for thoughtful young men, studying how their civilization had come to be, how their culture had developed, to understand how the Fascist takeover happened, how a free people permitted it to happen. They had faith, however, in their own destinies. There had always been violence and crude power in the world under one identifying label or another, and there had always been a need for diplomats; for heirs to the riches of the great minds of the past, men of poise and of detachment, men who spoke the languages of other men fluently and who took understanding of people from the study of their speech.

In May 1923, Don Battista went to Warsaw.

The appointment came on short notice. He was to act as secretary to the Apostolic Nuncio, Archbishop Lorenzo Lauri and his assistant, Monsignor Carlo Chiarlo. Don Battista was twenty-six, the youngest diplomat of the Church on active mission outside of Rome.

Warsaw was still bearing the scars of war and for Poland the war had never ended. The Treaty of Versailles had established highly unrealistic boundaries in re-establishing Poland as a nation and the people on those borders, Germans, Lithuanians, and Russians, did not submit to arbitrary assignment without conflict. Internally, the situation was similar. Nearly one-third of the people included within map lines drawn at the treaty table were non-Polish in speech, race, and culture. Earnest, patriotic Poles, living in the fulfilled dream of freedom from the domination of foreign powers, were contending with overwhelming difficulties in trying to hold the Polish republic together; not the least of which was the fact of Communist-oriented men in key positions.

Achille Ratti, now His Holiness Pius XI, had created an enduring legend in Warsaw and one had to go to Poland to hear it. The Bolsheviks invaded Poland during his tenure as Apostolic Nuncio. At the beginning of August 1920 their invading army was on the banks of the Vistula, practically at the gates of Warsaw, and all of the diplomats fled, save Archbishop Ratti. He was the only accredited diplomat left in the city and he walked the streets nonchalantly, showing no fear in a time of terror. He offered high Mass in the cathedral, but he neither exhorted nor assured; he merely prayed with the people and left the rest to God. Unaccountably, the Bolshevik advance bogged down where it was, within sight of the city and the crisis which lasted ten days was over when the French and Poles under General Maxime Weygand counterattacked, routing an enemy which had seemed invincible until then. There was a Te Deum sung in the cathedral and the people talked of the Miracle of the Vistula.

That is how the story was told to Archbishop Lauri, Monsignor Chiarlo, and Don Battista Montini. It was told with an odd pride in the telling which made Pius XI, in a sense, the son of Warsaw, Poland's pope.

Don Battista liked the Poles and he studied their language

with intense concentration. He was working in close contact with an archbishop and he was behind the curtain of events. Communism was a real threat, a daily reality, and the Church through its representatives was acting in behalf of its own people. It was a rewarding experience, this being one of those representatives. Don Battista celebrated Mass in strange foreign churches. He indulged a hobby he had developed when he came to Rome, the searching out of postal cards for his friends, cards that would be treasured later for that simple signature: *"Don Battista."*

At the end of six weeks, his conquered cough returned. He fought it doggedly through the summer but in the fall it defeated him. He was forced to take to his bed and a Polish doctor advised that he be sent home.

It was one of the abysmally low points of a career which was pitted with them. He had put health problems behind him and he had moved out on the firing line of the Apostolic Church, and now he was back again with his big diplomatic opportunity behind him. He had lasted little more than six months.

8

THE WAY OF ST. PAUL

THERE were people who ascribed to Rome one of the worst climates in the world; Don Battista Montini was not one of them. Rome restored him and reassured him. He regained his health and his sense of well-being when he returned to it. He had lost an opportunity in the foreign service and there was no recovering that, but there were tangible gains apart from the postcards he had collected. He continued to study the Polish language and he resumed work in the State Department of the Church.

He had been deposited gently at the foot of the ladder and the work assigned to him took no account of his experience in Poland. He was ranked as *apprendista* and assigned to a clerical cubicle in the Vatican, beyond the area of magnificent corridors, staircases, and apartments, a tiny room with shabby furniture and dull walls. It was one of a number of similar cells and he punched a time clock when he climbed the stairs to it and when he left.

This was the Roman Curia, one facet of it. He was a unit in the institution. It was not a popular institution. People damned it without knowing anything about it. When Don Battista entered it in 1923 the popular term for unwieldly bureaucratic processes was "red tape." Reputedly, the Curia strung miles of it around even the simplest affair. The Curia was obstructionist, too, according to its critics, and conservative, indifferent to objectives, and interested only in methods, living in a maze of filing cases, rubber stamps, and wastebaskets. The wastebaskets, it was darkly hinted, existed for the sole purpose of receiving reasonable requests and intelligent suggestions sent in by priests and bishops of the working Church.

To Don Battista in those early days, the Curia was a cubicle with leprous walls to which any dull and unimaginative job came when it was spurned in more highly ranked and elegant places. He read the dullest of the reports which were delivered to the Vatican and made digests of them for superiors who were thus spared much dreary reading. He answered the least interesting, innocuous mail and he performed any other task that required a minimum of intelligence. He was not justifying the time spent at Accademia dei Nobili Ecclesiastici in the work that he did, but someone had to read those reports and write those letters. That was the whole point of any Curia discussion.

The Roman Catholic Church sent men and women to teach all nations in the name of Jesus Christ and at His expressed command. Those men and women, priests, nuns, and laymen, were in cities and towns and country places, in jungles and deserts and low rice-paddy regions, in populous, highly civilized, ancient countries, and in new and dangerous nations. They were all held together by chains of command which stretched back to Bishops and archbishops and ultimately to the Holy Father. Those chains of command were also chains of need and want and necessity, sometimes of desperation. By the nature of the Church, established in vast areas of earth and speaking in many tongues, there had to be paperwork. There had to be bookkeeping, recordkeeping, archives.

The archives contained the files of ten centuries and there were items dating to the third century. Someone had to care for those precious letters and manuscripts. When new filing cabinets or typewriters or index cards were needed, there had to be someone who kept catalogs of such things and who knew where to buy them, and how much they cost; a purchasing department. If someone wrote a letter to the pope in Arabic or Urgandese or Nigerian or Hindustani, there had to be someone around who could translate it, and answer it.

All of that added up to bureaucracy and it was only a small part of the work which engaged approximately 2500 people in twelve congregations, three tribunals, and five offices. It annoyed many people in the Church that all of these people, most of them clerics, were in Rome and working in their hives and ant heaps so diligently that they had to be crisp and businesslike and stereotyped, sounding in correspondence like dehumanized machines. The whole papal establishment under the pope seemed cold and indifferent, hence full of its own self-importance, and there was always someone of high rank and higher dudgeon insisting upon a Curia reform, overhaul, refurbish, and massive shakeup.

Younc clerics such as Don Battista had, actually, very little sense of their own importance. Neither surroundings, condition of servitude, nor income contributed anything to false pride. A plebiscite among Vatican inhabitants would result in an overwhelming vote for more people rather than for less.

There were Curia cardinals in command positions, of course, who lacked tact and others who were known as crafty or belligerent. A man fought with the weapons that he had in order to hold what was his. A bishop or a cardinal, already straining to meet demands from outside and inside Rome, could not be expected to accept submissively a suggestion that he reduce a staff already overtaxed. The Curia was a professional operation and the professionals shuddered when amateurs, in their happy ignorance, proposed change in procedure without understanding what they proposed. This resistance to innovation and to change was classified impatiently as hidebound or conservative and the pastors of procedure knew it, classifying the classifiers in turn as progressive only in their itch to change the color of the grass in another man's domain to their own peculiar shade of green. The differences could not be expressed in the political terms of right and left, however, and, although it would be an exaggeration to say that all of the hierarchy loved one another, neither were they at one another's throats.

Don Battista and his contemporaries in the uncarpeted cells were content with Webster's dictionary definition of their condition in life: "Curia Romana: The body of congregations, tribunals, and offices through which the Pope governs the Roman Catholic Church." It was very simple when you put it that way. Each one of them was a cell in that body, and he hoped that he was a brain cell. The work that each man did, the humblest man, was work that came to the Holy Father and that he, as one man, could not handle in addition to all else demanded of him. Each man contributed then a living something in word, deed, or decision to the mind of the Church, helping to shape it perhaps in infinitesimal degree, being shaped greatly in turn by that which he shaped. Since they were not solidly Italian, these Curia creatures, but French, German, Belgian, American, many nationalities, it might not be an exaggeration to say that when they all added up to the working mind of the Church, that mind was properly catholic in the universal sense.

Inside the Vatican, or outside, the bureaucrats in the Roman collars were priests. They sought pastorates, however limited or temporary those pastorates might be.

Don Battista Montini became assistant chaplain for C.U.C.R. (Circolo Universitario Cattolico Romano) a club for Roman Catholic university students, at the University of Rome similar in plan to the Newman Club of the United States. It was work to be handled in his own time, apart from his position at the Vatican. The chaplain was Monsignor Amleto Giovanni Cicognani, the younger brother of Archbishop Gaetano Cicognani, Papal Nuncio to Bolivia, who would, theoretically, work with the older students and those engaged in postgraduate work while Don Battista worked with the younger men; actually, as they both knew in advance, there would be much overlapping and a need for close teamwork.

The long years of conflict between the government of Italy and the papacy had weakened the Catholic roots of young people who still considered themselves Catholics and had left them with little defense against the intense Fascist drive to control young minds. They had to be reinforced in knowledge of their own faith and they had to be taught how to pray if they were to survive. The Holy Father was concerned for them and he had expressed that concern to those around him. Any project which would extend a helping hand to them or provide a means of attaching them firmly to the Church would be a project close to his heart.

Don Battista was fortunate in his assignment to the University of Rome and fortunate in the opportunity of working with Monsignor Cicognani who had acquired much wisdom in his forty-one years without losing his own youthful spirit. From the outset the two priests worked well together.

There was the problem of a meeting place. It had to be convenient for the students yet suggest a departure from the secular environment. The University of Rome at that time was housed in the Sapienza Palace which had been built under the direction of Borromini in 1557. It had a beautiful courtyard with a loggia on three sides and on the fourth side, at the back of the court, there was an old church which had fallen into disuse and which served only as storage space. The member of the faculty responsible for it was Dr. Del Vechio, a Jew. He consented immediately to its reconversion into a church when he learned that students wanted a place for the discussion of religion and the worship of God. He was not a lover of Fascism.

"You plan a good use of this building," he said, "and you will disturb only some old maps."

There were maps, certainly, to be disturbed, thousands of them, and many other odds and ends which were covered with dust, but the students cheerfully undertook the moving and cleaning. Don Battista spent every minute that he could spare, working with them in the common task before he faced them as a priest. The mutual friendship and respect engendered made it easier for priest and students to work in other less tangible fields when the task was completed. Don Battista's interest in the priest-worker movement later in his career may have grown from seeds planted at the University of Rome where he was, for a time, a priest-worker himself.

The ancient Church of St. Ivo emerged from the dust and the old maps, a church of blind arches and convex curves, of a small dome making spirals out of light. The sophisticate in Church lore could find its odd dimensions, a geometrical figure of two interwoven triangles, suggestive of a bee; hence to be identified with Pope Urban VIII of the house of Barberini. Few of the young men who came to meetings of C.U.C.R. were interested in hidden symbols or in esoteric architecture: they were seekers of they-knew-not-what. Many of them were half-convinced that the Fascists were right, that there was, at least, an honest doubt about the existence of God.

That doubt, subtly or bluntly planted, was the enemy which Don Battista faced in this, his first real pastorate, and it was the enemy which terrified many of these young people who were reaching once more for aid before letting go. For these, the young people with the greatest need, C.U.C.R. did not in Don Battista's judgment, offer enough. Evening meetings and a Sunday Mass, no matter how carefully the sermon was prepared, did not provide sufficient close contact between priest and doubter. Fascism created massive moods which swept people out of their own reality into a psychological whirlpool in which everything spun and in which there was no individual orientation, no personal stability. There had to be a powerful force exerted in order to rescue young people from such a maelstrom, a force such as no single priest could hope to generate in an hour, or in a series of spaced hours. Don Battista discussed the problem with Monsignor Cicognani. The older man looked into space for a few moments.

"How about weekend retreats?" he said.

Don Battista organized the weekend retreats. Since the semi-fallen-away and the doubters and the spiritually illiterate had inspired the idea, he carefully handpicked his first group. He took them on the long streetcar ride to San Paolo fuori le Mura (St. Paul's Outside-the-Walls) and they met the Benedictine abbot, Alfredo Ildefonso Schuster, O.S.B., tall and lean, the ideal model for what he was. The body of St. Paul was here. The spot where he was martyred, marked by the Cistercian Abbey and the churches of Tre Fontane, was only a trifle over a mile away.

The retreat lasted through the weekend, two clock days, in which the rhythm was set to the rule of St. Benedict and the sermons preached in the idiom of St. Paul. Don Battista followed every hour and observed every rule with his boys of C.U.C.R. He walked in the evening, in the silence of the cloister, reading his Office, and this was an experience that he was never to forget; St. Paul speaking across the centuries in this holy place where his earthly body had lived and died.

9

FUCI

THE decade of the 1920s in the United States earned many adjectives from its historians and its novelists, lurid and melodramatic adjectives, on the whole, as befitted the times they were used to describe. There were poor people and simple people living unglamourously in that era of quick riches and of glamour but the spotlight of attention did not seek them.

In Italy the decade of the 1920s was the decade of Fascism. Benito Mussolini, Il Duce, reigned and ruled although the King existed as a ceremonial adornment to government. Young people belonged to youth organizations and wore uniforms; or accepting a certain drab quality in a lively martial era as an act of faith, wore ordinary civilian clothes. The uniform "haves" habitually attacked or harassed the "have-nots." The cities of Italy, and particularly Rome, experienced a face-lifting, a rejuvenation. The fiat of the dictator removed in one breath an old castle, a block of houses, any obstruction to a desired new boulevard or a monument to dictatorship. In the old days of government by the people, improvements were the subjects of endless debates and the destruction or removal of old things a slow process obstructed by legalism; now the city was renewed overnight. A dictator did not waste time on argument; he did what had to be done. The half-million unemployed of pre-Fascism had been reduced to a negligible few, the red-ink spattered railroads were making money now and running trains on time. Italy was great and would grow greater. There was bread and there were circuses and luxury abounded for those who could appreciate luxury and who would acknowledge the lavish hand which spread it o'er the land.

It was a bright new world in the mid-1920s. Germany, of course, was suffering from the effects of ruinous inflation which had wiped out savings, ruined business and industry, caused frightening unemployment. Russia was recovering slowly from famine and civil war, experiencing power convulsions at the head of the Soviet government. No one in the fortunate nations worried about such gloomy neighbors.

Pope Pius XI proclaimed 1925 a Holy Year and the Fascist government of Italy turned a benign smile upon religion and the ancient Catholic faith. Roman Catholicism was really a charming old institution which had built delightful churches all over Italy. The government of Italy would do everything possible to make a visit to Italy in the Holy Year memorable for any tourist. The prayers of the pilgrims would ascend from the shrines and the dollars, francs, or pounds-sterling would descend into the Italian economy, and everyone would be happy.

The Fascist gift of dissembling which produced pious expressions for world-wide visitors to the Holy Year observances concealed the real field of battle between Church and State. Dictatorship could afford to permit ceremony and worship, open churches and free speech up to a point; provided that dictatorship had control of education and power over the minds of youth. This generation would pass and the next generation, thinking thoughts which would rise no higher than their sources of information, would not cause any trouble.

The long delayed, gallant Catholic foray into politics, in the meanwhile, had proved to be of short duration. Giorgio Montini was re-elected to parliament in 1924 for his third term but the election was a personal tribute, no more. There was no longer work for a legislator to do, none that he would be permitted to do, and the Populari had been outlawed with other parties

ANSA

[1] Giorgio Montini
Pope Paul's father

[2] Giuditta Alghisi Montini
Pope Paul's mother

Wide World Photos, Inc.

UPI

[3] Francesca Buffali, Pope Paul's grandmother, holding the future pope in her arms.
His brother, Ludovico, is at the right.

[4] Giovanni Battista Montini at
the age of eight with his brothers
Francesco (left) now a doctor
and Ludovico now a lawyer.

[5] These natives of Concesio are pointing to the shuttered window of the room in which Pope Paul VI was born.

[6] Baptismal font in the Church of San Antonio where Battista was baptized.

[8] Battista's report card for the term 1909–10 at the Collegio Cesare Arici. The highest possible grade in any subject is 10.

[7] Collegio Cesare Arici in Brescia where Battista studied as a youth.

[9] A rare family portrait taken in 1922. Front row, left to right; Don Bonfadelli, Giorgio Montini, Teresa Alghisi (cousin of Giuditta), Giuditta Montini. Standing, left to right; Ludovico Montini, Francesco Montini, Giovanni Battista Montini. Woman standing and gentleman seated at right unknown.

[10] Father Montini in 1920, the year he was ordained.

[11] Msgr. Montini at the time he was serving in the Vatican's Secretariat of State.

[12] Msgr. Montini and Msgr. Domenico Tardini confer on a diplomatic matter.

[13] Msgr. Montini at the signing of an accord between the Holy See and Poland in 1939. Seated, left to right; John Szenbek, Polish Undersecretary of State, Cardinal Maglione, Papal Secretary of State, Stanislaus Janikowki, Polish Ambassador. Standing, left to right; Msgr. Meysztowicz, Ecclesiastical Counsel at Polish Embassy, Msgr. Domenico Tardini, Secretary for Extraordinary Affairs, and Msgr. Montini, Undersecretary of State.

[14] Msgr. Montini with Pope Pius XII.

[15] Cardinal Montini with Pope John XXIII in the Vatican in December 1958 immediately after His Holiness had named the then Archbishop of Milan a cardinal.

[16] Archbishop Montini kisses the soil of his new diocese on his arrival in Milan in 1955.

[17] The office of Archbishop Montini in Milan in 1956 after a bomb had been thrown into it by an unknown terrorist.

[18] Archbishop Montini carries a cross in a procession in Milan in sympathy for the Hungarian Freedom Fighters killed in the Hungarian uprising in 1956.

[19] Archbishop Montini wears a cycling cap at a bicycle racing meet.

[20] The Archbishop of Milan visits the coal miners of his archdiocese.

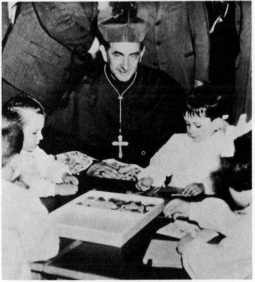

[21] The Archbishop of Milan visits with workers' children at a factory nursery in Milan.

[22] Cardinal Montini attends an official reception accorded Queen Elizabeth of England and Prince Philip by city officials on Her Majesty's visit to Milan in 1961.

[23] Cardinal Montini at the 115th annual commencement of the University of Notre Dame in 1960. The cardinal and President Dwight D. Eisenhower received honorary degrees. Very Rev. Christopher J. O'Toole C.S.C., superior-general of the Congregation of Holy Cross is walking behind the cardinal and Father Theodore M. Hesburgh C.S.C., president of the university is at the far right.

opposed to Fascism. Don Luigi Sturzo, creator of the party and co-ordinator of Catholic Action went into exile in England, with the permission of his bishop, after several serious threats of assassination.

"In 1919, I was elected to the House," Giorgio Montini wrote, "and there I remained, without blame and without praise, for three Legislatures."

It was Giorgio Montini's farewell to politics and his modest political epitaph. He was not, however, silenced. He had retained an interest in *Cittadino di Brescia* after his resignation as director and he returned now to his typewriter after a long lapse. He was fighting once more for the cause he had served years ago when the enemy was different in name and method but alike in purpose. The Fascists, like the radical group of his youth, wanted control of education and of the young.

Don Battista Montini was enlisted in the same cause that his father served. His work with the C.U.C.R., at the University of Rome was definitely counter to the Fascist youth aims. He was not only conducting an active apostolate with his group, he was writing articles for the national publication of the organization which included it: Federazione Universitaria Cattolica Italiana (Federation of Catholic University Students), better known by its initials—FUCI.

Don Battista had a warm feeling of personal friendship with the boys and young men who came to him at St. Ivo's. They tested, challenged, and fulfilled his priesthood through the spiritual need which they brought to him and they gave him in return the boyhood and the youth he had missed in his growing. He learned from them the special language, the camaraderie, the jocular attitudes of youth which he had never learned firsthand. Older than they were, he could still be one of them because he was discovering life on their terms. His students sensed that and liked him for the indefinable quality which he had and which was, perhaps, themselves reflected.

There was a spring outing of the Catholic University group at Ostia beside the sea. Don Battista was invited and he acted as referee or umpire for the games. After judging several races, he suddenly entered one, tucking his cassock into his belt and racing with long legs and surprising speed. When he came through the tape first, he laughed; then, as though he enjoyed the sensation of laughing, he threw himself down on the ground and continued to laugh.

It was a startling experience for his students who had never heard him laugh before. They heard him again that day when he joined them, sockless, with his trouser legs rolled up and his cassock in his belt once more, running in the water along the beach where the tide was rolling in.

"He acts as though he'd just discovered wading," one of the young men said.

It probably was exactly that; a discovery to Don Battista. Certainly the sharing of acts and deeds performed for no solid or useful purpose was new to Don Battista. Humor, too, the jests and exchanges, insulting terms used as friendly greetings, baffled him. He had no humor. As with music, however, he was capable of recognizing a deficiency in himself, a lack, the absence of something with which others were endowed. He watched and noted and studied the words, turns of expression, attitudes and actions which others found amusing. Ultimately he reached the point where he could anticipate the amusement of others in a given situation and, anticipating it, share it. It was not a sense of humor, nor even that lesser gift which so many possess, a sense of comedy; but it was a unique quality of his own, one which people were to find mystifying, a quality gained through patience and earnestness and effort, as were most things in the life of Don Battista Montini.

The two lives of the young priest moved in parallel, not meeting or touching except in his personality. At the Vatican, he advanced to the rank of Minutante. His new working cell was slightly larger than the old one and the walls were white. He had an extra table on which the in and the out work was deposited. The work which came to him was more interesting, with some editing and writing added to the other run-of-the-day assignments.

Under the heady spell of advancement, Don Battista moved from a room or apartment on Via Aurelia, which no one has described, to obviously more luxurious quarters on Aventine Hill which a friend described as "small, mean lodgings." He continued to live on the Aventine after he received the papal communication appointing him a domestic prelate with the title of Monsignor. He bought a violet cassock and montelleto which looked very well on him.

A second communication from Pope Pius XI named Monsignor Montini National Moderator of the Italian Federation of Catholic Students (FUCI). It was, on a national scale, the same task that had challenged him and absorbed him at the University of Rome, but on that national scale, the task called for a different approach. Monsignor Dominic Pini, his predecessor, had been a human dynamo type; hearty, outgiving, extrovert, a man of tremendous energy who sent a wave of that energy ahead of him when he entered a room. Monsignor Montini could not do that but he had the gift of eloquence, little challenged until now. He faced his first audience of Catholic youth and Catholic youth leaders in Italy's oldest university at Bologna, where Petrarch and Copernicus had studied, and his deep conviction, his enthusiasm for the work of Catholic Action powered his words. The introvert, still shy and diffident when not called out of himself, stirred his audience so deeply that he was besieged for personal interviews and group meetings afterwards.

One of his auditors, Padre Bevilacqua, wrote of the new director of FUCI: "He spoke to the young with his faith nourished by the riches of the gospel and the liturgy, addressing himself to the whole of the human condition. Because Don Battista loves the creative spirit of man under all of its aspects, art, thought, culture, science, technology, he saw everything through the eyes of the young, following them into each new undertaking with undiminished freshness and imagination."

The whole of the human condition to which the young monsignor addressed himself was poverty of material goods and poverty of the soul, ignorance of one's cultural inheritance and ignorance of one's spiritual inheritance, honor, and distinction in time, honor and distinction in eternity. Whenever a human good existed he looked at it from the aspect of its service to man and the aspect of its service to God. Under his direction, the FUCI chapters in the various cities and towns became study groups for Catholic young people who trained to be leaders in their communities, challengers of those who brought false accusations against the Church; as co-operators with the Societies of St. Vincent de Paul they went among the poor and the ill; they obeyed their government, served where they were called upon to serve but insisted upon God's prior claim and upon their right to serve Him. Theirs was a lay apostolate in formation, seeking ways in which to function as the lay arm of the clergy.

One of Monsignor Montini's essentials to a successful FUCI program anywhere was the retreat. He insisted that members should make one weekend retreat a year and he offered as a model the retreat pattern still followed in Rome at the Benedictine Abbey of San Paolo fuori le Mura. Abbot Alfredo Ildefonso Schuster was one of the men upon whom he drew for inspiration and for advice. His superior, Monsignor Cicognani was also a sound advisor and guide, as was Monsignor Giuseppe Pizzardo who had first suggested Montini's name when the post of National FUCI Moderator was open. The young monsignor was prescient in his advisers; they were three future cardinals.

The 1926 Congress of FUCI was planned for Macerata, a charming mountain town, with a seventeenth-century Church of St. Paul, and a nineteeth-century university built around the original of 1543. A Fascist Youth Organization, however, was strongly entrenched in Macerata. There had been many violent clashes between the two groups, FUCI and Fascist, in various sections of the country throughout the year. The Fascists threatened to summon a conclave of their own in Macerata if the Catholics came there so Monsignor Montini decided reluctantly, and against much argument by the membership, to change the convention base to Assisi. FUCI had not been organized for fighting and while violence was avoidable, he would avoid it.

"If today we cannot go with unfurled banners," he said, "let us work in silence."

It was a foretaste of the underground.

10

***

THE ROUGH AND THE SMOOTH

IGINIO RIGHETTI, a professor, was national president of FUCI and the Rome section operated under various leaders, including Ciro O. Scotti and Ugo Piazza, two future doctors. FUCI was a lay organization, existing to provide a forum for young people who wanted to study their faith and to associate with other young Catholics in cultural activities and charitable enterprises. It was not political in purpose or aim or, under fascism, even in potential; but it did hold promise of apostolic activity. In many situations, laymen could wield influence with other laymen, or young people with young people, where a priest could not. They were not proselyters so much as they were guardians of the faith, helping others to hold on when the totalitarian flood threatened to sweep them away.

Monsignor Montini as National Moderator was adviser, chaplain, and guide, but FUCI made its own rules, elected its own officers. Don Battista had not been able to resist the opportunity of starting a magazine, or naming the one he started, or becoming the star contributor. The FUCI magazine was named *Studium* and the letters which came to the editor from readers provided contact with members outside of Rome, throughout Italy. Monsignor Montini answered every letter personally. There were, too, the visitations which he inaugurated. He, Iginio Righetti, and other members who could afford the time traveled to nearby towns and cities to meet with FUCI chapters and give them moral support.

Monsignor Montini assumed the pastorate of the Rome group when Monsignor Cicognani was assigned to the intricate and demanding assignment of codifying Oriental canon law. Monsignor Geremia Pacchiani became assistant. "When we were having conventions or visitations," he says, "it was my responsibility to go around to the Vatican and drag out Montini. It was always a big problem because someone always had extra work for him to do and they were reluctant to let him go. Also, of course, we did have a reputation for attracting trouble. We didn't seek it but when we walked in groups on Rome streets or visited other places, the Fascists called us names and ran along behind us, kicking us."

One of the most dramatic incidents occurred at Macerata, the town from which the convention had been moved to Assisi. Monsignor Montini and his group visited there to encourage the local FUCI who were low in morale.

"We Fucini were in danger immediately," Monsignor Pacchiani says. "The police did not want anything serious to happen so they tried to protect us. We came to the meeting place like a column of prisoners between two rows of carabineri [police]. Montini and Righetti were in the lead. The Fascists were hidden behind bushes near the church and they leaped out with clubs in their hands. There were too many of them. The police could not handle them and we couldn't do much, either, but we fought back before they scattered us."

That week the Holy Father granted his annual audience to the members of FUCI and as he moved around, talking to various groups, he stopped before Ugo Galli who had his head bandaged.

"What happened to you?" he asked bluntly.

Galli, now a dentist in Rome, was disconcerted, very self-conscious in the presence of the pope. "It is an incident," he said, "an incident that happened at Macerata."

Pope Pius XI turned to Monsignor Montini. "What was this incident?" he asked.

There was no avoiding of an answer although up to this point, FUCI had prided itself on handling its own problems, not involving any other organization, or outside individual, in group problems. Monsignor Montini summed up briefly the running feud between Fascist and Catholic youth. The Holy Father turned to Monsignor Pizzardo, Substitute Secretary of State, who was the guiding spirit behind Catholic Action.

"Why are these things not told to me?" he asked.

"Your Holiness shall have a report," Monsignor Pizzardo said.

Monsignor Montini did not see the report and he did not know what action was taken by Pius XI but the police were more diligent after that about breaking up groups of troublemakers and Fascist youth in uniform ignored the existence of the Fucini.

Another problem came to take the place of one that was lost. There were Catholic young women at Rome University who wanted to identify with FUCI and who advanced the reasonable argument that their problems were similar to those of the young men since there were Fascist organizations of women and their objectives were the same since they were trying to maintain the faith under difficulties. Monsignor Montini was not sympathetic with the idea that they should be admitted to meetings and other activities and he did not have the time to take care of two separate organizations. The girls organized without encouragement, called themselves FUCINA and came to meetings.

Monsignor Montini told Iginio Righetti that this was his problem as president, or the problem of the president and other officers, not the chaplain's problem. Iginio shook his head sadly.

"Father, we do not know how to handle this, either," he said. "It is a thing we must learn."

The impression spread that Monsignor Montini had adopted a narrow attitude which was dividing young Catholics and another Catholic Action chaplain characterized his attitude as "austere." The Fucini and the Fucina without their austere chaplain, staged a party meeting at which wine was consumed. Someone took photographs described as "Fucini delegates with their arms audaciously around Fucina delegates," and sent them to Monsignor Pizzardo at the Vatican. After that the two organizations were firmly divided and the Fucina provided with their own chaplain.

"We knew, of course, that we were only separating two groups officially to avoid possible scandal," Monsignor Pacchiani said. "We proposed no such grandiose idea as the separation of two sexes."

Monsignor Montini expressed his relief fervently when that problem quieted. He knew, as his assistants did not, how easy it would be to cripple or destroy FUCI from within. There were many people at the Vatican, some of them in high places, who frowned on the entire Catholic Action program as unnecessarily provocative in a time of sensitive politics, as needlessly placing in the hands of laymen the power of embarrassing the Church. They dismissed the incidents of violence as inevitable, the physical clash of young men pitted against each other by the setting up of opposing concepts.

"We must not forget," one elderly monsignor said, "that many of these Fascist youth are Catholics, too, as much our people as are these Fucini."

That was, of course, true. On the evidence up to that time, there was reason to believe that Fascism and the Church could find mutual living space in the same world. "We have endured many heads of government," a bishop said, "not involving ourselves in the changing of the government. Our best times have been when we pursued that policy, our worst with involvement. We have the centuries. We can be patient. Time changes governments."

There were many points of view. In some quarters, Monsignor Montini was looked upon as a liberal, quite possibly a leader of movements, a type who would have to be watched, perhaps held down. Monsignor Pizzardo, who was heart and soul in Catholic Action and who had projected Don Battista into it, was grimly cautious himself but he dismissed all criticism.

"We have passed the point of argument," he said.

11

THE LATERAN TREATY

THE Holy See and the Italian government, through negotiators, were working out a final settlement of the Roman Question.

Monsignor Montini, who had grown up in the home of a writer devoted to the subject, knew the Roman Question from many angles and elevations. He sympathized with Pope Pius XI and, as he was to demonstrate decisively, Monsignor Montini not only sympathized with the situation which the Holy Father had faced; he understood it.

Achille Ratti had been a priest in a black cassock, without rank, until he was fifty-seven years old. He had been a brilliant student in his youth, with three doctorates at twenty. He was appointed to the great Ambrosian Library in Milan and, with the self-effacement typical of librarians, he worked there for twenty-eight years. He wrote a number of books including a life of St. Charles Borromeo, written for the tercentenary of the saint. When a vacancy occurred, he was the logical choice to be Prefect of the Vatican Library and Pius X appointed him, raising him to domestic prelate with the rank of monsignor. Achille Ratti did not want to leave the Ambrosian Library nor Milan, but the voice of the pope was like the voice of God. He bowed to authority and came to Rome where he again sought anonymity among books. Without attempting to do so, he impressed his learning on those who used the Vatican Library.

"He cannot conceive of knowing any subject superficially," one awed prelate said.

Because he understood Poland and the intricacies of its makeup after World War I, Benedict XV sent Monsignor Ratti there as Apostolic Visitor, later raising him in rank. He was sixty-one when that happened and, again, he bowed to authority against his own desires. He was a cardinal at sixty-four and elected pope at sixty-five, eight years after his first advancement from the plain black cassock.

He chose his name with a certain irony, trusting librarians if no one else to read its significance, his acknowledgment before history that he knew what he was called upon to do. The Roman Question had been created under Pius IX and the hand of history had moved around the full circle of the clock. It was time to undo what had been done, to reverse the earlier Pius, and by reversing the Roman numerals, he symbolized the task ahead.

There was no question or doubt that the "Prisoner of the Vatican" chapter of history was over. Each pope since Pius IX had removed a little of the obstruction which he had erected during his long reign. It was time now for the papacy to sweep away the last debris of artificiality and to proclaim in action what it had long accepted in fact, that the realm of the pope is spiritual, not temporal; his parish, the world, not just a few Papal States of Italy.

Pius XI was not a mystic come to the throne, as Pius X had been; he was a hard-minded, direct man with a richly informed, questioning mind. No man, however, can come up through the priesthood to the papacy without accepting and deeply holding many mystical truths, among them the certain knowledge that each pope is selected to carry a cross. Pius XI saw the size and the shape and the weight of his.

He was confronted with the modern counterparts of the antagonists of Pius IX, a strong man, and a King; Mussolini and

Victor Emmanuel III in the roles of Garibaldi and Victor Emmanuel II. Pius XI could not reverse Pius IX, could not undo what Pio Nono had done, unless he had the will and the courage, facing the same problem, to resolve it differently. Pius IX had maintained that he could not deal with Victor Emmanuel without acknowledging Victor Emmanuel's right to negotiate and, with that acknowledgment, tacitly approve all that had been done to establish Victor Emmanuel in power. He took the position that to acknowledge the government of Italy would be to condone evil.

Pius XI faced a new government of Italy, a new strong man, and he was not deceived. Mussolini wanted peace with the Church because he was personally ambitious and because he needed the cloak of respectability to cover the callous ruthlessness of his rise to power. Camillo Benso Cavour, who had brought statecraft to the Italian revolution, had stated that the man who solved the Roman Question would be hailed by history as Italy's greatest statesman. Benito Mussolini wanted to be that man. He had become premier, and virtually dictator, of Italy in 1922, the year in which Pius XI ascended the throne of Peter. History from the onset, then, had linked the two men. In that first year, Benito Mussolini, through trusted emissaries, had felt out the Vatican on the possibility of settling differences.

Pius XI could open the door to the negotiators of Fascism and enter into agreements with Benito Mussolini and his government, but if those negotiations strengthened the position of Mussolini in the world, he, Pius XI, would be labeled by some historians a collaborator in whatever evil might ensue. The alternative was to close the door, revert to Pius IX, remain a "Prisoner in the Vatican" and confront another generation of Italians with the awful question: How can I be Italian and Catholic? When that decision was thrust upon Italians earlier, too many of them, out of the demands of Army service, the need for bread, the pressure of the Communists, decided to be Italian.

The descendants of those who made that bitter choice were

many and they were only nominally Catholic, if Catholic at all. They were spiritually illiterate because they had been raised without the knowledge of God. They were a receptive people to any super-state philosophy because they had been taught that all good flows from government.

Pius XI had been quoted as saying that he would negotiate with the devil if the salvation of souls was at stake. He did not, however, consider the situation so extreme. He had a friendly interest in Benito Mussolini who, although a self-professed atheist, had declared that Italy was necessarily a Catholic nation. In November 1922, when he took over the government as premier, Mussolini spoke to the parliament and said: "May God help me! May God help me to carry to a victorious end my arduous task." He was the first Prime Minister of modern Italy to invoke the name of God publicly. Pius XI had hopes for him, hopes tinged with caution but, nevertheless, hopes.

On October 4, 1926, Signor Francesco Pacelli, general counsel for the Holy See, and Signor Domenico Barone, Italian Privy Councilor met. They continued to meet for two and a half years.

Those years were fateful. There were other heavy problems weighing upon the Universal Church besides those of Italy. Many of them came, at least in bits or fragments, across the desk of Monsignor Giovanni Battista Montini, who decided no policy, made no important decision, influenced no attitudes.

The French Church was Monsignor Montini's main concern. He was aware, however, of other situations: the grim persecution of Catholics in Mexico, the continuing crises in Poland and Slavonic Europe. In the United States, a Catholic, Alfred E. Smith, was contending for the presidency with Herbert Hoover. There were several Americans in Curia cubbyholes, among them an ebullient, cheerful, irrepressible young monsignor named Francis Spellman.

Monsignor Spellman had been involved in the building of Rome playgrounds with Knights of Columbus funds and, in the course of it, he seemed to meet and know everyone in Rome.

Monsignor Montini had had casual contact with the Bostonian on youth work and Catholic Action. Although they worked with different age groups, and the American was older than he was and much more confident, they had been congenial. Spellman was one of his guides in trying to understand the United States.

The New World was baffling to Italian minds. Despite Columbus, there was no tradition, diplomatic or commercial, linking Italy to America. The great emigration had been mostly from the southern part of Italy, less articulate and less influential as far as public opinion was concerned than if it had represented the north. The United States, seen from a distance, was a Protestant nation and, except for technological skills, a backward one. It did not maintain diplomatic relations with the Vatican and, although it was the heaviest financial contributor of all the powers to Peter's Pence, it made no contribution culturally. Americans, on the whole, spoke no European languages. It was only a short time, the reign of Pius X, since the United States ceased to be mission territory.

Monsignor Montini and other young Italian priests learned much about the United States from Monsignor Spellman but he did not succeed in explaining American politics. There was no marked furor for Alfred E. Smith and his cause in Rome. No one seemed to know him. Several of the cardinals knew Herbert Hoover from the days of his mercy missions during, and after, World War I, liked him and respected him. His election caused neither consternation nor surprise. No Italian was startled or outraged at the anti-Catholic bias which had crept into the 1928 campaign, embarrassing Americans; it seemed quite a normal political element, certainly to be expected.

Monsignor Montini was studying English but his work, and the interests of his young men at FUCI, demanded much of him in French. He translated a book of Jacques Maritain, the first to be translated in Italy and his own first published volume. Inspired by the FUCI congress at Assisi, he did extensive research on St. Francis and wrote a life which was never published.

He started another book which was eventually published, *The University Conscience.*

On February 7, 1929, the Vatican announced that an accord had been reached with the Italian government after 329 meetings and twenty-one rewritings of the proposed treaty. Pius XI had been hard and immovable, standing firmly on the Church demand for sovereignty, firmly established within the temporal order and accepted by other states, with no dependence upon the benevolence of the Italian government. Church property was restored, harsh and restrictive laws repealed and indemnity over a period of years arranged. Accompanying the treaty, and essential to it, was a Concordat assuring the rights of the Church in ministering to its people, educating its young, and conducting its affairs within the state without molestation.

Many of the cardinals first informed of the treaty felt that more land and more indemnity should have been given the Church. Pius XI had tears in his eyes. "No," he said. "I felt like a father negotiating with his own children. I could not be too hard on them."

In cold type, the agreement seemed one-sided in favor of the Church to many observers but the gain to Mussolini was world prestige and an easing of tensions at home. The accord was hailed internationally and Il Duce was praised as one of its authors. In Italy his popularity swept to a high point. The Italians, always responsive to eras of good feeling, staged parades and processions in the cities and in the towns.

On a day of fog and rain, February 11, 1929, the actual signing took place in the Lateran Palace. Benito Mussolini and his aides appeared for the King; Pietro Cardinal Gasparri and his aides for the pope. The Roman Question was answered.

Monsignor Montini walked in the procession which celebrated the treaty-signing when Pope Pius XI formally left the Vatican for the first time on the Feast of Corpus Christi, July 25, 1929. It was the most elaborate ceremony in which he had ever participated. Pope Pius XI was carried on a ceremonial throne, wearing a richly embroidered gold robe. He held the monstrance aloft with both hands above the heads of the people who sank to their knees in waves as though a strong wind was passing over them.

The two bronze doors of the Vatican, and the main doorways of the noble families linked to the papacy, were open wide for the first time since 1870 and papal troops in uniform, a token force but symbolic, marched again. There were an estimated 300,000 people in St. Peter's Square.

Among the casualties of conflict between the Italian government and the Vatican was the Benedictine Abbey of St. Paul's-Outside-the-Walls which was secularized. Abbot Alfredo Ildefonso Schuster was, to use the words of Pius XI, "elevated to the splendor of the Roman purple" on July 15, 1929, replacing the learned British Benedictine, Francis Cardinal Gasquet, who had died on April 5. The Holy Father then appointed the new Cardinal Archbishop of Milan, second in importance only to Rome among the dioceses of Italy.

Monsignor Montini was present for his friend's reception in Rome and for his consecration in the magnificent cathedral of Milan. There was glory in it and happiness, but a touch of sadness, too. There would be no more retreats outside the walls, no more sermons on St. Paul, no more long talks in the hushed and holy abbey. All things were changing.

Monsignor Montini had written an analysis of the Lateran Treaty, with a summary of its historical background, for a Catholic magazine after the signing. The article was published in the week following the Corpus Christi procession. Monsignor Pizzardo congratulated him on it and suggested that he seek an audience with the Holy Father.

Pius XI received Monsignor Montini in his library. He looked no older than at their first meeting in the Lombard House. His hair was still black, sprinkled with gray, and his skin was firm, smooth, ruddy. There was complete repose in him although he sat straight. His eyes measured the young man before him. He did not find it necessary to smile; he had a friendliness of manner rather than of expression. He asked the young Monsignor several questions about himself and about his work and about FUCI, then he rose.

"I have read your article," he said. "You have brought rare understanding to a difficult affair."

That was all. It was enough. Praise from a pope is rare in any strata of society and in the life of a young cleric too impossible even for his dreaming. Pius XI had already said to Monsignor Pizzardo:

"This Monsignor Montini is one of the few who has truly understood the direction of our work."

12

TO THE CATACOMBS

THE time of accord between the Vatican and the government of Italy was pleasant while it lasted, all the more pleasant in retrospect because the time was so short. Mussolini presented the impressive Chigi Library to the first librarian pope with a speech of gracious compliment. Members of the Catholic hierarchy made friendly, laudatory remarks about Mussolini and about the King who replied in kind. World opinion approved this harmony. Mussolini was esteemed abroad, a colorful swashbuckler of a type forever popular with crowds. The youngest of the world's sovereign powers, the 160-acre Vatican State, was the center of intense interest. Together, the swashbuckler and the world's smallest state made news.

By order of Il Duce, the crucifix was restored to public buildings in Italy and to the classrooms of the schools. A new edition of the history volume approved by the government for school use carried a picture of Pius XI. The Catholic clergy, of high rank and low, relaxed. In view of the threat posed by godless communism, a strong Catholic state was a blessing to the world.

The people of his former archdiocese of Milan presented Pius XI with an American automobile, a Graham-Paige, the first automobile ever owned by a pope. He drove in it to take formal repossession of the basilica and palace of St. John Lateran, the cathedral of the Bishop of Rome.

There was a powerful Vatican radio station, then, donated by Guglielmo Marconi himself, with an oddly solemn Monsignor Spellman translating into English for the microphone, the half-hour Latin speech of Pius XI. This was the first time any pope had spoken into a mechanical or electrical device.

The Vatican science age touched Monsignor Montini only obliquely with the microphone performance of his contemporary, Monsignor Spellman, but it moved directly into his life when he received a new typewriter for his cubicle. There were adding machines and dictating machines going into offices of the Vatican and, most miraculous of all, the telephone system was being completely modernized. Until 1929 there had been only four telephones for the more than one thousand offices, rooms, and apartments.

The American stock market crashed in October 1929, during the period of goodwill and refurbishing in Rome and Vatican City, but only the bankers took the distant event seriously. Among the clerics in the Vatican State Department offices the big news was the return of Archbishop Pacelli from Germany where he had served as Nuncio at Munich and then Berlin from 1917 to 1929. He was the hero of their craft and guild, the most discussed, the most colorful, the most distinguished diplomat of the Holy See.

Monsignor Montini saw the legendary Pacelli several times from a distance during the week after the Nuncio's return and he had the fabulous luck of an invitation to the Sistine Chapel for the Public Consistory of December 16, 1929, which elevated Eugenio Pacelli to the cardinalate. His invitation came from his friend and sponsor, Monsignor Giuseppe Pizzardo.

There were six archbishops raised to the cardinalate; Their Excellencies Emanuele Goncalves Cerejeira, Luigi Lavitrano, Carlo Dalmazio Minoretti, Jean Verdier, Joseph MacRory, and Eugenio Pacelli. The man whom everyone watched was Pacelli. He was a cardinal out of fiction, out of theatre, out of the Renaissance. He was tall, elegantly tall. He walked gracefully, his spine straight but he created no impression of military bearing.

His face was boldly carved, Roman, a head for an ancient coin. He had compelling eyes, eyes with no readable expression, that seemed to exist for absorbing impressions rather than for revealing thought. There was an air of gentleness about him, which was odd, since he had served the Church on its least gentle front among people to whom gentleness is a weakness, the people of international diplomacy. He had never had a parish.

Monsignor Pizzardo presented Battista Montini at the reception and when the young monsignor turned away the eyes of the diplomat followed him. "I like that intense young man," Cardinal Pacelli said.

"So do I," said the Monsignor, relating briefly Montini's experience with the young men of FUCI and with their leader at the abbey outside the walls. Eugenio Cardinal Pacelli listened and remembered.

That winter was productive of rumors as winters usually were on Vatican Hill. Cardinal Gasparri was going to retire now that he had the Lateran Treaty as a monument, rumor said, and Bonaventure Cardinal Cerretti, whom Monsignor Montini knew well, would replace him. The inspired guess was only half correct. Cardinal Gasparri did retire, with his three parrots, to a villa on the outskirts of Rome but his veteran assistant, recently Nuncio to Paris, did not move up into his place. Eugenio Cardinal Pacelli became Secretary of State. He chose the American, Monsignor Spellman, as his secretary and took him with him when he went to Switzerland on vacation.

If Monsignor Battista Montini cherished a hope that his compliment from the pope or his meeting with cardinals would immediately change his own fortunes, he was disappointed. He probably did not waste much time on hoping. His work at the Vatican was demanding and he was busy with both national and local FUCI.

Dr. Ciro O. Scotti of Providence, Rhode Island, one of his Fucini at St. Ivo's, recalls his preaching at this period: "As he expounded on the words of Saint Paul with spellbinding, passionate acuteness and fervor, Saint Paul's words came alive and the presence of Christ within the church a reality. . . . His preaching was brief, clear, intense, reduced to the essentials, filled with a poetic and prophetic quality."

Archbishop Sergio Pignedoli, Apostolic Delegate to West-Central Africa, was a later member of the group at St. Ivo's. "If in Italy today there are men, including those in government, who are prepared to enter the external battles of life without timidity," he says, "it is due to that decisive and uncompromising conscience that was formed in them during the years of FUCI. Monsignor Montini was for many of them a spiritual director of unique firmness."

Battista Montini could not look into the future and see the fruits of his apostolate. It must have seemed to him that he was overworked and that each task well done attracted another responsibility. No one of that period of his life can recall that he ever pleaded overwork, however, when called upon for counsel, guidance, or aid in a project. He had a habit then which he continued throughout his life; when called upon to make an appointment with anyone, he chose a church as a meeting place. He did this as naturally as another man might choose a hotel, a bar or one of Rome's many fountains or piazzas, and he liked small or obscure churches unknown to the guidebooks. If a friend was late for an appointment, he would find the Monsignor kneeling in one of the pews or before one of the altars.

In the spring of 1931, the era of good feeling between the Church and the Italian government seemed to be approaching a twilight. Fascist leaders complained to the Vatican that Catholic lay organizations under the pretense of religious activity were indulging in politics, a violation of the Concordat.

Pope Pius XI received Monsignor Pizzardo and Monsignor Montini in his library, a room of dull crimson with tall windows shaded in olive and draped in white. The Holy Father looked severe, the lines on his face emphasized by the tightness of his mouth.

"What is our reply to this?" he said.

"They would make Catholic Action a political party because

we have banners, badges, and identification cards," Monsignor Pizzardo said. "They mention those things in their complaint. It is ridiculous. Organizations of all types have banners, badges, and cards."

Pope Pius XI looked at Monsignor Montini. "What of you? Have your young people been engaged in street fighting lately, or offering any incitation to violence?"

"None, Your Holiness."

Under the probing questions of the Holy Father, Monsignor Montini admitted reluctantly that there had been some baiting of FUCI youth by Fascists of late, after a long peace: cries of "rabbits" and "candle jockeys" and other derisive terms. The Fucini had ignored them. There had been no reprisals.

Monsignor Montini left the library of Pius XI without receiving any hint of what the Holy Father proposed to do, but Pius XI was angry, controlling his anger with obvious effort, and he acted promptly. He rejected the protest of the Italian government with the statement that his investigation had not revealed any support of their charges; that, on the contrary, Catholic groups in all categories were working within the terms of the pact and avoiding political activity.

The Catholic newspapers published the Holy Father's statement on their front pages and supported it editorially. Benito Mussolini ordered the dissolution of all Catholic Action groups and all societies, even those which were for women exclusively, the closing of all clubhouses and meeting places, the shutting down of the five Knights of Columbus playgrounds in Rome. The entire Catholic press was suppressed, forbidden to publish.

It was a frightening display of power, the other side of dictatorship which could do benevolent and worthy things speedily without the annoyances of due process. Italy's dictator was demonstrating the fact that he could take away any right of a citizen as easily as he could remove a row of houses to make a boulevard. Pope Pius XI replied, threatening to void the Concordat.

Fascist retaliation was swift and savage. Fascist groups, in uniform or mob mufti, raided the headquarters of Catholic Action groups in Rome, Milan, Pavia, Benevento, Venice, Trieste, and Verona. Books, records, and files were destroyed, athletic equipment broken, typewriters and office machines smashed. In some cases, the headquarters of Catholic groups were burned. Catholic newspaper offices were flooded, type scattered, presses broken. Once started, the violence spread swiftly all over Italy.

Monsignor Montini was conducting a meeting at St. Ivo's the night that the first attacks came. The Fascist youth waited until the Fucini left the Church, then charged. They were in overwhelming superiority numerically and the Catholic young men were knocked down, kicked and beaten. It was not until girls came, attracted by the noise, crying out their protests, that the Fascists withdrew.

Monsignor Montini had his wounded brought into St. Ivo's. Wounded, was literally accurate. The Fucini were bleeding, brutally bruised, some of them with broken bones. Many of the Fucini were medical students and they took care of one another until University of Rome doctors took charge.

There were Catholic youths killed in other places but the authorities played down the violence, minimizing it and attributing it to clashes between rival youth groups.

Monsignor Montini went home to his room on the Aventine Hill in a mood of deep depression. He was concerned for the young people who had been hurt, humiliated that survival had depended upon the screams of women and personally disturbed that the fury, the action, the violence had swirled around him, leaving him untouched. He had not been attacked and he had not been able, as a priest, to attack, even if his unpracticed attack would have accomplished anything. He did not have a bruise or a wound. He was young and he was male and the absence of a combat stripe when his companions were hurt was a humiliation.

On the following Sunday, at his direction, the members of his FUCI chapter met him in the catacombs, traveling singly to their destination. He said the Mass for them where other Christians, hunted and beaten for their faith, had taken refuge in the first centuries of the Church. His statement of an earlier time —"If today we cannot go with unfurled banners, let us work in silence"—no longer seemed melodramatic.

There were many weeks of Masses in the catacombs and there were many catacombs, Catholic and Jewish, under the city of Rome; underground cemeteries cut out of calcareous tufa, a porous rock. There were chapels and assembly rooms and long corridors, the walls decorated with paintings of the very early centuries, carved in some sections with the names of those who had taken refuge or who had buried their loved ones in these depths.

Monsignor Montini changed the meeting place each week and his followers became familiar with the lives of the early Christians; more important, they identified with them. They were learning what it was like to contend with swaggering Romans and to go under the earth in order to worship God. In this identification with those other Christians of unquestioned glory, the young men of FUCI regained their strength and their pride.

On the grounds of the University of Rome, Fascist youth made bonfires out of material taken from Catholic youth headquarters all over Rome, and out of huge piles of *Osservatore Romano*, the one newspaper which Fascism had been unable to suppress since it was published in the sovereign precincts of Vatican City.

His Holiness Pope Pius XI wrote his encyclical, *Non Abbiamo Bisogno*, which he dated June 29, 1931, and released on July 5 in the *Osservatore Romano*. This was his statement of the case against the Fascist government of Italy and he was laying it before the world. Despite the fact that he had a powerful radio transmitter at his disposal, access to the world through diplomatic pouches of all the leading powers, and the Vatican newspaper to present his text without alteration, Cardinal Pacelli suggested to him that the Fascists would be able to keep the papal message from the world. Cardinal Pacelli sent his own secretary, Monsignor Spellman, to Paris with a copy of the encyclical to be released through the international news services.

In that encyclical, the anger of Pius XI is apparent but the facts are marshaled by a scholar, without emotional distortion. He sets forth the points raised in the political activity charge of the Fascist government, submits the results of his own investigation, relates an account of the violence done to Catholic institutions and ends with expressions of alarm at the portent for the future. The following highlights from the encyclical reveal its mood:

"There has been an attempt to strike unto death that which was and always will be dearest to our heart as Father and as Shepherd of Souls. . . . It has been for us an exquisite satisfaction to see the Catholic Action organizations of all countries . . . all expressing their astonishment and grief in seeing Catholic Action societies persecuted and assailed here in the very center of the apostolic hierarchy . . . these organizations have refrained . . . absolutely from any and every kind of political party activity. How many insults in the press, how many injurious words and acts against things and persons, not excluding ourself, preceded, accompanied and followed the carrying into effect of the lightning-like police order . . . The history of documents prepared not in the service of truth but in offense of truth and justice is a long and sad story. But We must say, with a certain deep dismay, that in our many active years as a librarian, rarely have We seen an article so tendentious and so contrary to truth and justice in its references to this Holy See, to Italian Catholic Action, and particularly to the associations so harshly treated. . . . And it is with a grief inexpressible that We saw a real and true persecution break out in this our Italy. . . . A conception of the State which makes the young generation belong entirely to it without any exception from the tenderest years up to adult life cannot be reconciled by a Catholic with the Catholic doctrine, nor can it be reconciled with the natural right of the family. . . . We have reasons to believe, it is determined not to permit our Catholic youth to reunite, even silently, unless the directors are threatened with bitter

122

punishment! What new thing, therefore, We ask Ourself, does the future prepare and threaten?"

There was shock in the ranks of Benito Mussolini's government when the indictment of Pius XI was spread before the world. "The Church must not mix in politics and politics must not mix in the Church," Mussolini said. "His children are fooling the Holy Father."

Nevertheless Il Duce appointed a commission to confer with representatives of Pope Pius XI and to seek a means of resolving misunderstandings. The violence came to a halt and ultimately an agreement was drawn which spelled out more precisely what the government interpreted as political activity and what the Church insisted upon as necessary freedom to teach and to worship.

In the eyes of some critics, Pius XI lost the final battle because he made concessions to, and accepted concessions from, Benito Mussolini; but, in the eyes of a realist, that end was inevitable from the beginning. The government of Italy existed in fact and it was not the imperative of the Church to change governments but rather to find a means of existing with them; provided that means recognized the mission of the Church as the guide and guardian of souls.

The imbroglio between Church and State was not finally set at rest until Benito Mussolini appeared at the Vatican for a 10 A.M. audience with Pius XI on February 11, 1932, the third anniversary of the signing of the Lateran Treaty.

The two men conferred for an hour. After the conference, Benito Mussolini, wearing his dress uniform, knelt in prayer with Pius XI at the tomb of St. Peter; which was, perhaps, the ultimate concession.

Monsignor Battista Montini was happy with the tribute to Catholic Action and the recognition of youth work, in the encyclical *Non Abbiamo Bisogno* (literally, "We do not need it"; popularly, *On Catholic Action*). It was recognition from the highest source of a cause and of an activity into which he had put the young, eager, enthusiastic years of his life. It came when new responsibility was awaiting him.

On September 8, 1932, Monsignor Francis J. Spellman was consecrated auxiliary bishop of Boston by Cardinal Pacelli. There was a reception in the Borgia Rooms of the Vatican, the six-room suite of the iniquitous Alexander VI. Monsignor Montini attended but he was not quite part of it.

The American monsignor had moved up and soon he would be sailing home, after he and Cardinal Pacelli had a planned holiday first at Cannes. Monsignor Pizzardo and Monsignor Borgongini had been co-consecrators at the ceremony in the morning, closely linked before that. At the reception they seemed like members of an exclusive club. Monsignor Montini went home early. He had no presentiment that he was about to become a member of that exclusive club.

Eugenio Cardinal Pacelli called him in for a conference after his return from Cannes and talked to him for an hour. When Monsignor Battista Montini walked out of the study of the Secretary of State, he had until the first of the year to clear his other work and his commitments. He would then join the personal staff of the Secretary. Only one regret attached to that. Cardinal Pacelli had not spoken one word of praise or blame in connection with Monsignor Montini's work with FUCI but he had suggested gently that a faculty position at Accademia dei Nobili Ecclesiastici, which he would arrange, would be more in harmony with a position in the Vatican Department of State than was youth work on the Catholic Action front.

A priest accepts more easily, perhaps, than other men the hard fact that he is not indispensable, that he can be replaced without serious damage to the Church. It was, however, a wrench for Monsignor Montini to say farewell to FUCI. It was difficult for the men of FUCI, too, to accept the fact that he was leaving them. In behalf of the group, Iginio Righetti, the president, addressed a petition to the Holy Father, lauding the accomplishments of Monsignor Montini and expressing the hope that a way would be found to extend his service in the work that he did so well.

The Holy Father replied with brevity and forthrightness rather than with tact: "Monsignor Montini has such gifts that he is destined to render service to the Church at higher levels."

An index to the feeling of Monsignor Battista Montini at this point of change in his life is best obtained from a paragraph which he wrote before the event, a paragraph from his early writing which was revelatory of his yearning for pastoral duty:

"If there is one thing of beauty which fills with joy the heart of the pope and of the bishops, it is a poor priest with worn-out cassock and torn buttons who has around him a group of boys who are playing, studying, thinking about life with him, and who esteem and trust him."

It was his dream of the priesthood and he had had it at St. Ivo.

BOOK II

The City and the World

13

THE LONG TWILIGHT

GIOVANNI BATTISTA MONTINI moved from his attic cubby-
hole to a large office with green walls and carpeting on
the floor in 1932. He abandoned his quarters on the Aventine
Hill for a small apartment in the Belvedere Palace in 1933. The
moving, changing, advancing were in the spirit of the time.
Other men, too, were moving into new positions in those years.

Eamon de Valera became President of Irish Free State in
1932 through coalition with the Labor Party and gained full
power the following year when he went to the country. Engel-
bert Dollfuss became Chancelor of Austria in 1932 and dictator
the following year. The new republic of Spain which had replaced King Alfonso XIII in 1931 was expelling Jesuits, burning churches, schools, and convents in 1932 and the following
year. Adolf Hitler became a political force in Germany in 1932
and absolute dictator in 1933. Franklin Delano Roosevelt,
elected President of the United States in 1932, was inaugurated
in 1933. The Soviet Union started a new five-year plan and was
recognized by the United States early in the new administration,
1933. Great names had arisen in the world, names that, beside
the already established Stalin and Mussolini, would dominate
the news for many years.

Monsignor Montini was not a great name and he had not
risen to power but in 1932 and 1933 he stood in the wings of

history while the drama was enacted on stage. He was a staff member, however lowly in rank, of the Vatican Department of State, diplomatic arm of the Holy See. His immediate superior was Monsignor Domenico Tardini but the department, all of it, belonged to one man.

Eugenio Cardinal Pacelli, Papal Secretary of State, was in some moods like a disembodied spirit rather than a man; beautiful at prayer, rapt in meditation, awe-inspiring in his saying of the Mass. He was suave, smooth, flawless in manner and speech in private audience; gracious and kind and gentle in public audience; an exacting, demanding, perfectionist to those who worked under him. He respected his own high position and he expected others to respect it. He was humble before the Holy Father, granting him a deference that seemed, at times, exaggerated, but bowing his will to the office rather than to the man. He was precise in all that he did and he demanded precision from others; the exact word, the properly placed punctuation marks, the clearly expressed thought. Time was his constant companion. He rose, dressed, dined, prayed, exercised, and slept exactly on schedule, never a minute late for an appointment, never tolerant of another's tardiness. He was a hard taskmaster, more severe on himself than on others. He believed, and perhaps not unreasonably, that his own dedication to the responsibility placed upon him justified the demand which he made upon his subordinates. He served well and they were extensions of himself.

Battista Montini was several long steps away from the magic inner circle of Cardinal Pacelli but within the circles of discipline. He learned, by doing and redoing, to be precise and exact in all that he put on paper. He learned to dress well, within the limitations of clerical garb, and to move with grace, to avoid unnecessary gestures, to eliminate mannerisms, to control facial expression. All of which was part of a great discipline, not a process of dehumanizing. There were compensations, many of them, and relaxations and, of course, the intangible rewards of discipline which translate into morale and honest pride and confidence.

He took his pride and his confidence and his distinguished bearing to Accademia dei Nobili Ecclesiastici where he conducted his classes. He was as far above these aspiring diplomats as the Secretary was above himself, and he held them firmly to lines which he drew; knowing that it was good for them to be held and to be compelled, knowing that human personality is a firm element rather than a limp one, needing the regimen of strength for its development, not the coddling of weakness.

He had learned, and he was still learning as he taught, that diplomacy is the art of negotiation, concerning itself with tactics rather than strategy, advising and providing information but never formulating policy. He was in a position where he could see such a textbook concept become living reality. The many papal diplomats around the earth pooled their observation, their knowledge, their advice through the Vatican. Cardinal Pacelli created policy out of that pool and submitted the policy to the final judgment of His Holiness, Pius XI. The approval of Pius XI could not be taken for granted. He was not a figurehead, a passive signer of the pronouncements of other men; he was a vital, virile, short-tempered, strong-willed man of great courage and determination, little patience with sham or hypocrisy. Pius XI wrote policy in terms of accepting realities without changing the names of those realities.

It was stimulating to work in the atmosphere created by two such strong personalities as Pius XI and Eugenio Pacelli and it was rewarding to face the diplomatic tomorrow of the Church in the classroom. Of this experience he was to write later:

"I liked teaching. I looked forward with anticipation to the classes and to the stimulation of contact with young minds. I thought often that to teach would be a rewarding way of investing one's life if one were called by God to that great responsibility."

Giovanni Battista Montini was called to a different responsibility, but the ends of Vatican diplomacy were the ends of priesthood; the salvation of souls, the spreading of God's word among men, fidelity to the words of Christ. Men in their diversity devised governments and theories of government, differing from one another in form and in their manner of balancing contending human forces. The Church, through its representatives, dealt with those governments, seeking protection for its people in their God-given rights, seeking justice and charity, seeking peace, watchful and suspicious of movements which enslaved the minds and wills of men, of philosophies which fashioned false gods or which sought to lure men to the lonely dark crypts of godlessness and materialism.

Catholic diplomacy is concerned, too, with material things; the critic says: with property and with money. To which Monsignor Montini and his students, and his superiors in the State Department, would offer only agreement. In nations, ancient and new, there are churches, convents, abbeys, monasteries, schools, and hospitals erected and maintained with the money of self-sacrificing, devout, charitable people. The Church, nominally owning these properties, actually holds them in trust for the people, living and dead, whose money they represent, the people, present and future, whose welfare they are designed to serve.

In defense of property, in defense of rights, in performance of its commission from Jesus Christ, the Roman Catholic Church deals with governments through its diplomats. Its diplomacy is second to none on earth in skill and subtlety, older than any in its history and its traditions.

Giovanni Battista Montini was called to a diplomatic career on the eve of one of the world's darkest nights, the beginning of an era of intense hatreds, savage cruelties, an abandonment of God.

The Nazi Party under Adolf Hitler assumed power in Germany with the usual promises, after the usual period of revolutionary violence. In many ways it resembled the Fascist rise in Italy, with its uniforms and parades and elaborate salutes; promises and bright hopes for a people weary of inflation, unemployment and an inept bureaucracy in power. There were differences, however, under the surface but menacing. Adolf Hitler had written *Mein Kampf* and it was a warning.

The Vatican State Department was wary of the initial Hitler statements which proclaimed Christianity as "indispensable to the moral renascence of the German people." Cardinal Pacelli, who rarely betrayed his feelings, was visibly disturbed. He had gone to Germany in 1917 as Apostolic Nuncio to Bavaria and in 1920 was appointed Papal Nuncio to Berlin. He had served in Germany until November 1929. He had countless friends there, Catholic and non-Catholic. He had many memories, the memories of maturity. He had been forty-one when he arrived in Munich. He had shared good times and bad with the German people, hardship and hazard. He knew the elements which composed Hitlerism and he could see only disaster in permitting them power.

Cardinal Pacelli had signed Concordats with Bavaria in 1925 and with Prussia in 1929. A Concordat was, in effect, a treaty, an agreement, a definition of terms under which Church and State could act within their own spheres of influence without conflicting with each other. Hitler expressed a desire for a Concordat similar to those previously concluded with German States and sent his Vice-Chancelor Franz von Papen to Rome to negotiate it. Von Papen held court at Rome's Hotel Eden, entertained press and politicians, made his formal calls to the Vatican and signed a Concordat with Cardinal Pacelli.

There was justification for the easy, relaxed feeling in the Vatican after Von Papen went home. The new government of Germany had proved more conciliatory than anyone had dared to expect. The agreement between Vatican and Reich, among other provisions, promised noninterference by the government in the printing and distributing of pastoral letters, protection of priests in the performance of all priestly offices, free functioning of the Catholic school system and of Catholic youth organized for purely religious ends and purposes. The Church granted the right of the German government to veto any candidate for episcopal honors and agreed that its clergy should not participate in politics or seek public office.

Monsignor Montini was particularly interested in the provisions affecting youth organizations and Catholic Action. When details of the agreement with Germany were published in *Osservatore Romano*, he had dinner with Iginio Righetti, his comrade and co-worker in FUCI, and with Padre Bevilacqua, a dangerously outspoken priest who had fled the Fascists in Brescia and whom Don Battista had hidden in his Via delle Terme lodgings on the Aventine. In the company of these men, there were no formalities. He was Don Battista as he had always been.

"The Nazis will never keep the agreement," Padre Bevilacqua said. "They sign it to fool the world. It is a proof of their pure intention and high ideals. When they break it, they will charge us with breaking it. If they introduce sufficient confusion into their charges, people will give up trying to understand the issue and these Nazis will be exonerated."

"You should be a diplomat," Battista said.

"I am. I am a diplomat in spirit, but I have no patience. These Nazis, because they are Germans, will be worse than the Fascists. They will be more like the Russians."

"They are the enemies of the Communists. That is how they came to power," Iginio Righetti said.

"Ah, yes. And now they *have* power. They can be anything," Padre Bevilacqua said. "They need no longer hate Communists."

It was an odd quirk in the Oratorian priest that he could see greater potential for evil in the distant totalitarians than in those near at hand, from whom he was in hiding. Monsignor Montini had arranged a post for him as secretary of the Society for Preserving the Faith, a sinecure that kept him out of a pulpit where he endangered himself with denunciations of the Fascists. Tonight, to anyone who did not know him, he might seem a defender of Fascism rather than one of its victims. It was an Italianity which bewildered foreigners, this objectivity about things Italian; many Italians had it to the point of belittling even the evil of their own land as not quite first rate.

At fifty-three Padre Bevilacqua was not so old as he seemed to Don Battista who was thirty-seven and Iginio Righetti who was younger but he was at least partially responsible for the "old man" attitude which they adopted toward him. He had a Polonius quality of advising and lecturing, particularly to Battista whom he treated, rather absurdly, as a son.

"Catholic Action and the youth groups always provide the targets," Iginio said. "If we do not give people like the Fascists an excuse to fall on us they will invent an excuse and have no difficulty in convincing the majority of people. People are conditioned to believe anything charged against youth."

"It is difficult to find leaders who will not overdo things," Battista said.

He had been through that, and so had Iginio, making their own mistakes and seeing mistakes made. It was essential that the Church hold and interest its young people, kindle their loyalty and guide them in the difficult adjustments that must be made, and made again, between the spiritual, the physical, the material. Young people could not be held in static roles, listeners to lectures, nor enlisted in perpetual rounds of sports and entertainments. To interest young people and command their resources of mind and body, there had to be work, objectives worth struggling to reach, difficulty to overcome. Catholic Action, by frankly seeking to enlist apostles, could be the perfect answer, and seldom was. The human elements, clerical and lay, were unpredictable of themselves or in combination.

"I'd like to see this movement in Germany," Iginio said. "It may take the same course as our own experience or it may be different."

"It will be different only in being German," Padre Bevilacqua said, "but that is a great difference."

Battista walked home with the priest after Iginio Righetti left. Padre Bevilacqua rested a hand on his arm. "Work less," he said. "Let other people have a share in the work of the world.

You are too involved in problems. Life makes another problem from the stuff you spill in mending the problem you have. These youths in Germany? They are not your concern. You have other work. This Catholic Action in Italy, these Fucini, they are no longer your responsibility. There are others to worry about them. Give them your blessing and go home to bed."

"One never entirely ceases to be what one has sincerely been," said Don Battista.

Within a week, the Nazi government had broken the Concordat with passage and publication of their sterilization law. It was the first violation of many and in its wake came news of clashes between Hitler Youth and the Catholic groups. A familiar pattern was unfolding. The Vatican protests and the evasive treatment of the protests were familiar, too. The Nazi government existed in fact, as the Fascist government existed, and the Communist. The Vatican had to deal with governments as they were, protesting where protest was justified, condemning where the stronger course became necessary, always mindful that its strength was drawn from the loyalty of the faithful, and dependent upon their freedom to implement that loyalty. The Pope, as Stalin said, had no "divisions," no troops; he had, apart from whatever supernatural help was granted him in the wisdom of God, only his moral force, his power to stir the conscience of the world. One used such force and power as he had with discretion.

The protests against violation of the Concordat were dispatched to the Nazi government and another duel began. There was still hope that the revolutionary violence which had brought the Nazis to power would lose momentum and that other elements in Germany would provide balances. Italy under Fascism continued to provide grave problems for the Church, but again the situation was not impossible. The one implacable enemy at that point was communism.

The Church could not make Concordats with the Soviet Union, latterly claiming respectability in its recognition by the United States and in its acceptance as a member of the League

of Nations which followed that recognition. Communism acknowledged no god but the State and no religion which did not
permit its tenets to be twisted into State worship. Communism
was a ruthless persecutor, a destroyer of all that opposed or that
stood in its way. There was no middle ground on which to meet
it. The fascism of Mussolini was easier to understand. Count
Carlo Sforza, an uncompromising anti-Fascist, said that Fascism
had copied its ideas, laws, and methods from Napoleon III.
Mussolini, in short, was a tyrant and the Church had dealt with
tyrants in every century of its long history.

Hitler? That was the grim question mark. If he could be
contained, if he followed the traditional patterns of revolu-
tionaries come to power, or of tyrants, the Church could be
patient up to a point while opposing him every step of the way.
If he proclaimed the State a god, then he could protest his
hatred of communism and still be no more tolerable than the
system which, theoretically, he opposed.

Pius XI had eloquently stated the dilemma in the fateful year
1932, in his encyclical *Caritate Christi*:

"Profiting by so much economic distress and so much moral
disorder, the enemies of all social order, be they called Communists or by any other name, boldly set about breaking through
every restraint. This is the most dreadful evil of our times, for
they destroy every bond of law, human or divine, they engage
openly and in secret in a relentless struggle against religion and
against God Himself; they carry out the diabolical program of
wresting from the hearts of all, even of children, all religious
sentiment; for well they know that, when once belief in God has
been taken from the heart of mankind, they will be entirely free
to work out their will. Thus we see today, what was never seen
before in history, the satanical banners of war against God and
against religion brazenly unfurled to the winds in the midst of
all peoples and in all parts of the earth."

The effort which Pius XI was exerting received recognition
from an unexpected source in 1935 when Great Britain, for the
first time since Henry VIII, sent a Minister to the Papal Court.

The momentum of events, however, was violent and beyond the braking power of any man's effort.

The neopaganism of the Nazis was loosing savagery on all religious groups. The anti-Semitism which had been seemingly a rabble-rousing political device in the beginning had become fanatical. Pius XI made his oft-quoted statement and made it sternly: "It is not possible for Christians to take part in anti-Semitism. We are Semites spiritually."

Bishops and priests in Germany were condemning the segregation of Jews and the cult of blood-exalting paganism from their pulpits but requesting Rome to move slowly. The old familiar charge, that Catholics are aliens owing allegiance abroad had been raised in the land and it was considered better for the Church, and for people of all faiths, if protest against things German came from German lips. Michael Cardinal von Faulhauber and Bishops von Galen and von Preysing had been courageously outspoken. They were making common cause with the Protestant groups under Pastor Martin Niemöller and they were optimistic about the chances of an early Nazi crackup. There seemed to be dissension in the ranks and there were rumors of a *coup*.

On June 30, 1934, the leaders of the celebrated S.A., brownshirt storm troopers, in Germany were liquidated by the Reichswehr (the Regular Army) with Hitler's consent. Rumor said that he was slated to die with his brownshirts, but that he had saved his life and his place of power by sacrificing them. In reasserting his power, Hitler disbanded the Catholic Youth organizations.

"As long as youth follows me," he said, "I don't mind if the old people limp to the confessional."

Monsignor Montini went to Concesio and Brescia for his vacation during that uneasy summer. He had become accustomed to matters of great moment, the sense of a world resting uneasily upon a volcano rim, and it was almost shocking to move among people who were unaware of crises, who seemed happy about the state of the nation, reasonably prosperous and proud of evident and obvious progress, a new road here, a new building there. Toward trouble in other lands they were not indifferent but hadn't it always been so in those other lands?

Old neighbors were a little diffident with the young man they had once called Battista, then Don Battista. He was no longer quite so young, his hair was thinning slightly. He had always had a grave and solemn look but now it was a little more than that: he was distinguished and looked what he was, an associate of the Holy Father in the Vatican Palace. He could not hurdle that fence they built around him until an old man leveled it for him in Verolavecchia.

The old man was a well-remembered neighbor, more than a little senile now, but still walking well without a cane. Don Battista met him in the road that runs through the village. The old man was carrying a basket of eggs. He blinked and then, as recognition came, he would have gone down on his knees if Battista had not prevented him with a swift grip upon his arm and a reproving: "There is no reason why you should do that."

"They told me you were a bishop," the man said.

"Indeed not."

"Then you must pray for me if you are only a priest. I would kiss your ring if you were a bishop."

The man dipped into his basket and handed Don Battista an egg. Other eggs followed and there was nowhere to put them. He did not want to hurt the old man's feelings so he put the eggs into his hat. Not until he was walking away did he realize that a small knot of villagers had gathered and that they were watching him with amusement.

After that day there was no more rigidity in his relations with the villagers of Verolavecchia. They smiled when they met him and if the smiles meant, as they undoubtedly did, that the neighbors liked him better when he proved that he could be slightly ridiculous, then he was pleased with his hatful of eggs.

Monsignor Montini returned to his labors refreshed, having

discovered that there were still simple people living quite uncomplicated lives and capable of deriving joy from small events.

In October, Eugenio Cardinal Pacelli went to Buenos Aires as the Legate of His Holiness Pius XI at the International Eucharistic Congress. There were four cardinals, seventy-five bishops, thousands of priests, a million laymen at the Congress and Eugenio Pacelli was priest, diplomat, Secretary of State. In vestments and cope, he offered the white Christ of the Monstrance to the million worshipers. He moved easily at receptions, meeting and talking to people, and in schools, convents, the halls of politics. He listened to the cardinals and the bishops and he returned to Rome.

"The people of the Americas, North and South," he reported to Pius XI, "are not concerned, nor yet indifferent, to events in Spain, in Germany, in Russia, in Italy; they merely fail to comprehend the reality of those events."

While Cardinal Pacelli was away, the Italian Army had invaded Ethiopia and aroused the protests of governments if not of people. Benito Mussolini had brushed those protests aside.

"Invasion of sovereign rights has been in progress for centuries," he said. "Where is the nation today which during its history has not invaded the sovereign rights of others? Take the United States! How did it push its frontiers back?"

Later, to newspapermen, he said, "These righteous people who are criticizing me would make morality a matter of time."

Throughout Italy there were families with boys in the Army who were fighting in Ethiopia. They prayed in their churches for the safety of their sons. They lighted candles and vigil lights before the altars and they sought the prayers of their priests. Young boys on short leave home before going to the front knelt before their parish priests for blessings. The Church blessed and the Church prayed for its sons and the Church sought to build diplomatic dams against the torrents of violence which might flash-flood from any direction on the totalitarian triangle.

Monsignor Giovanni Battista Montini, working on the edge of

events and not too close to the center, prepared a paper for his class. It is, he demonstrated, as unfortunate to have strong diplomacy serving weak policy as it is to have a strong policy nullified by weak diplomacy.

14

EUGENIO CARDINAL PACELLI

Edward VIII succeeded his father as King of England in January 1936 and the shadow of his ultimate abdication hung over him. He was never crowned. In March the Nazis marched into the Rhineland and the world attitude was shocked surprise rather than effective protest.

Monsignor Giovanni Battista Montini became Papal Undersecretary of State.

Eugenio Cardinal Pacelli informed him of his promotion in a private conversation that was no less formal because it was friendly. He complimented Monsignor Montini on having merited this promotion and on the opportunity of service to Christ which the promotion afforded. His hands were as expressive as his features when he spoke of the problems that lay ahead. He had a remarkable quality of communicating interest in, and affection for, the person with whom he conversed. He wanted the man he faced to be happy in the work that he was called to do, but his happiness was relatively unimportant as long as his work served the greater honor and glory of God.

Cardinal Pacelli, if he had lived in the thirteenth century, might have been a cathedral builder, one of the great guild of those who wrought wonder in stone and marble and glass, who wrought anonymously, refusing to put their names to their work lest in glorifying themselves they might diminish, by even a particle, the glory belonging to God. Anonymity, of course, was not asked of Cardinal Pacelli. He lived in a spotlight, he wielded power. Yet he had come the way that Monsignor Montini had come: the sickly childhood, the missed school companionship while he worked with tutors, the humble jobs of a Curia clerk. He had accepted all that, giving richly of himself, studying, developing the gifts of tongues and of presence.

Monsignor Montini did not have that gift of presence, that awesome dignity, that effect of other-worldliness. He did not have the same background, either, despite similarities. Eugenio Pacelli had been born within sight of St. Peter's. He had been able to raise his eyes in the midst of childhood play and look across the Tiber to the great dome of Michelangelo, under which he would experience incredible drama in his manhood. The Vatican tradition was in the Pacelli family. Eugenio's grandfather, Marcantonio Pacelli, was the nephew of a cardinal and Undersecretary of the Interior for the Papal States under Pius IX. He was editor of *Osservatore Romano* after that. Felippo, one of Marcantonio's many sons, the father of Eugenio, was dean of Consistorial Advocates of the Vatican. Francesco Pacelli, Eugenio's brother, was Chief Consistorial Advocate at a later date, the man who drew up the Lateran Treaty for Pius XI.

Giovanni Battista Montini had had FUCI and there was no equivalent of that in the career of the older man. Cardinal Pacelli had never been a parish priest. As Secretary of State, he considered all of the world his parish. He could talk to the least, or the greatest, of his parishioners and convey interest, concern, sympathy. He inspired the warm liking of Battista Montini and the loyalty which that liking inspired was to last long, to serve greatly under tremendous difficulties.

"There are many decisions before us," Cardinal Pacelli said.

Monsignor Montini left him, knowing that the great decisions ahead would be made across more important desks than his own but that now he would contribute to the making. The post of undersecretary was an unobtrusive one but, for the first time, he represented the State Department in social and routine matters below the top levels. He worked with the secret codes used in diplomatic exchanges and he prepared memoranda of a highly confidential nature. Ascending to this new desk was like the ascent to the dome of St. Peter's. The horizons moved back as one climbed and the world grew large, with increasing areas of it within view.

A German diplomatic report on changes in the Vatican staff mentioned that the new undersecretary was familiar with the Polish language and had been known to read Polish books and magazines.

Monsignor Montini would have been surprised if he saw that report when it was written because he did not consider Polish one of his languages. He had had too little time to use and speak it. Among his correspondents was Bishop Angelo Roncalli who had served as Apostolic Visitor to Bulgaria and who had made himself fluent in Bulgarian, a language spoken in few other places. He had been transferred and now, as Apostolic Visitor to Turkey and Greece, he was studying Turkish. Papal diplomacy demanded many things of many men. Battista Montini's current language study was English.

Archbishop Amleto Cicognani, his old mentor, friend, and superior at St. Ivo was now Apostolic Delegate to the United States and Don Battista corresponded with him, officially and unofficially. Bishop Cicognani was convinced of the growing importance of the English language and, despite the frightening military might of the totalitarian countries, he believed that the future would be shaped by the English-speaking nations. In Rome, with the secret and the open dispatches flowing across one's desk, one had some grave doubts about the future and one trusted to prayer.

The Italian Army completed the conquest of Ethiopia in May. There was great jubilation in Italy, less for victory than for peace. Benito Mussolini announced that King Victor Emmanuel III would be crowned Emperor of Ethiopia. Victor Emmanuel did not matter actually. Il Duce was building an empire. He was jealous of Britain in the Mediterranean, *mare nostrum*, and determined that Italy's King would stand as high as England's. He was jealous, too, of Hitler and alarmed by him. He had treated the Nazis patronizingly at first, considering them imitators of his Fascists, but they had developed fast and they stood for different values, a different philosophy. Mussolini was critical of their racial theories, their anti-Semitic measures.

"Anti-Semitism does not exist in Italy," he said. "The Italian Jews have always behaved well as citizens and fought bravely as soldiers. They occupy eminent positions in the universities, the Army, the banks."

Pius XI, without any illusions whatever about Mussolini's morals or Mussolini's opportunism, seemed to have a gruff liking for him. It was more difficult to assess the thought or feeling of Cardinal Pacelli who had made himself the instrument of the Holy Father and who submerged himself in the role. The submerging, of course, was not abject. The Secretary of State had his own stature. Much of the information on which Pius XI based his decisions cleared through him.

Eugenio Cardinal Pacelli recognized no boundary of hours on the work that he had to do, nor on the work which he demanded of his staff. He rose precisely at six each morning and he moved through his day on a rigid timetable, but he placed no limitations on the night. He worked and he walked and he worried in the dark night hours. He prayed in his private chapel. Often he tapped on a typewriter, writing to clarify his thoughts. He would call an assistant at any hour if he wanted information from that assistant or if he had an idea to transmit which required careful interpretation. Whatever the hour, he tolerated no informality. The man whom he called presented himself to the Papal Secretary suitably attired.

Cardinal Pacelli was an austere man in appearance at these nocturnal conferences, as a rule, straight-backed, straight-lipped, solemn. He never apologized for calling a man at an unseemly hour, but he did not waste anyone's time. His mind was astonishing in its range of knowledge, its capacity for reasoning in depth, its intuitional quality which verged on the gift of prophecy.

"Hitler will go into Austria," he told his staff after the Rhineland occupation. "Then they will have Danzig, Memel, the Polish Corridor, Sudetenland, and Bohemia. The only doubtful point now is the chronology."

No one at the Vatican accepted Hitler as a possible barrier to the spread of communism, although that faint hope had existed when he first came to power. His revival of ancient paganism, his obsession with blood and attraction to barbaric ritual spelled religion rather than revolution. This was another cult of the State, a god from the womb of Politics, before whom human sacrifices would be offered as they were offered in Russia and in Spain. The total of priests, nuns, and laymen slaughtered by the Communist government of Spain now exceeded 14,000.

On July 19, 1936, General Francisco Franco's counterrevolution was launched in Spain.

The lights burned late in the Vatican.

Monsignor Montini never knew when he would have time to himself, or how much time, but when he did, he had space and comfort in his Belvedere Palace apartment. He had a record player with an automatic changer and he liked to play records while he wrote. His favorite composers were Chopin, Mozart, and Beethoven. He wrote in a great many fields, essays for magazines under his own name, lectures and sermons for men in the Curia who outranked him and whose identities he protected carefully. His personal correspondence was heavy, much of it from former members of FUCI. His usual signature on the personal mail was still "Don Battista" but his State Department signature was "G. B. Montini." When he wrote in English, as he frequently did, he signed "J. B. Montini."

He was forced by the pressure of work to resign from the teaching faculty of the Academy of the Noble Ecclesiastics but he clung to parish work. The Church of St. Anne, just inside St. Anne's Gate in Vatican City, was very old and residents of Vatican City considered it their parish church, as did many people from the shabby neighborhood on the Rome side of the wall. Monsignor Montini heard confessions in St. Anne's on Friday and Saturday nights, often saying Sunday Mass and preaching a sermon.

Eugenio Cardinal Pacelli sailed for the United States on the *Conte di Savoia*, September 29, 1936. Ostensibly, the Papal Secretary of State was taking a holiday and becoming acquainted with the United States, but he traveled with two assistants and two secretaries and he undertook a schedule that would have killed him if he had been as frail as he appeared. In one month he traveled 16,000 American miles, visited twelve of the sixteen ecclesiastical provinces in the United States and talked with seventy-nine bishops. He accepted honorary degrees from Fordham, Georgetown, and Notre Dame Universities and spoke to the members of the National Press Club in Washington. He crossed and recrossed the paths of Franklin Delano Roosevelt, campaigning for a second term as President of the United States, and Alfred M. Landon, his Republican opponent. Cardinal Pacelli avoided and ignored politics. Not until after the election did he show an awareness of the campaign. He called on President Roosevelt then and had luncheon with him at Hyde Park.

Catholics and non-Catholics liked, and responded to, Cardinal Pacelli. He had had a reputation as a charming host in Munich and in Berlin, a delightful and much-sought guest. The qualities which had won that reputation traveled with him. He had a natural courtesy, was grateful for even the smallest favor and was gracious with compliments. He exhibited no competitive or superior religious attitudes, but nothing that he said or did could be interpreted as ingratiating. His physical appearance was striking. As many thousands of people would say in the future, those who met him in 1936 said that he had the look of a Saint.

Battista Montini won his diplomatic service stripes during that fall. Demands were heavy on a department that had been understaffed at full strength. Incidents were increasing in Germany, some of them violent, many of them calculated official harassment. Cardinal Pacelli normally dealt with German problems himself, usually through Cardinal von Faulhauber. The Spanish Civil War was itself a grave problem and it was creating problems elsewhere. France had a Socialist government under Léon Blum in June and the Soviet Union staged a mass execution in August of alleged plotters against the life of Joseph Stalin. Cardinal Pacelli on tour kept in touch with all developments and his cables flowed in steadily, each requiring action of one kind or another.

Pius XI showed a preference for Monsignor Montini when he had orders or directives, trusting him with the wording and the execution. He was seriously ill and in great pain, pain that was obvious when he moved, but he refused to see a doctor and he would permit no one to mention his health.

Cardinal Pacelli returned to Rome on November 16, 1936, and two days later the Italian government recognized the Franco government in Spain. German recognition followed immediately.

It was obvious now that Pius XI could not go longer without medical attention and the Secretary of State had the authority of manner and skill of approach to succeed where others had failed with the Holy Father. The old man's face was white and there was sweat on his forehead.

"I will hear your report first," he said.

It was his ultimate concession. Cardinal Pacelli's report was confidential, of course, a secret report for the Sovereign Pontiff. He made other reports to his staff and his tour was well covered by the press. There is no great mystery about what he heard in the United States and what he observed there. There was no American sense of involvement in political developments which were seen as "European" and not as "World." Mussolini was popular, ridiculed by some of the press for his bombast and love of uniforms, but respected as the creator of the "new Italy" which had become a world power. Hitler was underrated. There was a widespread dismissal of Der Fuehrer as "ridiculous" and a comfortable American assumption that Germany was a hollow shell, unable to maintain its showy Army in the face of any threat. The anti-Semitic policies of the Reich had not aroused any widespread concern. There were many firms and business-men pleased with the Nazi government for pulling Germany out of its slump, wiping out unemployment and putting the na-tion back into the world markets.

The Spanish War was a real divider in the U.S. as elsewhere. The Vatican State Department had been aware for more than a year that the propaganda line of the Comintern to party ad-herents in all nations had been the ignoring or playing down of Soviet Russia, the playing up of its seedling, "the Spanish de-mocracy." In the United States, there was strong anti-Franco feeling on the part of the left wing, intellectual, and nonintel-lectual, a majority of newspaper people and many honest lib-erals. The people around Roosevelt, too, seemed to favor the Spanish republic but the weight of public opinion did not sup-port them. The American people did not want to become in-volved in Spain and certainly not on the side of the government which many people, including the majority of Catholics, refused to call a republic or a democracy, a government which they frankly labeled "Communist" or "Red."

During the visit of Cardinal Pacelli, the *New Republic* stated: "The Communist menace is about as real as the Japanese men-ace."

American newspapers were, on the average, good newspapers but Americans did not seem to understand communism, na-zism, or fascism as Europeans did, or in any comparable terms.

The American economy was not yet healthy. There was alarm-ing unemployment and the government would be concerned with domestic issues for a long time to come. President Roosevelt had received an overwhelming vote on Election Day, which indicated that he had won the confidence of the voters in his first four years. He was a confident, magnetic man but he had a naïve idea that he could settle any issue or dispute, diplomatic or otherwise, through personal conference: "horse trading" as he put it.

The Catholic Church in the United States was strong, hurt by the depression as all American institutions were, but recovering steadily. Rome and the Holy Father were almost abstractions to the average American Catholic. There was no direct link. The papal encyclicals were not read from pulpits and the percentage of Catholics familiar with them was small.

Pius XI heard Cardinal Pacelli's report and went to bed under medical treatment. He was suffering from varicose leg ulcers, myocarditis, general irregularity of blood circulation, and asthma. His doctors did not expect him to leave his bed again but he was up to broadcast his Christmas message in which he indicted communism as the source of the many evils which infected Europe. He returned to work, postponing nothing that he had to do except the public audiences which he had never liked. He filled all vacancies promptly and announced proudly in 1937 that every See in the United States was filled for the first time in many years. He was approaching eighty and he had to rely on wheel chairs and bed desks but he refused to concede to the obvious pain of his ailments.

"Pain is a privilege," he said. "It admits us to participation in the agonies of Our Lord."

Monsignor Montini was often with the Holy Father for hours at a time and he formed a close attachment with Cardinal Pacelli during this period of almost constant concern for the stubborn, gallant old man under whom they both worked.

The Cardinal Secretary of State slept only a few hours of the night, an hour of siesta. Don Battista learned to anticipate his needs and watched him carefully without being obvious about it. Eugenio Pacelli seemed to require just that. He never carried money or pens or pencils. He carried nothing. At the moment when he had a need, someone had to be present to pay his bill, to hand him a pen, to make a note. Battista, reading the despatches from the world of Catholicism, knew by instinct what to brief and what to leave intact. Often that instinct told him that a seemingly insignificant item, a trifle, was exactly what Cardinal Pacelli would want to see on that particular day. He was seldom wrong. The cardinal never seemed to notice that such things were caused, that they did not merely happen, and he never acknowledged thoughtfulness on the part of those who served under him but he drew Battista more closely into his confidence. He talked to him sometimes about events in the world and he invited the young Monsignor to pray with him, which was the richest sharing.

Through the first two months of 1937, Pius XI labored on his encyclical to the Germans. He had signed a Concordat with the Nazi government which Cardinal Pacelli negotiated and he told them how and why he signed it. "In the summer of 1933 . . . We accepted the offer made by the government of the Reich to institute negotiations for a Concordat . . . We were guided by the solicitude incumbent on Us to safeguard the freedom of the Church in the exercise of her apostolic ministry in Germany . . . In spite of many serious misgivings at the time . . . We wished to spare our faithful sons and daughters in Germany . . . anxiety and suffering. We have done everything to defend the sanctity of a word solemnly pledged."

Pius XI stated solemnly that the solemn pledges in Germany were broken and proceeded to his indictment of Nazi paganism. "He who replaces a personal God with a weird impersonal Fate supposedly according to ancient pre-Christian concepts denies the wisdom and providence of God . . . He who takes the race, or the people, or the state, or the form of government . . . out of the system of their earthly valuation and makes them the ultimate norm of all, even of religious values, and deifies them with an idolatrous worship perverts and falsifies the order of things created and commanded by God. . . . Our God is the personal, superhuman, almighty, infinitely perfect God, one in the Trinity of persons, threefold in the unity of the divine essence, the Creator of the universe . . . Who suffers and can suffer no other god beside Him."

He lashed out at the racial superiority claims with: "Only superficial minds can lapse into the heresy of speaking of a national god, of a national religion; only such can make the mad

151

attempt of trying to confine within the boundaries of a single people, within the narrow bloodstream of a single race, God, the Creator of the world . . . Only blindness and pride can close their eyes to the treasures of instruction for salvation that are in the Old Testament. He who wants to see the Biblical history and the wisdom of the Old Testament banished from the church and school blasphemes the Word of God."

He titled his encyclical *Mit Brennender Sorge* (*With Burning Anxiety*).

The German Catholics would suffer for that encyclical. It put them on the front line of the Church. It would be easy to spare them, to rationalize the situation, to accept violation of the Concordat as inevitable; to blink at the evils of the master race philosophy; to reason that since the Catholic Church still functioned in Germany and had vanished in Russia, a compromise should be reached with the system which still tolerated it. Pius XI could not accept that kind of pragmatism. A terrible evil was developing in a nation where the Church had voices with which to speak and to denounce. It was the duty of the Church to name that evil. Only incidentally did he mention the Jews, the people of the Old Testament, because only incidentally did he have the right to speak for them. He was not their chosen spokesman. He could not put them on the firing line but he did denounce the evil which menaced them.

The encyclical was dispatched to Germany with instructions that it be printed and that it be read from the pulpits on Passion Sunday. There was a feeling of tension, of waiting, in the Department of State, of bracing for shock. Cardinal Pacelli, who was emotionally involved with the German people, seemed more pale than usual and pallor was normal to him. Monsignor Montini said the Rosary with him and at the end of it he knelt for a half hour motionless, silent.

. In Germany, the pastors, with a very few negligible exceptions, read the encyclical of Pius XI denouncing the Nazi philosophy, the bad faith of the Nazi government, and the evil inherent in the cult of race and blood and destiny. Their shocked, stunned parishioners listened to them. The editors of Catholic newspapers published the Pope's message. There it was. They still had priests and churches and a Catholic press under the Nazi government but Catholicism was meaningless if it had to become the co-conspirator with a system which negated it, the possible partner in the denial of Christ. Pius XI asked much of the German Catholics and their pastors, and they gave him obedience.

The Nazi government struck promptly.

On May 28, Joseph Goebbels, in a savage speech, announced that a death struggle with the Catholic Church was beginning. The German Ambassador to the Vatican was recalled and more than one thousand priests and monks in Germany were placed under arrest on various charges. Catholic newspapers were suppressed, Catholic youth organizations disbanded, the presses on which the papal encyclical was printed in Germany were confiscated.

Don Battista, Ugo Piazza, Ciro Scotti, and Iginio Righetti had dinner together during the height of this persecution. Friends of theirs had been swept up by the Nazis in their drive against Catholic youth. Ten priests who were leaders, chaplains of their groups, were in prison and so was Righetti's opposite number, Franz Steber, the president of the German equivalent of FUCI. Battista's opposite number, the spiritual leader of German youth, Reverend Karl Kramer, had also been arrested.

"It is more important today than it was last year," Battista said, "and the year before, that young people hold firm to Catholic ideals, that they have companionship in that holding firm, that they understand those ideals to which they hold."

Monsignor Montini was Don Battista again in his concern and in the intensity of his feeling. The other three men were emboldened to offer a suggestion which they knew was outrageous.

"Father," they said, "if we organize a FUCI Alumni Society, composed of men who have absorbed the ideals and known the companionship, will you be our chaplain?"

"What would your object be?"

"We are older. We could offer guidance. We could let young people know that FUCI does not stop at a given year, that it has a continuing purpose."

Monsignor Montini had more demands on his time than any man could meet within any decent limits on a day, but he accepted this new post. It would be impossible for such a group as that proposed to meet frequently but by coming into existence it proclaimed the vitality of the Catholic youth movement which fed leaders into the lifestream of the community.

The Nazi punishment of German Catholics continued and in July it was extended to Protestants with the arrest of the Reverend Martin Niemöller, Berlin pastor, and 115 of his supporters.

Eugenio Cardinal Pacelli read the news from Germany tight-lipped, without any betraying expression, and despite the burden placed upon him by the uncertainty of the Holy Father's health, he increased his devotions, his periods of the day devoted to prayer.

He was, because experience and responsibility and environment had made him so, German in part, allied in sympathy to those who suffered, whom he had not spared and for whom he had not argued compromise or appeasement.

15

THE ALTARS OF CHAOS

THE Department of State of the Vatican was a listening post, a place of vantage, a combat zone into which men moved without weapons. The world around it seemed to be flying apart, erupting here and there, separating, splitting into zones and fragments. Monsignor Montini was a vital figure on the papal island in the middle of chaos and everything that happened to him there, everything in which he shared, marked him, shaped him, narrowed and expanded him.

Pius XI, followed his encyclical to the Germans with one to the world on atheistic communism which he titled *Divini Redemptoris*. It is clear, incisive, without ambiguity, and deserves to be read in full. Two significant paragraphs illustrate his approach, the earnest attempt that he was making to explain to the world an enemy with which he was familiar, one which he considered the enemy of all mankind.

"The communism of today, more emphatically than similar movements in the past, conceals in itself a false messianic idea. A pseudo-ideal of justice, of equality and fraternity in labor impregnates all its doctrine and activity with a deceptive mysticism, which communicates a zealous and contagious enthusiasm to the multitudes, entrapped by delusive promises. This is especially true in an age like ours when unusual misery has resulted from the unequal distribution of the goods of the world."

"The doctrine of modern communism, which is often concealed under the most seductive trappings, is in substance based on the principles of dialectical and historical materialism previously advocated by Karl Marx, of which the theoreticians of Bolshevism claim to possess the only genuine interpretation. According to this doctrine there is in the world only one reality, matter, the blind forces of which evolve into plant, animal, and man. Even human society is nothing but a phenomenon or form of matter, evolving in the same way. By a law of inexorable necessity, and through a perpetual conflict of forces, matter moves toward the final synthesis of a classless society. In such a doctrine, as is evident, there is no room for the idea of an eternal God; there is no difference between matter and spirit, between soul and body; there is neither survival of the soul after death nor any hope of a future life. Insisting on the dialectical aspect of their materialism, the Communists claim that the conflict which carries the world toward its final synthesis can be accelerated by man. Hence they endeavor to sharpen the antagonisms which arise between the various classes of society. Thus the class struggle with its consequent violent hate and destruction takes on the aspect of a crusade for the progress of humanity."

Pius XI was within weeks of his eightieth birthday. He was dying slowly, painfully, but he saw the world that he was leaving in sharp focus. He defined the twin dangers which menaced civilization and he called men to God. He could do no more. He was too much of a realist to expect a mass movement to God, even on the part of the professedly religious. The sacrifices and the risks would appall all save a courageous few, but such a movement could inundate the totalitarians and all that they had built. The Holy Father could write but each man who read would read the meaning within the limitations of his wisdom, his experience, and his conscience.

The world of 1937 paid little attention. Each statesman brewed his own magic, burned incense to his own wisdom.

There was unreality to the streets of Rome when Monsignor

Montini walked on them after a day at the Vatican. The streets said: "Italy is great! All is well with the world!" The unsightly old structures between Castel Sant'Angelo and Piazza San Pietro had been thinned out and a wide swath driven through Borgo Nuovo and Borgo Vecchia. A broad boulevard to be named Via della Conciliazione was coming into being, leading to St. Peter's and the Vatican and proclaiming by its name, "Conciliation," that all was well in Italy between Church and State.

The people, too, reflected a state of well-being. There was prosperity and people were at work. Everywhere one walked in Rome there were improvements; new subways being built, excavations to free the ancient monuments from the accretion of centuries. Ancient Rome was shining in glory again beside the glory of modern Rome.

St. Ivo's was slipping back into the neglect from which FUCI had rescued it. The University of Rome had expanded, moving from the old Palazzo della Sapienza to large, modern, new buildings. One could walk in any direction and the evidence submitted to his eyes proclaimed the success of Fascism, the boundless future of Italy.

Mussolini and Hitler were supporting Franco in the Spanish Civil War. Soviet Russia was supporting the so-called republic. Mussolini was swaggering more since his reception in Berlin, talking in more grandiose terms than ever, but he had less authentic arrogance. He had slipped quite definitely into second place, behind Hitler in their joint operations. Hitler was the more dynamic figure now in world opinion. Il Duce did not like it and could do nothing about it. Italy was not ready for another war. Raw materials were not stockpiled in sufficient quantity and Italian industry was inadequate for the support of a big war machine.

Eleven days after Hitler entered Austria, another army crossed a frontier, an army without guns. Delegates from all over Europe, and from overseas, arrived in Budapest for the 34th International Eucharistic Congress on March 23 and they were courageous people. The Nazi Party had been suppressed in Hungary only a month before and now the Nazis, in armed might, were next-door neighbors. The people of Budapest lived in a danger zone and their visitors entered a danger zone voluntarily.

Monsignor Montini, to his great surprise, was selected to accompany Cardinal Pacelli who was the Papal Legate. There had been little travel in his life and that little had been mainly within Italy, yet he was an inveterate sight-seer, a lover of pictorial souvenirs and guidebooks and maps. Despite the gravity of the situation which framed the Eucharistic Congress of 1938, he brought personal and priestly excitement to it as personal letters to friends and former Fucini attest.

The train which brought Cardinal Pacelli and Monsignor Montini into Budapest was decorated with papal flags and bunting in the papal colors. The locomotive carried a large cross. High dignitaries of Church and State met the train and the party drove through streets hung with bunting, under triumphal arches, between masses of spectators lining the way. Another delegation was waiting at the historic Church of the Incarnation and Cardinal Pacelli occupied a seat on a reviewing platform with the Regent of Hungary, Admiral Miklós Horthy.

In his address, Cardinal Pacelli said: "Are we surprised, in a world in which the idea of the fear of God is lost and the teachings of Christ are not applied to the practice of real life, to see suspicion rule between class and class, between man and man, between nation and nation, between people and people, suspicion which has arrived at such a degree that its brutal force threatens every moment to cause a catastrophe, and that in any case it covers with dark clouds the horizon of today and the near future?"

The clouds lifted briefly for those in attendance at the Congress. Cardinal Pacelli offered the pontifical Mass and the papal benediction. His inner conviction that this was very nearly man's final appeal to the Almighty for release from the horror which threatened was in his face, the supplicating gestures of his magnificently expressive hands, the rich timbre of his voice.

The people responded to him and to the event and to the presence of Christ upon the altar. The atmosphere of the Mass was charged with emotion which flowed along the streets when the Blessed Sacrament was carried in solemn procession.

Christ was walking the streets of Budapest where the sacred hosts had been scattered and spat upon during the Communist regime of Béla Kun.

Don Battista said Mass at St. Stephen's. He assisted Cardinal Pacelli, of course, at his Masses and he was beside him during ceremony and audience and the blessing of the delegates. He was with him, too, in relaxed moments, closer to him than he had ever been, patient with his impatience, touched by his gentleness. It was an odd relationship. Cardinal Pacelli did not find in Battista Montini the companionable qualities which he found in Monsignor (later Bishop and Cardinal) Spellman because he did not meet him on a companionable basis. The Cardinal Secretary of State was a stern autocrat to whom the work done is more important than the man who does it; he was also a priest with a sensitivity to the presence of Christ in a room, a hall, a city street, wherever he might be. His attitude toward Battista Montini was stern, and again gentle. There were marked similarities, physical and temperamental, between them and equally sharp divergences. Eugenio Pacelli had a paternal feeling for all the people of the world, a pastoral paternity, which became particularized in the case of Battista Montini so that, after the trip to Budapest, he often treated him as a man might treat a son.

They stayed an extra day in Budapest when the Eucharistic Congress was over in order to participate in the feast of St. Stephen. School children, boys and girls, paraded, wearing native costumes and the streets were brave with color.

Sharing the train ride to Rome, the Cardinal and the Monsignor knew as diplomats that, barring a miracle of God, the city and the nation they had left would be engulfed in the totalitarian tide, that the human choices confronting Hungary's leaders did not include the perfect, the ideal, or even the desirable. As priests they knew that if God in His mercy did offer man peace at this point, or the means of achieving peace, man would reject the offer. The hatreds, greeds, ambitions, and prides of the great and the small, their weak compromises and cowardly acts of self-interest, their sins of omission and commission, were all in the chalice which the witch doctors of neo-paganism offered at the altar of chaos. It was a common cup.

Monsignor Carlo Confalonieri, secretary to Pius XI, was delighted at the return of Cardinal Pacelli, and of Monsignor Montini who had been of immeasurable assistance to him during the long illness of the Holy Father. No one knew Pius XI better than Monsignor Confalonieri. He had been his secretary when Pius XI was Cardinal Archbishop of Milan and he had come with him to Rome. He was a Milanese and only a few years older than Monsignor Montini. The two men worked closely and well together. Monsignor Confalonieri was concerned about Pius XI who had put a heavy strain on his ailing heart during the absence of Cardinal Pacelli, worrying about the tightening world situation and composing a new encyclical. Other men might share duties, responsibilities, problems, and conflicts with the Supreme Pontiff but Monsignor Confalonieri shared his mind uniquely.

"He is becoming pessimistic in outlook," he said, of Pius XI, "and that is not his nature. I solicit good or hopeful news for him."

The news was neither good nor hopeful. In July, despite his previous disavowals, Benito Mussolini approved an anti-Semitic law drafted by a joint committee of Italian and German jurors working to co-ordinate legislation between the two nations. The law excluded people of Jewish birth from schools and the faculties of schools, from learned societies. Jews of foreign nationality were ordered to leave the country. Native-born Jews were forced to exchange property under unfavorable circumstances and to accept government bonds in payment.

Pius XI was incensed and outraged. He condemned the law

swiftly and angrily as "an unfortunate imitation of Germany's," knowing well how Mussolini hated even an inference that he was an imitator. He wrote personal letters to King Victor Emmanuel and to Mussolini, pointing out the fact that the new laws prohibiting mixed marriages between Jews and Christians were in opposition to the doctrines of the Roman Catholic Church and in violation of Article 34 of the 1929 Concordat.

The anti-Semitic law was unpopular with the Italian people and was immediately dubbed the "Nazi law." Count Carlo Sforza called anti-Semitism "the Socialism of imbeciles." Mussolini had not done a more unpopular thing since he came to power, nor anything which cost him more in world influence and respect.

Men of good will were still trying to find a way in which to deal with the frightening belligerency of Hitler's Germany without opening the European gate to the equally frightening might of the Soviet. Soviet Russia was quiet save for the cannibalistic purging of its own people but quiet only in the sense that it had completed its programs of antireligion before the later tyrants came. The Russian Jews were dispersed or in exile, the churches closed, the lingering traces of religion controlled by the State and rendered meaningless.

Neville Chamberlain, Prime Minister of Great Britain, was one of the men of good will. In the idealistic sense he was willing to accept humiliation rather than release evil on the world through the open door of war; in the practical sense he needed time in which to prepare Britain's defenses against a menace which was already bristlingly prepared. He opened negotiations with Adolf Hitler and he went to Munich.

"Peace!" Pius XI snorted. "One cannot talk peace in a forest of bayonets."

Nevertheless he dared to hope again. The Hitler-Chamberlain conference was scheduled for September 29. The Holy Father drew upon his last reserves of strength and energy for a radio address which he broadcast to the world, eloquently pleading for peace and for the intervention of God that the peace achieved would be a lasting one.

It was his last effort but one. He had two heart attacks after that, but stayed stubbornly alive. He had been living for years with all the medical odds against him and now he had one more goal. He had an encyclical to write that would crown all of those that he had written, a plan for peace.

Hitler at Munich obtained all of the border territory in Czechoslovakia in which German majorities lived and immediately took them over. Poland, disappointingly, took advantage of its neighbor's distress to slice off territory. Having done so with impunity, Poland returned for another slice.

In Paris a seventeen-year-old Polish Jew assassinated Herr Ernst von Rath, a German diplomatic official on November 7. There was no evidence that he was the instrument of a conspiracy or acting out of any compulsion except some crazed notion of his own but Hitler's Reich condemned all Jews for that one shot. Eleven hours of rioting in German cities destroyed Jewish stores and homes, killed and injured Jewish people. The government then imposed the harshest laws to date and levied an enormous fine against the Jewish community. The shocked protests of the leading nations and of the Vatican had no effect. The fanatical anti-Semitism crossed the borders into German-held territory.

Pius XI issued a summons for a convocation of the Bishops of Italy and set the date as February 11, 1939. It was the tenth anniversary of the Lateran Pact and he was writing his special encyclical for it. He had chosen the Bishops as his audience. He was fading fast physically and his heart was giving him trouble. He rested in bed but he couldn't rally this time and he knew it. He prayed, and he asked those around him to pray, and he told his doctors: "I must have two more days."

The doctors could not give him those two days and God did not. At 5:31 A.M., February 10, 1939, Pius XI died. His encyclical was never delivered. As is customary, it was locked up for the archives with other unfinished projects of the reign. The throne of Peter was vacant.

Giovanni Battista Montini knelt once more at the bier of a pope and kissed a dead hand. He had been very close to this man and had learned much from him.

16

THE HOLOCAUST

T HERE was an immense crowd gathered in Piazza San Pietro within the enfolding arms of the Bernini colonnades. They had seen the plume of white smoke rise and they were awaiting the name of the new pope. Monsignor Montini sat alone at his desk. The phone rang and he answered it. He knelt then with the phone in his hand.

Eugenio Cardinal Pacelli had just told him that the College of Cardinals had chosen him and that his name would be Pius XII.

Giovanni Battista Montini was the first one to know the identity of the new pope outside of the locked rooms of the Sistine Palace, recipient of the first blessing of the Sovereign Pontiff, a blessing over a telephone and oddly appropriate to the era.

There was no truce with time, no leisurely establishment of routine. Pius XII appointed his immediate staff before his coronation: Luigi Cardinal Maglione, Secretary of State; Monsignor Domenico Tardini, Chief of the Foreign Office; Monsignor Carlo Confalonieri, secretary, the same post he had held with Pius XI; Monsignor Montini retained his title as Undersecretary of State and only Tardini outranked him under the Secretary. Tardini was short, squat, aggressive, tougher in manner than in reality. Don Battista had known him and worked under him for years. Despite his appearance and his manner, Monsignor Tardini was a skilled diplomat. He had been Don Battista's predecessor on the faculty of the Noble Ecclesiastics but the two men had little in common save experience.

Cardinal Maglione was a contemporary of the new pope, one year younger. He had been the expert on French affairs under Pius XI as Cardinal Pacelli had been expert on the Germans. A strikingly handsome blond Italian, Cardinal Maglione was one of the Vatican's best personal contact men. He wrote his itinerary of the trips he planned to take in the immediate future before he had been in office twenty-four hours.

There was a sense of urgency behind the scenes at the Vatican while arrangements proceeded for the solemn ceremonial rites which symbolized the timeless and the eternal.

Pius XII was crowned on March 12, 1939, and three days later, Hitler's troops took over what was left of Czechoslovakia. Adolf Hitler entered Prague in triumph and with cynical indifference to the violated treaty on which Neville Chamberlain had based his hope of "peace in our time."

The Spanish Civil War ended on March 28 with the forces of Francisco Franco victorious. Hitler was exchanging angry notes with Poland which was being encouraged to resist by Britain and France.

Cardinal Maglione left Rome on a trip which took him to London, Paris, Berlin, and Warsaw. Archbishop Amleto Cicognani called on President Roosevelt, then came to Rome. The pope had no divisions but he mobilized his forces, offering his influence to anyone who would work for peace.

Pius XII had taken on a new personality with the papacy. He had been tentative as Secretary of State, now he was confident. He was no longer the executor of another man's policy; he was policy. He talked to the visiting cardinals individually before they went home from the conclave and he subordinated every other interest to peace. Plans and projects would be meaningless if war came, so war must be averted. He spoke, publicly and in private, as though confident that war could be averted.

He planned his moves as though the problems of totalitarianism and war had just come into the world, as though his pontificate had been born with them, having no continuity with the reign of Pius XI. He could not have felt that but, for the time, he created the impression and he lifted hopes.

He had never been more impressive than in those first weeks of his primacy. He was over six feet in height and straight of spine. His height and his magnificent detachment awed visitors and his own staff. He had given to the Vicar of Christ a respect and deference that at times seemed exaggerated when he was next to the throne as Secretary of State, and he paid that same respect and deference now that he wore the ring of Peter. He did not relax any of the elaborate ceremony of approaching and addressing a pope even under the stresses of international conflict, nor diminish the great and awesome dignity of the office by any act or concession. He had ascended to the throne but he was not the papacy. The papacy belonged to all of the popes who had been and all of the popes yet to be. It was difficult for people to understand that quality of sublimation that he had; the quality of separating his personality from the highest throne in the world, of which he considered his personality unworthy. Unless one did understand it, Pius was that incomprehensible paradox, a humble egotist.

Monsignor Montini brought rare understanding to Pius XII. They were sufficiently alike for him to comprehend perfectly the sublimation and to anticipate the needs and the wants of the man who had moved into utter and complete loneliness in gaining the heights to which he had, unquestionably, aspired. That was another of the factors that was seldom weighed with Pius XII. He was, beyond any doubt, the best qualified man in the world for the office when the conclave elected him Pope in 1939. He knew that he was the best qualified and he wanted the opportunity to use his knowledge, his experience, his many skills in the service of the Church at a time of crisis. It was a form of ambition which Giovanni Battista Montini could understand and serve. He served well, wearing for a long while the literal robe of anonymity, which was sublimizing of a kind.

Through the cardinals, through nuncios, through special envoys, through his traveling Secretary of State, Pius XII sent personal messages to the bishops of all the nations, urging them to exert their own influence and to solicit that of others in behalf of a drive for peace, for declarations of world unity that the dictators would recognize. It was idealistic but it was not impractical. Pius XII was a diplomat of long experience and he knew the value of mobilized public opinion, the weight exerted by unexpected combinations of nations not normally in alliance. There was fear in the world that might result in alignments of potential force sufficient to halt further aggression before it started.

Pius XII lost his gamble for peace because the Nazi diplomats reasoned as he did and saw as a danger the possibility which Pius saw as a hope. To cancel out the threat of unusual combinations against them and the menace of a possible multi-front war when they moved aggressively, the Nazis entered into discussions which led to the least probable, in world eyes, of all alliances; the German-Russian nonaggression pact of August 21, 1939.

The Vatican State Department knew through secret channels that the pact was in prospect five weeks before it was signed. There was no one in the hierarchies of Nazidom or Communism who could be influenced by the Roman Catholic Church, or any other religious organization, with an appeal in behalf of world order or the welfare of mankind. Pius XII, however, continued to appeal for peace over the Vatican Radio. Poland was doomed unless a miracle happened and he was refusing to concede. Through Cardinal Maglione he asked for a fifteen-day truce in the German-Polish dispute, a temporary halt to preparations for war, and a conference of the leading world powers.

On September 1, 1939, the Nazi legions hammered their way into Poland and set an avalanche into roaring motion.

The Vatican received its first word of the unleashed German might through a phone call from Archbishop Cesare Orsenigo, Papal Nuncio at Berlin, to Cardinal Maglione at 6 A.M. Cardinal Maglione broke the news to the Holy Father who immediately invited him to kneel in prayer.

The shocking news was circulating fast through Rome when Monsignor Confalonieri introduced the subject of the day's audience. There was an audience scheduled for the afternoon, a mixed group of people, mainly tourists. Pius XII said that he would not disappoint the people. He would hold the audience. His secretary mentioned then the fact which worried the Maestro di Camera who was responsible for audiences.

"There are fifteen German soldiers invited to the audience, your Holiness."

Fifteen German soldiers! They were on leave and traveling, no doubt. Tourists, but in uniform. They would have no other clothing. Catholics in all probability, spending a leave to visit the greatest shrine in Christendom. They would be unpopular. Everyone who looked at them would be reminded of their comrades who had invaded Poland today, bringing war to the world. Anyone who had anything to do with them would be suspected of sympathy for the Nazi cause. Pius XII could look further ahead than most men and see more clearly, but he did not ordain his actions to please men.

"We shall see these soldiers," he said. "They have been promised an audience." His voice softened. "Who in these days stands more in need of a blessing, and of our prayers, than does a soldier called by his government to battle."

There was immediate criticism from neutral nations and from England and France when the story of the audience was published in the press. Reynolds Packard of United Press went to the Vatican for comment and according to his report of the resulting interview:

"Monsignor Giovanni Battista Montini, one of the foreign affairs experts of the Secretariat, confirmed the truth of the story and appeared disturbed that it had caused such international repercussions. He explained that the pope was always disposed to receive all people whenever possible and that 'all people, regardless of their nationality are beloved by the Holy Father.'"

It was a truth which the Vatican could attest at all times but which was not acceptable in wartime by people whose emotional conditioning demanded even of God no less than partisanship.

The house of peace that men had tried to build of words and treaties, and pacts and compromises, came tumbling down. Britain and France immediately declared war on Germany. The Russians poured into Poland over the opposite border as agreed with Germany, partitioning the country. Russia attacked Finland despite protests from the United States, the Vatican, and the League of Nations. Their separate protests and mutual concern at the violent trend of events ahead made allies, in spirit at least, of the Vatican and the White House. The relationship had been, of course, consistently cordial despite the fact that the United States was the only one of the great powers, with the exception of the Soviet Union, which was not represented by an Ambassador to the Holy See.

Pope Pius XII and President Franklin D. Roosevelt had met when the pope, then Cardinal Pacelli, toured the United States. As a friendly gesture, President Roosevelt sent Joseph P. Kennedy, United States Ambassador to Great Britain, as his personal representative to the coronation of Piux XII. Ambassador Kennedy was accompanied by his wife and eight of his nine children. It is a curious footnote to history that Monsignor Giovanni Battista Montini met the Kennedy family before the coronation ceremonies and again briefly later; thus bringing together at that crowning a future President of the United States and a future pope of the Universal Church.

On December 23, 1939, the President of the United States sent a personal letter to the Holy Father. It was one of a number of letters which he wrote to religious leaders of all faiths. He could invite Protestant and Jewish leaders to visit him in the White House but personal contact with the pope necessitated an intermediary. Myron C. Taylor, a prominent Protestant

Episcopal layman, consented to be that intermediary. The letter of President Roosevelt proposing this method of communication by personal representative delighted Pius XII. It could not have been more aptly phrased for him as even a few sentences will indicate.

". . . civilization today passed through war and travail. I take heart in remembering that in a similar time, Isaiah first prophesied the birth of Christ. Then, several centuries before His coming, the condition of the world was not unlike that which we see today. Then, as now, a conflagration had been set, and nations walked dangerously in the light of the fires which they had themselves kindled. . . . In their hearts men decline to accept for long the law of destruction forced upon them by wielders of brute force. Always they seek, sometimes in silence, to find again the faith without which the welfare of nations and the peace of the world cannot be rebuilt."

It was the kind of letter that Pius himself might have written. He read it to his staff and he summoned many high-ranking members of the Curia to hear it. His reply was dated January 7, 1940. Again, a brief extract expresses the style and spirit of the letter:

"We have been particularly impressed by one characteristic feature of Your Excellency's message: the vital, spiritual contact with the thoughts and the feelings, the hopes and the aspirations of the masses of the people, of those classes, namely, on whom more than others, and in a measure never felt before, weighs the burden of sorrow and sacrifice imposed by the present restless and tempestuous hour."

Those two letters marked the beginning of a remarkable correspondence. Pope and President were much alike in their fondness for rhetoric, for ringing phrases, and in their penchant for personal diplomacy, for dispensing with advisers and cabinets. They preferred to dispense, too, with Secretaries of State.

The correspondence made history in its way and it introduced a dramatic sequence of events at the Vatican, a colorful grouping of people.

On February 27, 1940, Myron C. Taylor presented his credentials at the Vatican and a hand-written letter from President Roosevelt to Pope Pius XII. Myron C. Taylor, in writing of his Rome experience, mentioned Luigi Cardinal Maglione, Monsignor Domenico Tardini and Monsignor Giovanni B. Montini, "on whom it was always possible to depend for sympathetic and intelligent consideration of problems, whether burdensome or not."

On his part Monsignor Montini found in the American an interesting and stimulating personality, a highly successful businessman who had owned a house in Florence for many years and who was thoroughly at home in Italy.

Harold Tittman left the United States Embassy in Rome to assist Myron C. Taylor at the Vatican and he was another extraordinary individual, well known to the Department of State staff. One of the real heroes of American aviation in the First World War, Tittman had been shot down and so badly wounded that he never completely recovered. After twenty years in Rome, he was more Roman than American.

Don Battista liked him and spent much time with him; Myron Taylor naturally falling into the orbit of Cardinal Maglione. Tittman's wife, Eleanor, was a formidable woman, equally at home at a bridge table or on a golf course. Monsignor Montini, for all of a diplomat's poise and polish, was more than a little overwhelmed by her competence but he enjoyed the family and the contact with America. He had been briefed on Myron Taylor by Archbishop Cicognani who had had friendly relations with Taylor in Washington.

This Taylor mission to Pope Pius XII was a happy inspiration. It gave the small State Department staff of the Vatican a feeling of alliance with the powerful United States when all Europe was in flames. They had neutrality in common and they found common objectives with President Roosevelt's representatives. Myron Taylor had had experience with disaster problems, refugees and homeless people, orphans and people of lost nationality which were high on the list of Vatican responsibilities now and for indefinite time to come. The immediate objective, as contrasted to the continuing one, was that of keeping Italy neutral.

As early as August 1939, before he wrote to the Holy Father, President Roosevelt had written a letter to King Victor Emmanuel III of Italy "in behalf of the maintenance of peace," congratulating him on "the great achievements which the Italian nation has attained in the past generation." He concluded his letter with a passage in which he said: "The governments of Italy and the United States today advance those ideals of Christianity which of late seem so often obscured."

Pope Pius XII, too, had made his overtures to Italy. On December 21, he received the King and Queen at the Vatican, and Foreign Minister Count Ciano, Mussolini's son-in-law. More than that, he returned the visit to the Quirinal Palace, the first Pope to call on a King of Italy.

President Roosevelt wrote a letter to Mussolini at the beginning of the new year, 1940, and again after Myron C. Taylor arrived in Rome, friendly letters expressing his hope that Italy would continue to thrive and remain at peace.

In the meantime, Germany invaded Denmark and Norway, the Netherlands, Belgium, Luxembourg. In May, Belgium surrendered, the French Army collapsed and the British saved their Army from the beaches of Dunkerque in one of the most remarkable evacuations of history.

Mussolini was restless, a man with many uniforms and no war to fight. Hitler was a world figure, establishing dominion over the greater part of Europe, and Il Duce did not even have an excuse for a balcony appearance at Palazzo di Venezia.

Declaring that the destiny of Italy demanded an outlet to the Atlantic and freedom from her imprisonment in the Mediterranean, Mussolini's Italy declared war on France and Great Britain, June 9, 1940.

The Vatican was completely surrounded by a nation at war.

17

CLOAK AND DAGGER

G IOVANNI BATTISTA MONTINI became the central figure of melodramatic tales and legends during the war years. He was rumored to be the chief of an espionage network, the key figure in underground organizations, the master of Vatican Intelligence. He neither admitted nor denied anything that was said of him. He was adroit at turning a question which he did not want to answer and he avoided publicity, even in the most obvious affairs. He did not confide in anyone and he was notably discreet in conversation.

"You could make a huge collection of Montini photographs covering the war years," one of his contemporaries said. "In every one of them you would see him *listening* to somebody."

The State Department, under the Holy Father, retained most of its peacetime duties and responsibilities with many new tasks added by the war. Cardinal Maglione and Monsignor Tardini communicated with governments and their representatives, arranged for credentials of Vatican representatives to other nations and accepted those of people assigned to them. They handled the vastly complicated correspondence with Departments of State of warring nations involving Church personnel, property, and money both within the nations and in the countries which they invaded. The occupied territory of a sovereign State with its people, priests and churches presented many problems in any war; in World War II the very speed of conquest, the ruthless brutality of mechanized warfare, complicated and confused procedures.

Monsignor Montini did not deal with governments. His work concerned people. In normal times he maintained contact with dioceses and archdioceses throughout the world, with Catholic Action groups of all kinds from students to dispensers of charity. He corresponded with papal diplomats and nuncios about the projects which were his responsibility and the individuals in the nuncio's nation attached to the projects. He knew by correspondence the men and women working on future Eucharistic Congresses and other international, or large national, Church activities. The widening circles of his activity inevitably included Catholics and non-Catholics. War brought to a halt many of his projects, opened up others.

Monsignor Montini found himself confronted suddenly with the awful problem of refugees, of homeless, hungry people uprooted and tossed aside by armies which moved with numbing speed. Vatican diplomacy had expended its main effort on the preservation of peace as long as a hope of peace remained. Having failed to save these people from the terrors of conflict and the desperation of involuntary mass migration, the Church must now strive to rescue them.

The process was complicated. Monsignor Montini worked through existing agencies where he could, offering financial aid in some cases, personnel in others. Once the first shock of war had passed there were survivors in Catholic organizations with whom he re-established contact. He had worked quietly with some of them before the war broke in aiding the escape of Catholic youth leaders from Germany, Czechoslovakia, and Austria, and in rescuing Jews in those same countries. He had to impose even graver risks upon them now but the need was greater. He had, too, the agency which the Vatican had established in the First World War and which was immediately revived in the Second; the Information Bureau which sought the names of prisoners of war and war wounded, for transmittal to families.

This project was one close to the heart of Pius XII. When the reality of war supplanted the hope of peace, he held a number of conferences with Monsignor Montini, offering him everything that he needed to establish a humanitarian service in a war that might be of long duration.

"Uncertainty about the fate of sons, husbands, fathers, called to the battlefields is an immeasurable agony," the Holy Father said. "We must relieve it where we can."

Italy was not at war when the Information Bureau was established so office equipment was ordered in Rome. Space was assigned to the Bureau in the building of the Congregation for the Oriental Church and Monsignor Montini addressed himself to the problem of manpower. The English, Scotch, Spanish, Ukrainian, Rumanian, American, and many other colleges closed with the coming of war, some of them not until Italy entered it. Former faculty men became available, young clerics from the student bodies who were not returning home, and other priests made transients by the dislocations of war and politics.

The Academy of the Noble Ecclesiastics was still functioning but Pope Pius XII had changed its name to Ecclesiastical Academy. It was an unpopular change with traditionalists but the Holy Father, although formerly on the faculty, had never attended the academy. He said, in changing the name, that the "Noble" was pretentious and outmoded. The small conflict led the more conservative members of the Curia, most of them academy graduates, to look upon Pius XII as liberal, or leaning liberal. Monsignor Montini, who had attended the academy and served on its faculty, expressed no opinion.

Recruiting for Monsignor Montini's Information Bureau proceeded rapidly. Within an astonishingly short time, he had 130 men serving under him, clerics of all ages with only a very few laymen. They constituted a Bureau which obtained and prepared for broadcast the names of prisoners of war and war wounded on all fronts. Vatican Radio made broadcasts several times a day and in a number of languages. In the course of collecting these names, and other mercy information, Monsignor Montini's sources obtained much other information significant in itself or of a kind that could be interpreted significantly. He had to guard and suppress such data lest he endanger people on whom he relied or expose the Vatican to charges of breached neutrality.

The value of the Bureau increased as others used it. Radio station personnel in many countries monitored the Vatican broadcasts and repeated the names for their own listeners.

On September 1, 1941, two years after Germany invaded Poland, the Information Bureau was able to report that it had handled 364,409 requests for information and succeeded in locating the missing persons sought by the inquirers in 147,862 cases. This service was, of course, supplementary to the daily broadcasts and the contact work, by correspondence and other means, which produced the steady flow of names from the battlefronts.

There was an air of intrigue in this operation and it was in connection with it that Montini was first identified with undercover work. He was jokingly accused once of commanding "a white gestapo." One of his titles, Secretary of the Cipher, had a conspiratorial sound, too.

The Holy Father's obviously high regard for Monsignor Montini enhanced his reputation as a skillful manipulator of chess pieces offstage but it is doubtful that he had the authority or the influence with which he was credited, although he undoubtedly had the responsibility. The Supreme Pontiff remained supreme and he permitted few guiding lines to escape his fingers. He had a remarkable capacity for carrying in his mind the details, great and small, of the many papal problems, even those which he delegated to others.

Monsignor Montini achieved one brief visit home, in August 1940, to celebrate the forty-fifth wedding anniversary of his parents. Neither Giorgio nor Giuditta was in good health and the rigors of war were hard on them. Milan was bombed every night and there had been bombings of Bergamo and Brescia. The Church of Santa Maria dei Miracoli had been hit by bombs and was in a state of ruin. They heard bombers going over at night even when Brescia was not bombed. They did not want to leave home and live in the Vatican although their son could have arranged it.

"This is our home. This is where we belong," Giorgio Montini said.

He had given an interview to the paper a few days earlier. "We have had three sons," he said, "who have carried on well the family traditions. The eldest is a lawyer who divides his time between his profession and Catholic enterprises. He married fifteen years ago a kind and good young lady. The second son, ordained after his lyceum studies, went to Rome for degrees in philosophy, law and literature. He is caught up in the gears of Vatican diplomacy and is now substitute Secretary of State to His Holiness. The third is a doctor who devotes himself to his studies, to his patients and to works of charity."

Monsignor Montini visited with his parents, with his brothers and their families, with neighbors. He was Don Battista again for a while and the talk of his brothers was the down-to-earth talk of men who had to contend with war and the effects of war on a different level than his own, neither more nor less real. He stood with them and watched flashes on the horizon at night when the British bombers came over Milan, and he prayed.

He had to return too soon to his duties at the Vatican, but as an anniversary present, he took his parents with him. They lived for a week in his apartment and they had an audience with Pope Pius XII. During the audience the Holy Father used a subterfuge to send Monsignor Montini from the room briefly. He looked then at Giorgio and Giuditta Montini.

"I thank you for having offered a son such as this to the Church," he said. "He is very dear and very valuable to me. You cannot imagine how much more so he will be, for everyone, in the years to come."

In that first summer of the war, despite the smothering heat of Rome, Pius XII elected to stay at the Vatican rather than at Castel Gandolfo in the Alban Hills where he would normally go. Monsignor Montini made many trips to the papal summer palace that year although he did not spend any extended time there. It was said that he was concerned about the refugees hidden in the palace and the town, and expressing through his visits the concern of the Holy Father, lest the Fascists descend on the place.

Among the people who had found sanctuary at Castel Gandolfo were men who had incurred Fascist displeasure through Catholic Action programs and who, in wartime, might find themselves in grave trouble if normal opposition to political measures was interpreted as treasonable. Families who had fled the anti-Semitic persecutions in Germany and Poland as well as Italy, were also hidden there. It would be naïve to assume that the Fascists were deceived, but they had sufficient trouble without opening another trouble front with the Vatican. Monsignor Montini's regular visits were evidence of papal concern for Castel Gandolfo and its guests, so Fascist officialdom looked the other way.

Many of those officials, particularly the minor ones, were feeling the pull of religion again as were people all over Italy, the normally religious and the normally indifferent. The Italian people were not only attending Masses, they were in the churches at all hours, pouring out their grief and their fears in prayer as were other people in other countries all over the world.

The war had gone badly for Italy from the beginning. Mussolini had miscalculated when he anticipated a swift, decisive German victory after the fall of France, one in which he could share and in which his risk would be small. He was not prepared for a long war and he could not adequately clothe, feed, or equip the men he drafted to fight in Africa and the Balkans. He invaded Greece against the advice of Hitler and the Greeks threw his army out with heavy losses. The English beat him in Libya and Ethiopia. Italy's African empire was melting away and Italy was losing her sons on battlefields remote from any interest of Italy's.

The Germans thundered on, unchecked, but the Italian people felt no identification with their victories. They were the allies of Russia, Communist Russia. So, too, was Italy but it was difficult to comprehend. On April 13, 1941, while the Nazis were rounding off their swift conquest of Yugoslavia, the Soviet signed a five-year neutrality pact with Japan.

All of these confusions were the daily fare of the Vatican; its work and its conversation. The Vatican, like Castel Gandolfo, had become a sanctuary. Some fugitives and displaced persons reached it through the escape routes of other organizations and to them the Vatican was the abbey or the monastery of the Middle Ages, bound by rule to offer hospitality and such safety as was possible. There were routes by which they could be moved along, as there were routes entirely controlled by "the Church of rescue and of compassion" which was a way of designating the operation which rescued and hid the otherwise doomed; a Church of humble people who took enormous risks in the name of charity.

Monsignor Montini was responsible for this activity as he was for the names of prisoners of war, but no man took credit for such intricate enterprises involving clergy and laity in great numbers. He never discussed, or even mentioned, this movement of people, this gathering of names, in which he played a directing role. A small glimpse of the work done, the incredible detail to be handled and the risks to be run, is obtained from a report prepared by B'nai B'rith long after the war. In the Bulletin of the Anti-Defamation League for October 1958 the report reads:

"It is known today that, under Pope Pius XII's instructions, 15,000 Jews received asylum in Castel Gandolfo. In convents and monasteries, canonical enclosure was lifted so that Jews of both sexes might find security under Vatican immunity. More than 180 places thus made available a secret asylum given to over 7000 refugee Jews."

A full report would include people of all faiths who were caught up in the rescue net of compassion, the misses and the tragedies as well as the successes and the triumphs. Such a report does not exist in available form although the astonishing Vatican archives may make figures available in another century or two.

Within the Vatican, and apart from the furtive transients whom they never saw, were other guests of greater stability. At the outbreak of the war, the nations of the world were represented at the papal court by fifteen embassies, twenty-four envoys of ministerial rank, and one chargé d'affaires. Others were added later. All of these diplomats with families and staffs moved into tiny Vatican City, 162 persons at the outset. There were members of the Catholic hierarchy of conquered countries, and priests, many of them in only briefly for conferences and some for residence of indefinite duration. There were also laymen who were invited for one reason or another, or granted sanctuary. They comprised a relatively small but colorful population. Social life, restricted neccessarily, was interesting.

Once a month, except during Lent and during summer, the Secretary of State invited the diplomats accredited to the Holy See to dinner. A problem arose immediately with the war declarations. Protocol said that the diplomats should be seated according to seniority and there could be no departure from protocol. The Ministers of Great Britain and of Germany were of almost equal seniority so must sit beside each other. It would be obviously impossible to so seat them, with the war going as it was, even if they normally liked each other. Francis D'Arcy Osborne and Baron von Weysalker decidedly disliked each other. The answer, the only answer, was that protocol permitted a host to be seated anywhere at the table. Monsignor Giovanni Battista Montini, Undersecretary of State, was one of the hosts, so he was seated between the two hostile diplomats.

Monsignor Montini faced an obvious dilemma. If he was friendly, the two men might compete for his time and his attention, jealous in the way of diplomats and ready to take offense if he seemed to favor one or the other. There were no safe topics of conversation, either, when one sat between an official Englishman and an official German. Monsignor Montini solved the problem by remaining silent, scrupulously silent. His companions on either side could turn from his silence to people on the other side and converse but he had to assume the position of buffer, sharing the dinner interval with no one. He did this month after month, accepting the role which no one else wanted. The diplomatic set found the situation intriguing and the Undersecretary's endurance astonishing.

"How does he do it?" someone asked.

"Out of habit! He is like that when there is no situation," Monsignor Domenico Tardini said.

Another, lesser, figure in the Department of State answered the same question with: "It isn't difficult for Montini. He has his own voices, like Joan of Arc."

The impression that Battista Montini was by nature quiet, withdrawn, undemonstrative, a trifle cold, was widespread. His old tutor, P. Giuseppe Persico, S.J., is quite voluble on that subject.

"It is wrong," he said. "I have known him as a boy and as a man. He has a sweet nature. His affections are warm as are his loyalties. He is thoughtful and he values friendships as do few men. He did not have real friendships when he was a boy and he did not know how to establish them. When he discovered a friendship it was a jewel to him, something of great value."

Of the war years, Padre Persico says: "It was a great wrong to him to give him such work to do, secret work that he could not confide to others, that he must keep within himself. It took him many years to escape from within himself. He was locked in, you understand. It was a risk to force him back again when he had come out of himself into the world. If he did not have a strong will and the character of greatness, he could not have done this work which was of the sort which he should have avoided."

Montini, in these war years, was in his middle forties, thin and usually pale, a man with a fine profile and compelling eyes. If the problems of secrecy bothered him, he carried them well. No one who remembers him from that period seems able to recall his speaking at length on any subject, or dominating any conversations: but they do remember him as smooth and easy, relaxed in any company, not smiling often but smiling well. He was attracted to the odd flavor of American turns of phrase, American gestures, the terse manner in which Americans often convey profound ideas. He had a phrase that he used often himself, rather wryly, when he assigned some work and was asked when he wanted it; a phrase that may be translated as "relatively instantly."

The one-time Monsignor, now Archbishop, Francis J. Spellman, had taught him much about America and Americans, mainly by indirection, during their early years in Curia offices and there were Americans among the odd internationals of the wartime Vatican; Monsignors Francis J. Brennan of Philadelphia, Joseph McGeough of New York, Walter S. Carroll of Pittsburgh. There were, of course, the Tittmans. The diplomats included Hildebrand Pinto of Brazil, Mercado Batton of Bolivia, Casas Briceno of Venezuela, Marco Schreiber of Peru, Casimir Papee of Poland, Cheon Kang-sie of China and many more. Regular, or temporary or semidiplomatic, attached to embassies or legations, were authors, poets, painters, and composers who, with the artist's knack of antagonizing politicians, were fugitives from the warring world. The hosts included cardinals, archbishops, bishops, monsignori, unranked priests, and friars.

The conversation was remarkable.

Vatican City, a sovereign state which occupies less land than the average city park, 108.7 acres, was a tiny dot of peace and neutrality completely surrounded by death and destruction. The people who lived in it and the people who shared its hospitality were linked to the world disaster through families and other ties or emotionally involved in it. They showed their concern in many ways but they also sought ways in which to escape from

182

that concern, to maintain the balance upon which sanity depends.

Almost without any conscious planning, men pooled knowledge, resources and skills for the benefit of the group. Those who spoke unusual languages gave lectures, and taught the languages if interest developed. Men shared their knowledge of art, of music, of literature, of architecture, or archaeology. There were experts on early and half-forgotten ceremonies and rituals who revived them briefly, and other experts who taught strange chants to choirs. It was not a case of filling time; it was, perhaps, a necessity for finding something meaningful in years dedicated to destruction. Men, and the few women, gathered in small or large groups and shared what others had found interesting in life, had found worth the learning.

These temporary people of the Vatican were, with few exceptions, linguists. They spoke one European tongue and moved to another without a break in thought. They prized wit in any language and they enjoyed anecdotes with point. They were civilized people in terms of education, taste, experience, social discipline. Monsignor Montini enjoyed the varied activities, his restless, ever-curious mind reaching eagerly for these treasures of casual classrooms which represented mature seeking rather than a youthful submission to instruction.

Giovanni Battista Montini was one with these people but he was also a priest, and that was another order within the social structure of this island in war. Priests did not speak pietisms to one another nor move with the spirits of saints in the corridors which saints had known and walked. They accepted what they were, and what lay people were. They did not exhort in this palace of administration and communication because exhortation belonged elsewhere and was the function of other priests. Outsiders, knowing little of them, considered priests of the Vatican worldly, more sophisticated than spiritual. In a sense they were, but such generalities are difficult to define. They were priests and they prayed. They did not consider it enough that they said their morning Masses and read the Daily Office and participated in the round of Vatican rite and ceremony; they prayed at odd hours through the day, sometimes in pairs or in small groups.

Priests had a double identity with the war. They had given hostages to pain as the laymen had; relatives in the armed services or in the bombed areas, the invasion or defense sectors. They had also their own kind in hazard. They felt the deaths of many priests on the battlefields as losses in their own families, a diminishing of themselves. They prayed and none of them, perhaps, offered more voluntary hours of prayer than Pius XII.

Monsignor Montini continued to hear confessions at St. Anne's and he said Masses there and at Castel Gandolfo, and in the Sistine Chapel for the diplomats and their families. Most of the diplomatic corps lived in the Sistine apartments normally reserved for cardinals in conclave, so the celebrated chapel was their parish church.

"We never considered Monsignor Montini as a diplomat who said Mass," Count Vladimir d'Ormesson, French Ambassador to the Holy See, wrote. "We always considered him a priest who concerned himself with uncommon interest in Church diplomacy."

In mid-year, 1941, Hitler turned on his ally and the German Army launched its attack on Russia. The Russian Army crumpled and fell back as other armies had done, holding nowhere. This, in the minds of many people, was the ideal situation if the war could not be stopped; a death struggle between two godless systems, two tyrannies, two super-states, tramplers on human dignity.

The war did not narrow, however, nor settle into attrition between Nazis and Communists. In December the Japanese attacked Pearl Harbor. Germany and Italy, bound by alliance to Japan, declared war upon the United States.

Myron C. Taylor conferred with Pope Pius XII and made a report to the President on the papal ideas of a peace which would bear "within itself the seeds of longevity." Mr. Taylor's memorandum summed up those ideas of the Holy Father:

"A first requisite was that the relations between governments and their people, and between all governments and peoples, must be based on the fulfillment of contracts, on the observance of justice and law tempered by Christian charity and brotherly love, and on reverence for the dignity of the human person and respect for religious conviction. The worship of God must again exercise its due influence in individual and national life. The pope again states, as in earlier public utterances, that certain principles of right and justice have their foundation deep in the moral order of the universe, and that on such principles there can never be compromise. He was greatly heartened to know that the peace aims of the United States fully recognized these basic moral principles. These principles would unswervingly point the direction of His own path of duty."

The Vatican Information Bureau was frantically setting up its sources of information on the other side of the world, preparing to increase broadcast time for the added names expected. It was going to be difficult to import food now since the United States was in the war.

Monsignor Montini wore a worried look. The flow of refugees would probably increase.

18

THE ETERNAL CITY

THE year 1942 unwound before the anxious eyes in the Vatican like a newsreel of disaster. Men, women, and children died terrible deaths and human beings turned bestial in the face of fear, hunger, and privation. The tale of horror was long and human minds rejected it. Japan and Germany were scoring victories; Italy, allied to the victorious, suffered defeat after defeat. Mussolini had permitted the dispersal of Italian manpower and the use of Italian troops as auxiliaries by the Germans. The Italians had no spirit for the war, no sense of an objective, and conditions deteriorated on the home front as drastic shortages of food, clothing, and fuel weakened the morale of the people, most of whom were in mourning.

The Vatican, feeding an unprecedented number of people, was rationing, too, although food had been ordered from the United States and stockpiled before there was any emergency. There was no heat in the Vatican buildings and men moved in the beauty of the long corridors, the rooms rich in mosaic and tapestry, wrapped like eskimos.

Giovanni Battista Montini, with his long history of respiratory trouble and his susceptibility to colds, seemed impervious now to attack. Under the worst of conditions he seemed to thrive. More guests had been added to the Vatican international set, bringing fresh anecdote to conversation.

Among the newer guests was Pietro Nenni, political leader of the extreme Socialist left, fleeing for his life from the Fascists. Short, fat, voluble, Nenni claimed to be merely the friend of the Communists but opposed to them. He had been in Moscow and he had met Stalin. He liked Stalin, too. "I would not yield to him," he said. "I am a progressive democrat."

Already established in the Vatican as a resident was Nenni's natural opponent, Alcide De Gasperi, a Christian-Democrat who had been a prime mover in Partito Populare with Giorgio Montini and Don Luigi Sturzo. Slender, pale, with fine ascetic features and long-fingered hands, De Gasperi was a perfect contrast for Pietro Nenni. At opposite poles of thought, the two men had much in common. De Gasperi had spent years in Fascist jails and Nenni had spent years avoiding those jails.

Monsignor Montini often joined the two men, fascinated always by political discussion. The possible future of Italy was roughed out experimentally in these conversations. If there were no Fascism, where would Italy turn? These two men represented two alternatives and there was no area of compromise, but they were congenial in the Vatican discussions and seemed to enjoy the company of each other.

The Vatican as a powerhouse of prayer offered variety in ritual. Priests from various Congregations celebrated Mass according to a number of different rites: Greek, Russian, Ambrosian. There were vespers and benediction, chants in Latin and in many other tongues. Most of the Vatican inhabitants, Catholic and non-Catholic, attended when something unusual was promised, but Pietro Nenni avoided all religious observance. One evening several companions deserted him for a lecture by Father Augustin Bea who was a noted Scripture scholar and authority on the lands and the people of the Old Testament. Pietro Nenni was forlorn in his aloneness.

"I am in a preposterous situation," he said, "but I am consistent. I remain a revolutionist."

Father Bea, a German Jesuit, was a friend of Monsignor Montini and had been for some years. They had been thrown to-

gether frequently during the pontificate of Pius XI. Father Bea
had collaborated in the writing of the encyclical to the Germans, *Mit Brennender Sorge*, as had the then Cardinal Pacelli.
He was the author of pamphlets based on lectures he had given
on the anthropological ridiculousness of the pure blood theory.
He favored an open Catholic mind to non-Catholic scholarship
in languages, ancient literatures, and archaeological evaluations.
He lectured well and he talked well. He was one of the good
companions of the war years and he was confessor of Pius XII.

The Russians, aided by American lend-lease and large ship-
ments of the latest model tanks, halted the German advance at
Stalingrad and the war in Russia was turning. The United
States and England combined in landing an army of huge pro-
portions in North Africa and American planes hammered the
port of Naples. The British continued to pound Milan, Turin,
and Genoa nightly. The Germans started occupying all of
France.

Like a frail and lovely ghost in all of this carnage and destruction, Princess Marie Clotilde, the daughter of Victor Emmanuel II returned to the stage of history. Her cause was introduced
for beatification on December 21, first step on the way to saint-
hood. Child of the King whom Pius IX excommunicated,
Princess Marie Clotilde was also the daughter of the Risorgimento, symbol of its sad conflict between throne and altar.
Practically unnoticed in this new age of conflict, she emerged
briefly from the deliberations of the Congregation of Rites, then
vanished again.

Monsignor Montini had a worrisome time as the year ended.
Heinrich Himmler and a horde of Gestapo agents moved into
Rome, impatient at what they called Italian carelessness about
security. It was more difficult to hide people from the efficient
Germans than from the Italians but those most in danger were
moved to the catacombs where elaborate escape channels
existed. Many of those so moved were Jews, but not all. For the
first time since FUCI days, Monsignor Montini said Mass in
the catacombs. He took physical risk to do so.

That Christmas season was the grimmest of Giovanni Battista Montini's life. Despite all that he could do, the Gestapo rounded up a number of the hidden people in raids on sanctuaries. Those who were rounded up vanished and not even the most skillful ferrets of information could discover what had happened to them. He had a personal concern, too, which weighed heavily on him.

Giorgio Montini was gravely ill. He had been operated on and was not responding. Travel was difficult, all but impossible, and hedged round by government restrictions, but Monsignor Montini reached Brescia. His father rallied and his mother drew upon hope.

"He draws strength from your presence," Giuditta said. "The grace of God came with you."

Battista said a Christmas Mass in Santa Maria della Grazie where he had said his first Mass and another in the duomo where he had been ordained. He spent as much time as he could with his mother and sat beside his father's bed. They listened together to Pope Pius XII when he delivered his Christmas allocution over the Vatican Radio.

The Holy Father spoke, that Christmas of 1942, of the dignity and the rights of the human person: his right to develop his physical, intellectual, and moral life; the right to provide education and religious training for his children; the right to worship God publicly and privately; the right to engage in religious works of charity; the right to marriage, to wedded society and home life; the right to religious vocation; the right to work and to earn wages; the right to the possession of material goods. He warned that wars were fought in vain if men were offered less when they were concluded and that wars were refought because victors withheld human rights from the vanquished.

There was eloquence and great sincerity and a love for mankind in Pius XII. He worked long hours composing messages of consolation and of hope, plans for peace, formulas by which men could come to an understanding of one another and achieve respect for one another. He spoke against the wind, with the words blown from his lips and scattered almost as soon as he uttered them. The insanity of war permitted no tolerance of sanity.

Battista stayed with his family as long as he could, but he was needed at the Vatican and he could not remain indefinitely. His father clung to life, feebly but persistently. At parting they both knew how near to impossible it would be for the son to return.

"The work of God comes before all things," Giorgio Montini said.

On January 12, 1943, he died.

The day of Giorgio Montini's death, Monsignor Montini called upon Count Galeazzo Ciano, Foreign Minister of Italy, at the suggestion of Pope Pius XII. It was obvious that the Fascist regime was in dire trouble and apt to blow wide open at any time. Persistent rumors reaching the Vatican linked Count Ciano to dissident elements who were anxious to remove Mussolini and make a separate peace with the Allies. Pius XII wanted to permit Count Ciano an opportunity to discuss any ideas that he had for peace and he wanted the circumstances of the meeting to be a guarantee of discretion. He chose his Undersecretary of State for the mission of inquiry as a gesture of informality that the suave Ciano could not fail to understand.

Ciano was Benito Mussolini's son-in-law, married to Edda Mussolini, and a tremendously wealthy man by inheritance whose fortune had increased through politics. He had commanded the Disperata bombing squadron in Ethiopia where he won two silver medals for valor. He had a reputation as a daring pilot, in and out of war, and he delighted in outdoor activities; swimming, riding, golf. Men liked him and he had many friends even among those who disliked and distrusted Fascists. The Vatican State Department staff had always found him obliging and good-natured even under difficult circumstances.

Count Ciano's account of his conversation with Monsignor

Montini appears in his published diaries and has been widely misinterpreted. It reads:

"January 12, 1943—A long conference in the Colonna residence with Monsignor Montini, who, from what is said, is a really close collaborator of the Holy Father. He acted prudently, reservedly and like an Italian. He did not express any opinion on the military situation but said only that in the Vatican they believe that the struggle will still be hard and long. He added that insofar as he is able to do anything in favor of our country, he is completely at our disposal. I spoke to him of the importance we must attach to the internal order in our country at all times and he agreed. The Church will always work in this direction. Though he is anti-Bolshevik, he nevertheless expressed admiration and surprise at what Stalin has been able to do. He said: 'One thing is important; whatever the future may bring, our people have given singular proof of strength, faith and discipline. These are qualities that will bring about a complete revival.'"

There is no better example available in public records of Monsignor Montini in action, facing a delicate diplomatic problem of utmost gravity. He was meeting with a man who was, allegedly, about to desert the existing government of Italy in favor of one that would concede a lost war and sign a peace treaty. To betray a knowledge that Count Ciano was contemplating such action would be tantamount to an accusation of treason against him. The problem was to make it easy for him to confide his intention, rationalizing it however he wished.

Monsignor Montini began obviously by brushing aside any discussion of the war in military terms. Two men who lived behind the scenes did not have to waste time in that way. There was no military situation that could be helped. Fascist Italy had lost its war. One could comment, however, that the war in terms of Germany and other powers would still be hard and long. Italy could be ground to powder in that war, gaining nothing. On that the two men had to be in agreement.

Monsignor Montini extended his invitation, then. Italy was

in a terrible situation and the monsignor personally, or the Vatican State Department was at Count Ciano's disposal if he had any ideas of anything they could do "in favor of our country." It was the moment when Count Ciano, if he had a plan for taking over the government and making a separate peace, should speak. Pius XII was hoping that Ciano would speak, that he did have a plan for a separate peace which he would confide and that the Holy Father would be permitted to act as mediator, perhaps through an act of personal diplomacy with his friend President Roosevelt. It would be an achievement to bring peace to even one area of earth and, perhaps, through that open door, let peace into the rest of the world.

The moment passed and Ciano did not speak. Monsignor Montini was aware of the political currents around the foreign office of Italy. If one sought a separate peace, one sought it where one could. The Vatican had access to the United States government without the necessity of placing faith in minor figures who might be double agents. Ciano probably lacked an American contact but was dealing with Italian Communists. If that were so, he might hesitate to discuss his activity with anyone from the Vatican, the uncompromising foe of communism.

Monsignor Montini had to reassure him on that score. The Church would co-operate with him in taking Italy out of the war even if his associates were Communists. The important thing was that the Italian people were still strong and disciplined. It would not do to wait till anarchy swept the country.

Ciano still did not speak. Monsignor Montini left him and there was disappointment in the Vatican. Pius XII paced back and forth.

"If only he would trust us!" he said.

Late that night the word came that Giorgio Montini was dead.

The following month, Il Duce removed Ciano as foreign minister of Italy and the Count fled for his life. He knew from experience that there was no more hazardous career than that of an ex-anything in a totalitarian regime. He declared himself

Felici Photo, Wide World Photos, Inc.

[24] His Holiness. Pope Paul VI

[25] Pope Paul VI is carried through St. Peter's Square to his coronation throne.

[26] Pope Paul, on his way to the Spanish College, greets crowds in downtown Rome.

[27] Pope Paul standing beside his papal throne just before his coronation in St. Peter's Square.

[28] Pope Paul VI prays before the tomb of his predecessor, Pope John XXIII.

[29] Newly elected Pope Paul VI with members of the Sacred College of Cardinals.

[30] Pope Paul VI receives a delegation from Nigeria.

[31] Pope Paul VI presents a replica of Michelangelo's "Pieta" to President John F. Kennedy.

[32] Pope Paul VI at work at his desk.

[33] Pope Paul addresses the members of the Diplomatic Corps.

[34] Pope Paul VI hails the movement for Christian unity in a speech delivered at an Eastern Rite monastery at Grotta-ferrata near Rome.

[35] Pope Paul, in an address to members of the Roman Curia on September 21, 1963, announces changes he plans for the Curia.

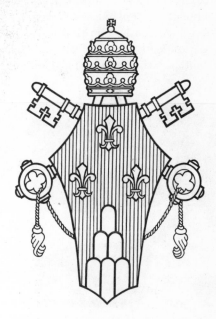

[36] Pope Paul's coat-of-arms. There are six small stylized mountains ("montini") in silver with three fleurs de lis in silver on a crimson field.

[37] Pope Paul VI receives congratulations from a group of cardinals shortly after his election. L/r are: Paul Marie Cardinal Richaud, Archbishop of Bordeaux, France; Juan Cardinal Landazuri Ricketts, Archbishop of Lima, Peru; Pierre Cardinal Gerlier (in foreground, talking with the Pontiff), Archbishop of Lyon, France; Augusto Cardinal Alvaro da Silva, Archbishop of Sao Salvador da Bahia, Brazil; Pope Paul VI; Stefan Cardinal Wyszynski, Archbishop of Warsaw and Primate of Poland; Paul Emile Cardinal Leger, Archbishop of Montreal, Canada; and Carlos Carmelo Cardinal de Vasconcellos Motta, Archbishop of São Paulo del Brazil.

[38] Pope Paul receives Francis Cardina Spellman, Archbishop of New York, i a private audience in the pope's privat library in the Apostolic Palace.

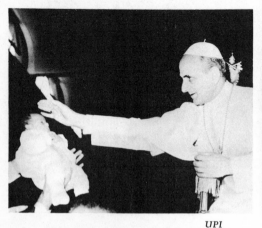

[39] His Holiness leans from his gestatorial chair to bless a small child.

[40] Pope Paul caresses a polio-stricken girl in the arms of her father during an audience for polio victims.

[41] Pope Paul VI reading an address to U Thant, Secretary General of the United Nations, in the papal library of the Apostolic Palace.

[42] Former United States Vice-President Richard M. Nixon receives a souvenir medallion from Pope Paul VI.

[43] Pope Paul receives President Antonio Segni of Italy during the President's first formal visit to the Pontiff.

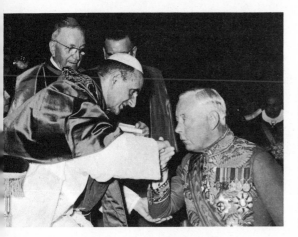

[44] The Duke of Norfolk, representative of Queen Elizabeth of England, kisses the ring of Pope Paul VI during an audience for the official delegations that attended His Holiness' coronation. Standing behind His Holiness is Amleto Cardinal Cicognani, Vatican Secretary of State.

[45] Pope Paul VI is carried into St. Peter's for the opening of the second session of Vatican Council II.

[46] The opening of the second session of Vatican Council II in St. Peter's. Pope Paul is being escorted to the papal altar in far background.

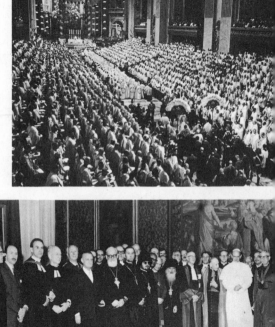

[47] Pope Paul VI addresses the Council Fathers at the opening of the second session of Vatican Council II.

[48] Pope Paul VI receives Protestant, Orthodox, and Anglican observers at the second session of Vatican Council II. He told these delegate-observers that "the best method for us is not to look to the past but to the present, and above all, to the future."

Ambassador to the Holy See and took residence in the Vatican where many men had preceded him, quite a few of them as enemies of the regime he had supported. He did not mention Monsignor Montini's call at the Palazzo Colonna.

The Vatican information service reported that 2943 Franciscans had been conscripted into the German army as combatants, 1200 German priests had vanished into concentration camps, more than 3000 priests had been executed in Poland.

In April, blossomtime in Brescia and the Valleys of the Po and the Adda, Giovanni Battista returned once more to the scenes of his childhood. Giuditta Montini had not had the will to survive her husband long. She was only briefly ill and slipped away swiftly.

It was the greatest loss of Battista's life. He had admired and respected his father, and he had tried, with a disqualifying physique and temperament, to emulate him. His mother, however, had been something precious in his life, an attachment beyond his powers of expression. Even years later, when he tried to speak of her, his voice broke and he could not continue.

Pius XII sympathized with bereavement and understood warm family attachments. Under his saintlike mask, his remoteness, his look of austerity, there was much sentiment, even sentimentality. He was concerned for his assistant in his double bereavement and he showed it. He said a Mass for Giuditta Montini.

"You should be closer to us," he said. "We face many crises which we shall have to meet together. I have ordered the Borromeo apartment prepared for you."

It was as casual as that, the gift of a magnificent apartment in the Apostolic Palace on the same floor as the Holy Father's own apartment. Pius XII knew, of course, that his assistant had a special devotion to St. Charles Borromeo and the apartment was the one which the saint had occupied when he was Secretary of State in 1559 under Pope Pius IV, the successor of Paul IV. The private chapel in the apartment was St. Charles Borromeo's;

perfectly preserved, as was the corridor with the frescoed walls along which he had once walked. There had been neither alteration nor restoration. The painting of St. John the Evangelist with St. Paul above the altar was an unusual combination of saints, the two being rarely associated. That, too, dated to the time of the great Charles.

"It was also the apartment of His Holiness, Julius II," said Father Bea when he heard about Monsignor Montini's move.

Luigi Cardinal Maglione was seriously ill and the Holy Father was placing increasing dependence upon his two Undersecretaries in this year of 1943. Monsignor Tardini knew how to draw lines on the amount of work that he would undertake and Monsignor Montini's field was more loosely defined; so the younger man was more often called upon to assume extra responsibilities which would normally fall to the Secretary of State.

On July 19, the Holy Father summoned his experts on Italian internal affairs for a conference in his library. He sat behind his large walnut desk with four men facing him. Directly behind him was a stained glass window depicting the Madonna and Child. The walls of the room were crimson and the draperies were drawn on two of the three tall windows which overlooked Piazza San Pietro. Monsignor Montini sat close to the desk, a file folder in his hands. The Holy Father was explaining that it would be interesting, but probably not advisable, to include Count Galeazzo Ciano, still a Vatican guest, in this discussion. He broke off as a sound like that of a great and distant wind intruded.

"What is that?" he said.

The sound increased in volume, deep and rumbling, sound that carried vibration with it. The windows of the room rattled and the floor seemed to shake. There was no longer any doubt about the identity of the sound but the volume was incredible, unbelievable, unlike anything that anyone in the room had ever heard before. Pius XII rose swiftly and crossed the room with long strides. He swept one of the draperies back and looked out.

An armada of airplanes covered the sky above Rome, seeming to leave only small slats and louvers for the passage of light.

There were 738 airplanes and they were American. No one could even guess the number at that moment, but their insignia identified their nationality. At a signal from the Holy Father, Monsignor Montini and the others crowded to the windows. The first bombs started to fall and the pope drew his breath in with an audible sound.

"San Lorenzo!" he said.

The railroad yards were there: nothing else of military interest. It was an area of tenements where laborers and the very poor lived. For two and one-half agonizing hours, the people of the Vatican watched from the windows and the roofs with the roar of airplane engines in their ears and the thunder of distant explosive violence. The Holy Father did not leave the window. His lips moved in prayer. When the raid seemed to be over, he turned to Monsignor Montini, gripping his forearm with strong fingers, deep shock in his voice.

"Gather all the money you have," he said. "We will have a car in the St. Damaso Courtyard."

Monsignor Montini needed no admonition to hurry. He packed two million lira, it is alleged, in a black bag and it is also alleged that this was an activity fund assigned to him for rescue work and for keeping escape routes open to the oppressed. Whatever it was, or how much, he raced with it to the courtyard where Pius XII met him in a Vatican car. They drove through empty streets and when they reached the Via Nationale they could see the flames under the rolling black smoke ahead of them.

There were barricades manned by police and by soldiers as they neared the disaster area. They left the car and the guards fell back as they recognized the Holy Father. He was wearing a white cassock and he stood tall above these other men, striding rapidly. Monsignor Montini stayed close to him, a few steps back. The smoke was dense and the streets piled with rubble and brick at which people tore frantically, seeking others buried beneath. There were skeleton walls where apartments had stood and, as they neared the Basilica of San Lorenzo, they could hear the cries of the wounded.

San Lorenzo fuori le Mura (St. Lawrence Outside-the-Walls) was an ancient basilica, parts of which dated to 330, the new part to 1216. It was the church in which the hapless Pius IX had willed that his body should rest. Bombs had shattered the church, tearing away the façade and ripping away the south wall of the Madonna Chapel. Priceless old mosaics were scattered in the debris and the Cardinal Freschi tomb, dating to 1256, was in fragments. The six Ionic columns of the façade and the carved figures were gone. There was a fire behind the building, the flames dancing in the background.

The Holy Father stood motionless and the people gathered around, falling to their knees and crying out to him. They were mostly women, some of them clutching terrified children. There were priests moving among the wounded which rescue workers brought to one side of the rubble-filled piazza. Pius XII blessed the crowding people and their panicky need seemed to settle him. He gestured to Monsignor Montini, a signal to distribute money, and he started praying aloud, calling on the women for response.

Monsignor Montini found the doctors, the leaders of rescue, the responsible citizens who were trying to bring order out of disaster. He gave them money without any means of estimating what was needed. There was a need. A man drew him aside, his eyes wide, his features contorting in a series of grimaces. He inclined his head toward the Holy Father, blessed himself and pointed in the direction of the cemetery.

"Campo Verano," he said. "Pacelli."

Bombs had fallen in the old cemetery and made a plowed field of it. It was the cemetery in which the Pacelli family had buried their dead for centuries. Monsignor Montini tried to protect the Holy Father from the knowledge of what had happened, but Pius XII knew. None of this area had been spared. Monsignor Montini walked with him when he went to the cemetery and there were more people there, weeping loudly. There was sudden silence as the pope walked to the spot where the Pacelli family plot had been and the Pacelli monument. Several men and women ran ahead of him, trying with bare hands to scrape sufficient earth for an earth cover on the exposed and scattered bones. The Pacelli graves had suffered a direct hit.

Pius XII stood with his eyes closed, praying: then he blessed the people around him and turned away. His mother and his father had been buried there.

A half-crazed woman with a child in her arms ran toward the Holy Father as he returned to the shattered basilica. She fell on her knees before him and as he raised his hand in blessing, she bounded up and thrust the child into his arms.

"Bring her back," she screamed. "Ask Christ! Bring her back."

Pope Pius XII stood helplessly with a small dead child in his arms and with blood running down the front of his white cassock until other women gathered around the frenzied mother and took the body of the little girl away from him.

He went back then with Monsignor Montini to their car beside the barricades. The smoke hung in the sky all night.

19

WINE AND ASHES

AMERICAN troops landed in Sicily and the Italians had no will to fight the army which included so many descendants of their own people. The United States was a symbol to the Italian. After the bombing of Rome, Count Galeazzo Ciano considered that his moment had come. He left the Vatican and appeared unexpectedly at a meeting of the Fascist Council, demanding the resignation of Mussolini. With this play he made obvious his reasons for remaining reticent in his interview with Monsignor Montini. He hoped to take over the government himself, Fascist still but under more intelligent leadership. If there had been any single note of encouragement from the Undersecretary to nurture a hope that the Vatican would support his ambition, Ciano would have confided. He made his play at the Fascist Council and lost. They would not support him. He fled to the north that night.

On the following day, July 25, 1943, Marshal Pietro Badoglio arrested Benito Mussolini in the name of the King and the Italian radio announced: "Fascism is over forever."

The Badoglio government made no attempt to work for a separate peace, its obvious goal, through the Vatican. It was in a dangerous situation with the Germans: dissembling and maneuvering for time. There were 400,000 Italian troops outside of Italy, most of them integrated with German troops under German command. There were half a million Italians working in German factories. The Germans mistrusted the new government of Italy, despite the hostages they held, and they started to move in, ostensibly as allies reinforcing Italians.

On September 10, the occupation of Rome was a fact accomplished and German troops were in Piazza San Pietro. General Albert Kesselring, the German commander, refused audience by Pius XII, conferred with Monsignor Montini. "I want only to offer reassurance," General Kesselring said. "We are here to offer protection to the pope."

"The Holy Father did not request protection," Monsignor Montini said.

"He cannot deceive himself that it is unnecessary. There are people who would kill him, who would burn the Vatican, in order to place blame on us before the world."

"Then you are protecting yourselves," said Monsignor Montini.

The Germans continued to protect themselves, and, incidentally, the pope and the Vatican. They made no attempt to invade the private quarters but there were soldiers constantly on guard in Piazza San Pietro and the Holy Father looked down upon the helmets and the olive green uniforms from his windows. St. Peter's was closed to worshipers from outside Vatican City and Pius XII protested that order through the German Ambassador. General Kesselring stood firm.

"He would make our task too difficult," he said.

There was a rumor that Adolf Hitler had offered Pius XII sanctuary in Liechtenstein after the Rome bombing. There had been an earlier, pre-bombing rumor that Archbishop Spellman had been the intermediary for a suggestion that the Holy Father move to Brazil.

On September 29, the Allies signed an armistice with the Badoglio government and accepted the Italians, not as allies but as co-belligerents. Italy declared war on Germany on October 13.

The German occupation of Italy was a grimmer thing after

Italy turned from the alliance and joined forces with the American armies driving up from the south. It was more difficult to keep fugitives hidden, very difficult to feed them, almost impossible to transport them. The Vatican was not molested, but it was restricted. The penned-up internationals were restive and unhappy. The new year of 1944 began with rumors and alarms, the fear that the Germans would destroy Rome and the Vatican before they left. The worry proved unfounded. The Nazis pulled out in May and the U. S. Fifth Army under General Mark Clark moved in on June 4.

The American occupation was exciting, a genuine liberation for those in the Vatican. The Holy Father gave audiences to great numbers of allied soldiers and delighted in it. On one occasion an officer mentioned to him that there were a number of Jewish soldiers in his group so he gave a blessing in Hebrew. The gesture was so well received that he made a practice of inquiring for soldiers of Jewish faith in later audiences.

On June 16, the Grand Rabbi of Rome, Dr. Israele Anton Zolli, thanked Pius XII for aid given to Jews during the Nazi occupation. Six months later, Dr. Zolli, his wife, and his children were baptized in the Catholic faith.

The Nazi grip was loosening everywhere. The Petain government fell in France and there were violent reprisals against French men and women accused of collaboration with the Germans. Archbishop Valerio Valeri, Apostolic Nuncio to France, was unpopular with the French because he had been assigned to Vichy. Pius XII recalled him and appointed Archbishop Angelo Giuseppe Roncalli to the post.

Monsignor Montini knew Archbishop Roncalli through his reputation and from his letters better than through personal contact. The Nuncio had spent little time in Rome, much time in Bulgaria, Turkey, and Greece. He arrived in Rome now, bewildered, and the Holy Father's schedule of audiences was heavy. Archbishop Roncalli was not on the list. Monsignor Montini saw him.

"There must be some mistake," the Nuncio said. "The Holy

Father has forgotten me or confused me with someone else. I am not the man for France. It is a sophisticated country."

"You speak French," Monsignor Montini said, "or am I mistaken?"

"Everyone speaks French."

The Undersecretary liked the broad-faced, heavy, uncomfortable Nuncio who had, probably, lived quite pleasantly in the Balkans and the Near East and who did not contemplate happily the formality of the French. He interceded for him and obtained an audience with Pius XII. He supplied with the audience invitation a word of counsel.

"Be resigned," he said. "You are going to France. In your place I would thank the Holy Father for sending me."

It was the beginning of a stanch friendship. The oddly humble Nuncio to France was a shrewd diplomat under the appearance of careless and carefree bonhomie, which was his normal character. Sound diplomacy is based upon the accurate appraisal of men and Angelo Roncalli made few mistakes in that regard. He was grateful to Battista Montini, less for the audience which he arranged, perhaps, than for the interest and concern which he had demonstrated in arranging it. There were many letters exchanged between the two men over a long period of time. Angelo Roncalli solicited the aid of the younger man when he had to express in words a matter of importance. He valued his own ideas but did not believe that he expressed them well.

The Nuncio to France became vitally interested in a movement known as Renouveau Catholique which was motivated by the philosophy of Thomas Aquinas as interpreted by Jacques Maritain; a group which studied the papal encyclicals as the basis of a sound society, leaning left but dedicated to the conversion of Communists rather than conflict with them. In writing of this movement to the Undersecretary of State, Archbishop Roncalli was writing to Jacques Maritain's first translator in Italy, a man who had urged his Fucini to study the encyclicals and who, by nature, leaned to the left in politics while remaining uncompromisingly opposed to communism and to Communist thought. Renouveau Catholique could not fail to interest Giovanni Battista Montini. It is quite probable that one result of the interest and of the correspondence was the series of diplomatic moves which later brought Jacques Maritain to the Vatican as French Ambassador.

It was difficult to find time for the writing of letters in 1944. The collapse of armies created social vacuums. People long under military government lacked the machinery for self-government and there were no leaders. The Communists were moving in fast wherever famine stalked or populations milled about in uncertainty, offering some relief but offering mainly the leadership of men trained in Communist academies who promptly liquidated any opposing leaders or potential leaders as soon as they were established in authority.

Italy was prostrate. Armies had fought across the country from Naples to Bologna and the damage was enormous: to cities, to towns, to the country from which the people drew sustenance. There were several million homeless people and large rural areas without seed or fertilizer, tools or electric power. Mob violence and the killing of former Fascist officials were routine.

German paratroopers rescued Mussolini and set him up in the north as the leader of a puppet Fascist government held together by Nazi force of arms. He made speeches in Milan but he was a pale echo of what he used to be. Count Galeazzo Ciano had not run far. His father-in-law's Fascists caught him at Verona and shot him.

"He might have had the courage of his convictions if he had ever discovered convictions," one of the Vatican internationals said.

Luigi Cardinal Maglione, Papal Secretary of State, died on August 22, 1944.

There was speculation in many quarters on his probable successor. In terms of seniority and prestige Undersecretary of State for Foreign Affairs, Monsignor Domenico Tardini had to be favored; but many observers pointed out that Monsignor Giovanni

Battista Montini, Undersecretary of State for Domestic Affairs, was closer to Pius XII, entrusted with more delicate missions, the obvious palace favorite. Tardini was short, thick-bodied, aggressive, abrupt, scornful of diplomatic niceties, a hard taskmaster on all those under him, in the Vatican and abroad. Montini was tall, slender, cordial if not effusive, tactful, exacting as far as those under him were concerned but considerate of the pride and dignity of those with whom he dealt. Either man could take care of a troublesome opponent; Tardini would walk over him and Montini would cut the ground out from under him. Tardini in a mood to enjoy himself had rough humor and a bluff heartiness; humor was always a problem for Montini and he could not tune in to boisterousness. Montini was probably more popular on all levels of Vatican life. They were both prodigious workers. They did not like each other too well.

Pius XII ended speculation by announcing that the post of Secretary of State would not be filled, that Monsignori Tardini and Montini would continue to handle the work that they were doing on a slightly extended pattern. Monsignor Tardini would be Substitute Secretary of State for Extraordinary Affairs; Monsignor Montini, Substitute Secretary of State for Ordinary Affairs. The Holy Father, then, was dividing Cardinal Maglione's routine work between two men and becoming, in authority, his own Secretary of State. Many of those who knew Pius XII well, without discounting his proven knowledge, experience, and skill as a diplomat, viewed this decision with misgiving. Domenico Tardini was frankly disappointed; Giovanni Battista Montini revealed nothing of what he felt and he may not have felt anything at all. He probably had not expected to be promoted to Secretary of State so had no reason to be disturbed by the decision.

The best picture of Monsignor Giovanni Battista Montini at this period is presented by Monsignor Sergio Pignedoli, Apostolic Delegate to West Central Africa. Monsignor Pignedoli was one of the Fucini from the University of Rome but he attended the university after Don Battista left FUCI. "His influence still lingered when I was there," he said. "He had an understanding heart for youth and special gifts for attracting them to Christianity." In 1941, while serving as a naval chaplain, Monsignor Pignedoli visited Monsignor Montini in the Vatican to ask his advice on some problems affecting university youth in the Navy. After the armistice in 1943, at Montini's invitation, he came to live and work at the Vatican. Speaking of Monsignor Montini, he says:

"His were the great qualities of the priest and the diplomat. He was still, after many years, attached spiritually to the university and to the problems faced by students. His feeling might be described as nostalgia which carried him, unaware, beyond the windows of his office. Even then, after all he had experienced, he looked at life with the trust of a young man, with freshness of eye and heart. He regarded the Church as does yesterday's convert, astonished and thankful that it exists, forever finding novelty in it."

Of Monsignor Montini's office manner and attitude at the Vatican State Department in the middle forties, his associate says: "For him the mass does not exist; each man is an individual. With unique patience, with extreme courtesy of manner, with open cordiality, and not lacking in good humor, he encourages relaxation, remaining tranquil even when confronted with the most unexpected visit. He invites visitors by his own ease to believe that he is completely at their disposal, although in reality his duties and responsibilities to the Holy Father are so many and of such variety that few men could manage them. If he had serious fault it was that he broke appointments and engagements on short notice. He accepted the blame for this fault, as he should, of course, knowing his own situation, but those of us who knew that he did not actually control his own time found it easy to forgive him."

The duties and responsibilities of the Vatican State Department were still heavily involved with war in 1945; displaced persons, long casualty lists and the confusing prisoner of war situation. There seemed no end to the refugees, many of them fleeing desperately and at great hazard from war zones to Italy because the armistice suggested peace and perhaps plenty; a cruel delusion. Despite the reality of these problems, the patient time they demanded, plans had to be made for a future already indicated. The war was moving to an exhausted finale.

The great figures, the men who had dominated events, who made the news of the world and who commanded lesser men to oft-unwanted destinies, were leaving the stage of history one by one. Franklin Delano Roosevelt died on April 12, 1945. Two weeks later Mussolini was captured by Italian Communists and shot, his body ravaged by a mob. Before the month ended, Adolf Hitler died by his own hand in Berlin. The only one of the three who commanded a message of regret from the Holy Father was the President of the United States. In a cablegram to his successor, Harry S. Truman, Pius XII said:

THE UNEXPECTED AND SORROWFUL WORD OF THE PASSING OF THE PRESIDENT BRINGS TO OUR HEART A PROFOUND SENSE OF GRIEF BORN OF THE HIGH ESTEEM IN WHICH WE HELD THIS RENOWNED STATESMAN AND OF THE FRIENDLY RELATIONS WHICH HE FOSTERED AND MAINTAINED WITH US AND WITH THE HOLY SEE.

TO THE EXPRESSION OF OUR CONDOLENCE WE JOIN THE AS-SURANCE OF OUR PRAYERS FOR THE ENTIRE AMERICAN PEOPLE AND FOR THEIR NEW PRESIDENT TO WHOM WE EXTEND OUR FERVENT GOOD WISHES THAT HIS LABORS MAY BE EFFICACIOUS IN LEADING THE NATIONS AT WAR TO AN EARLY PEACE THAT WILL BE JUST AND CHRISTIAN.

On May 5, 1945, the Germans laid down their arms except where confronted by Russians. Two days later they submitted to the "unconditional surrender" terms. The Pacific War ended in horror, a horror which was to remain in the world upon which it was released. On August 6, United States aircraft dropped the hitherto secret atomic bomb on Hiroshima, Japan, killing 60,000 persons and wounding 100,000. Three days later they dropped another on Nagasaki with casualties of 10,000 killed and 20,000 wounded.

The Vatican was inundated with demands that the Holy Father protest the use of the new weapon but Pius XII was a realist as he was a humanitarian. He was shocked and stunned by the enormity of the disaster to the two Japanese cities and at the loss of life. He was further saddened by the fact that the area which suffered was the most Catholic area of Japan; that priests, nuns, the churches, and schools in which they labored, were destroyed in the holocaust. No discussion on the morality of weapons, however, was possible except under one subhead to the main topic; the morality of war. There was no decent or humane weapon for killing a man violently; the bombs of Hiroshima and Nagasaki were merely the ultimate indecency, the ultimate inhumanity.

The only comment from ecclesiastical Rome on the bombings of the Japanese cities was the unofficial comment in *Osservatore Romano*: "The use of atomic bombs in Japan has created an unfavorable impression on the Vatican. This incredible destructive instrument remains a temptation to posterity."

On August 14, Japan surrendered.

It was all over now except for the rounding up and arresting of Axis leaders and officials, the mob actions and the suicides, the people wandering back to where their homes had been and finding only rubble. The lights were on again in European cities. Much was made of that and rightly so, but in the area beyond the lights, selfless men and women walked among the hungry and the homeless and the maimed. Many of those workers were Catholics, priests, members of religious orders and laymen, receiving aid directly from the Vatican which was feeling the financial pinch but which was not refusing aid where it was needed. The work of rescue and compassion could be openly carried out now, except in the Communist-dominated territories, and the newsworthy quality was missing from the effort, but human need was great.

In this busy and disheartening period, Giovanni Battista Montini found time to exchange views with Jacques Maritain, newest member of the Vatican diplomatic corps. The two men met on many areas of thought, common to both of them and they spent much time together. Monsignor Montini fulfilled, too, another ambition. For over a year he had been studying by extension, in a continuing correspondence course from the University of Milan, the subjects he had abandoned as a young priest when Monsignor Pizzardo drafted him into the diplomatic service. When the cessation of conflict simplified the problem of travel, he went to Milan to take his written and oral examinations, claiming no more consideration than any other postgraduate student. One of his examiners was the Most Reverend Adriano Bernareggi, Bishop of Bergamo, who said of Monsignor Montini:

"I still have the written examination and I retain that examination book as a rare memorial and as a lesson in humility. I, who was his teacher for a day, have taken, I hope, instruction from my pupil."

Pius XII had hoped that there would be an early peace conference, that he would be invited to participate and that a just and lasting peace would result from it. His hopes were not realized. There was no peace conference except a minor affair at Paris which dealt with the lesser nations and which was made ineffectual by dissension among the greater powers. Soviet Russia had swallowed up Estonia, Latvia, Lithuania, part of Finland, Poland, Rumania, North Prussia, Southern Sakhalin, Kurile Island, and Outer Mongolia. The Russians were not interested in any peace treaties which would take any of this spoil away but they gave wholehearted support to trials and executions of war criminals.

The Vatican faced its greatest enemy and saw that enemy built to strength beyond belief. The liberation of Europe was a fact only for those people and those nations who were not under the heel of Communism.

The triumphant nations drank the wine of victory but there was no peace. Men still rummaged in the ashes of war, seeking the values which they had lost; not finding them.

The words of Pius XII, which had called for peace during the dark, bombarding hours, were gone now as the smoke over bombed cities was gone. He did not hark back. He addressed himself to the future.

"The next decade will be ours if we pray," he said.

20

THE DAY AND THE DECADE

A DECADE, in terms of years, is ten. A man may live through the making of much history in ten years, may know many people, experience joy and sorrow, triumph and pain, may attain to heights or depths; more than anything else, however, a man experiences a day, a day typical of his own life which he repeats with only slight variations to the point where one might say, looking at it, that the day is his life, its variants mere digressions.

The day of Monsignor Giovanni Battista Montini, Substitute Secretary of State, began at 6 A.M. He rose and offered his first prayers of the day, usually standing at his window. He showered, shaved, and said Mass in his private chapel, in which St. Charles Borromeo had said his Masses four centuries earlier. He usually breakfasted alone but he had no set rule on that. A secretary or someone from his department might be invited to join him. He was more likely to skim through newspapers. He reached his office no later than 8.

The mail, the cablegrams, the appointment lists had to be digested and a summary prepared for the Holy Father. Pius XII descended on the lift, or via his private stairway at 8:47 and entered his office at 8:50. Watches could be set and set accurately on his entrances and exits. At exactly 8:59 he would press a button and Monsignor Tardini would march in, fully briefed and prepared, having done what his associate was doing, having

rounded up the latest messages, dispatches, news, and interpretation of his department. Sometimes, in certain circumstances,
Monsignor Montini would be the first one received, but not
normally. The bell summoning him rang at precisely 9:14 and
he would leave the office of His Holiness at 9:28, permitting the
Holy Father's secretary two minutes of preparation for the first
private audience of the day at 9:30.

Monsignor Montini had his own audiences, then, the people
whom he had to see, clerical and lay, in connection with his
own projects and the people delegated to him by the Holy Father. Some of the Vatican phrase-makers made a play on his
Substitute Secretary title and called him the Substitute Pope.
This was fairly accurate in some respects but he did not consider the remark amusing. They made a play on his name, too:
Montini, little mountain. It was easier to reach the little mountain, they said, than to reach the big one.

The Substitute Secretary had his own staff to see, too; undersecretaries and clerks to whom he had assigned responsibilities,
some of them continuing responsibilities which required period-
ical reporting. He had a schedule on his desk of the Holy Father's projected short talks and homilies on which research must
be done. The library work was parceled out to various individuals.

He tried to clear this routine by 1 P.M., so he could have lunch
but if the Holy Father wanted something in the course of the
morning audiences, his own schedule would have to be rearranged. Sometimes a bishop or a cardinal on his own list would
demand more time than his business justified and, however tact-
fully such situations were handled, they threw the timetable off.
There was the awkward matter of rank. Monsignori Tardini and
Montini had to contend constantly with cardinals and archbishops and bishops. The Holy Father would not consider sending
anyone as nuncio to anywhere without making him an Archbishop. Many of the nuncios were former students of either
Tardini or Montini. The rank question made social affairs difficult, too. The Substitute Secretaries were never seated with their

own contemporaries; they were placed with the lower echelons.

If all went reasonably well with the morning, Monsignor Montini had his lunch at 1 or 1:30. He liked to share it. He could discuss interesting subjects with interesting people and not have the subject funneled usefully to an objective. In times of exceptional stress or pressure, of course, even luncheon time had to serve the need of the moment but he tried to keep it clear.

In common with most Romans, he took a siesta after lunch if possible; seldom more than an hour in his case, an hour and a half for the Holy Father, two hours for most people.

The Holy Father would have an afternoon general audience or meet some special group or delegation. He might, or might not, want Monsignor Montini to assist in some way. One had to be in readiness and yet answer one's own mail and see one's own problem people. At 4 P.M. the Holy Father would take his walk in the gardens, precisely at 4, so that was the best time for the Substitute Secretary to do any errand he wanted to do in town or see anyone whom he wanted to see away from the Vatican.

At 6:30 P.M. Monsignori Tardini and Montini would arrive together in the presence of the Holy Father. Usually they would confer first for fifteen minutes or a half hour about the matters on the agenda. There were many places, naturally, where their work overlapped since they had the two halves of a job cut roughly down the middle. Any papers requiring the Holy Father's signature would be brought to this evening conference.

The Holy Father might be in an affable mood and relate experiences from the day's audiences, or comment on the news of the day, the personalities looming largest on the Vatican view screen at the moment. He might be in a mood to ask questions and he would be quite pleasant about that, too, but he would want merely answers, not advice; no obvious guidance, no interpretation which he did not solicit. A question period, however, did resemble a conversation. Sometimes, the mood was nervous, anxious, irritable, querulous, because this was a human being even though, as one Vatican comment ran, "every inch a pope, unfortunately." The quality of never quite relaxing with those closest to him in his official family was unfortunate for Pius XII. He did, however, in these evening sessions extract the meaning and the significance from the work of the day, and, sharing the immediate present with his two most valued assistants, he projected into the future with them and shared that, too.

The evening meeting ended at 7:45. The two Substitute Secretaries parted outside the library. Monsignor Montini dined at 8 in his own apartment or at 8:15, 8:30, or 9:00 in town. Rome liked late dining. He had many invitations, accepted relatively few. He represented the State Department at functions of one kind or another, sometimes alone, sometimes with Monsignor Tardini, rarely staying long. Engagements made under no compulsion save his own wishes were apt to be with politicians, literary people, former Fucini. He was still attracted to journalism but avoided journalists because it would not be discreet to gain a reputation, deserved or not, as a source of Vatican news.

Whether he dined out or not, Monsignor Montini had several hours of privacy that belonged in his day, usually at the end of it; the reading of his Office in his chapel, his private meditation and at least an hour devoted to writing letters in longhand, answers to letters received, thank-you notes for favors, remembrances of special days in the lives of friends. He played records while he wrote or while he read. He liked to read for an hour before he slept and he balanced his reading, with an honest liking for poetry and for novels.

That was the day, so often repeated that it represented the major part of a year, of a decade perhaps. There were variants, of course: days of ceremony at St. Peter's and special event days. Castel Gandolfo in the summer changed little except location: the work was exacting still and conducted on practically the same schedule. At certain periods, and over a measured space of time, new elements dominated those portions of the day not rigidly alloted to the Holy Father.

Such was the Italian election of 1948. That election attracted world attention. Italy became a battlefield in the new type of warfare which followed the cessation of armed conflict. In the campaigns of 1947 and '48, Giovanni Battista Montini became a general, decidedly a general. He planned strategy and tactics with Alcide De Gasperi, head of the Christian Democrat party and he provided help to De Gasperi where it was needed in that election. He granted no validity to charges that such political action was not the proper function of Church or clergy. The situation was quite a special one and the issue, beyond ordinary political definitions, was a world issue rather than purely Italian; as the world press recognized.

At the end of World War II there was only one obvious winner, the Soviet Union. The people of Europe did not, could not, overlook the frightening land growth of the Soviet Union, the obvious fact that no other power had the strength or resolution to demand the freedom promised to small nations, or that the Soviet keep covenants, or even that it stop at its outrageously stretched borders. The local Communists sprang up everywhere, capitalizing on the great triumphant position of the victorious Soviet, warning that the world would soon be all-Communist and that only those who joined early and voluntarily would be safe. The people of Europe had seen what happened to those who had opposed communism when the Communists took over. Fear was a great argument and there were other arguments.

Fascism and nazism, it had been often said, were reactionary systems which came into being as a reaction to established communism. It is a none too explicit generalization but if one may use it, one may say, too, that communism was a reaction to established fascism and nazism. When those two systems collapsed, the people who had lived under them were conditioned to totalitarianism. They were easily rounded up and controlled by the trained agents of the Comintern. The only known means for terrified people to prove that they were not Fascists or Nazis was Communist membership and the Communists did not bind people to them lightly; once a member, it was difficult to escape.

The blunt, hard, terrifying fact in Italy was that the people knew of no practical alternative to communism. They had had it hammered into them that there were only the two extremes, fascism and communism, left and right. It was shameful now to have any ties or connections with fascism, even those in the unchangeable past, and people wanted to disassociate themselves from that which was shameful. They were not offered democracy of the British or American kind as an alternative even by the British and Americans. They saw Milgov clear proven Communists fast from the taint of fascism. That clearance meant freedom from the fear of arrest, preference in jobs, in ration cards, in everything. The Americans and British had no ideology as far as Italians could judge. They had fought to destroy an evil rather than to establish a good. Having liberated the Italians from fascism and the rest of Europe from nazism, they wanted to go home with the sense of a job well done.

Italians of many political philosophies, men who had not ceased to think while living under a system which discouraged political thinking, tried earnestly to devise a form of government for Italy which would protect human rights and restore Italy to its place among the nations. Alcide De Gasperi proved to be one of the ablest and he became Prime Minister as early as 1945. Looking back on that period, the presidency of the Council of Ministers says in a carefully documented report on Italy's first ten post-Fascist years:

"The advent of De Gasperi as head of the government [1945] may be considered the turning point in Italian post-war politics, for this period, now universally known as the Period of National Reconstruction, bears the imprint of his ability and tenacity."

"De Gasperi showed great political ability, firmness of mind and acted with great courage yet never showed any signs of bragging over the successes he obtained. He concentrated on the material and moral reconstruction of the nation and was able to pilot it successfully to the first, free, democratic elections of the post-war years. These were held on June 2, 1946, and had two objectives: to determine the constitutional form chosen by the people, that is, a monarchy or a republic, and to elect deputies to the first free Assembly to be created after the Fascist period. The Assembly then had the task of drawing up the fundamental laws of the new democratic state: the Constitution."

To Monsignor Giovanni Battista Montini this period offered opportunities for which he had been shaped and trained, as he had been shaped and trained for the service of the Church. His life and his education and his self-expression in choice of reading and choice of companions, his family tradition: all came into balance in these first crucial post-Fascist years of Italy which were for the world, for other nations, no less crucial.

Alcide De Gasperi headed the Christian Democratic Party. It had developed as the successor to Partito Populare Italiano of Don Luigi Sturzo, the party which Giorgio Montini had helped to develop and to bring into existence, in which De Gasperi, too, had pioneered. There had been only ridicule and derision in the early days for the Catholics who were disenfranchised during the formative years of their nation by the *Non Expedit* of Pius IX and who made their way slowly and painfully into political life behind leaders like Montini and Sturzo, willing to work and suffer hardships with scant reward out of a great faith that the sacrifice was worthwhile. Those leaders of Partito Populare Italiano had never compromised with Fascism. Don Luigi Sturzo had accepted exile, Alcide De Gasperi had spent years in Fascist jails and Giorgio Montini had accepted the wiping out of his life work. The last editorial Giorgio Montini wrote for his paper was titled "Why I Cannot Accept Fascism."

There was a political alternative to communism, demonstrably non-Fascist, in the first year after the war because there had been men like Don Sturzo, Giorgio Montini, and Alcide De Gasperi. Giovanni Battista Montini could support that alternative, understanding what he had seen come into being, believing what he had learned as a boy, that conscience, duty and responsibility are involved in the casting of a vote.

Some 12,717,923 Italians voted for a republic and 10,719,284 for a monarchy. King Humbert II left Italy and the Prime Minister had the problem of holding the government together until a constitution could be submitted to the people.

There were many Italian political parties and the bewildering practice existed of merging and name changing. The Communists accepted frankly that designation, Communist, then absorbed the radical Socialists and other left-wing elements to become the People's Democratic Front (Fronti Democratici Populari). The Socialist Union united with the Italian Workers' Socialist Party and became the Union of Socialists. The Christian Democrats was the other major party, rated by many political observers as second in influence and following, or perhaps third, despite De Gasperi. Splinter parties ranged from Monarchists to Peasants.

The Communists, as a campaign tactic, attacked Pius XII and the Catholic Church, labeling both the pontiff and the Church "Fascist," the tag most likely to alienate the timid, the cautious, the fearful. To invite and shelter these there was a party called the Catholic Communist. Two new magazines appeared, *Don Basilio* and *Il Pollo*, obviously well financed, containing scurrilous attacks on pope and clergy in text and cartoon. Anticlerical movements started all over Italy. Churches were bombed, priests attacked, images defiled, walls covered with sacrilegious slogans. Communist orators asserted that these manifestations of public indignation at the Church which had betrayed them were spontaneous, the free expression of an awakened people. There were predictions in Italy and abroad that the Communists would sweep the election of 1948.

Monsignor Montini obtained permission from Pius XII to enter the lists against the Communists, to enlist the bishops and the pastors all over Italy in a countercampaign. He emphasized the fact in his letters and in personal contact that pietisms would not be enough, that communism, while denying religion, was itself a religion; that it must be forced into defending itself in its religious role which it sought to avoid.

A number of cardinal archbishops and bishops in the archdioceses and dioceses, individual priests and leaders of Catholic Action movements were already in the field against the Communists, of course, before the Substitute Secretary took the initiative in organizing scattered effort into one striking force, but they welcomed him. He worked quietly, as always, preferring to remain behind the scenes but he was tireless in staging conferences and in writing letters. From the outset he recognized the strong points of communism and its appeal to the people. The Communists were missionaries, many of them fanatics and many more idealists, who carried their religion of the all-wise State directly to the people, suffering for their faith if need be, bigotedly intolerant of any opposing faith. The Communists had their equivalent of a clergy, men rigorously trained in the Communist leadership schools. The Communist hierarchy made regular visits to Moscow as bishops came to Rome. Palmiro Togliatti, head of Italy's Communist Party, was no less than a cardinal in the Red hierarchy and had made his obeisances in the Kremlin.

With that concept of the issue, the Catholic Church entered without apology into the Italian elections of 1948. Conservative elements within the Church viewed with alarm, with misgiving, with disapproval. To some, this direct contact with politics was akin to touching pitch, to others it seemed a risk out of keeping with traditional Church caution and a gamble on which too much could be lost in Italy and in other nations of Europe. Criticism came into the Vatican from all over the world, some of it Communist-inspired, the inspired usually in blessed obliviousness of the fact that they were dupes. The world watched and international news coverage in Italy, at least briefly, was back to prewar strength.

The voting took place on April 18, 1948, with 89.1 per cent of the electorate going to the polls. The counting of the votes was a tense process and the result was:

217

Christian Democrats: 12,712,762
People's Democratic Front: 8,137,047
Union of Socialists: 1,858,346

Membership in the Chamber of Deputies resulted in: Christian Democrats, 305; People's Democratic Front, 179; Union of Socialists, 29. The Senate consisted of Christian Democrats, 149; People's Democratic Front, 72. De Gasperi remained naturally as Premier.

It was a stunning victory and scored at a perfect time. The Christian Democrats were established as a major political party which offered the voters an alternative to communism, a party which had an opportunity in power of demonstrating to the nation that it deserved to represent the hopes of the people. Monsignor Montini could withdraw from political campaigning at that point, and did.

One result of the election was a revival of wartime estimates of Giovanni Battista Montini as a director of Intelligence. His prestige soared with the victory although his name had been scarcely mentioned during the campaigning. He was mentioned cautiously in the press now as possibly the Vatican director of the Catholic sector of the cold war. His lack of rank was described as deliberately misleading. Catholic Action groups in other countries sought his advice and he was credited with considerable aid and counsel by the Christian Democrats in Germany who scored a notable victory on the Ruhr worker issue. He was in correspondence with anti-Communist political movements in France, Holland, and Belgium and his name was mentioned in connection with the Christian Democrat parties in those countries.

If he had the influence with which he was credited it was little in evidence at the Vatican. His normal day had been rearranged for a period but he slipped quietly back to reporting on the precise second to the Holy Father, answering his bells and anticipating his wants.

The Holy Year of 1950 was commanding time, thought, and

working effort a couple of years in advance. It was hoped that five million people would come to Rome in that year and the dazzling round of ceremony in prospect was not so smooth and natural and other-worldly in the planning stage as it would be ultimately in the solemn and holy round of the days.

A continuing subject in the files of Monsignor Montini was identified simply as *Mission de France*. It was a fascinating subject and potentially explosive. It dealt with "Worker Priests."

At the end of the war the Church in France was in, perhaps, more trouble than in any other nation. To the common problem of communism, France had the bitter issue of collaboration. The Vichy government had been headed by Marshal Henri Petain, a Catholic. Only historical perspective and passionless scholarship could pass a just verdict on a regime which either saved France by providing a government to treat with the conqueror or betrayed France by so treating. In the contemporary heat, the Vichy government was hated and much of that hatred struck directly or obliquely at the Church. In Paris, it was said, only 15 per cent of the Catholic population attended Mass and the average was no better than 30 per cent for the nation as a whole. The Communists were active, especially among the workers, and the worker-priest movement was expanding to combat them. The Vatican was alarmed and Archbishop Roncalli, Nuncio to France, appealed to Pius XII to withhold judgment for a while and give the movement a chance. That appeal drew Monsignor Montini into the admittedly delicate situation.

Mission de France came into existence to bring the Catholic faith and its teaching to Catholics grown indifferent and to Catholics fallen away. Seminaries were established at Lisieux and Limoges for priests of a special vocation who would share the work of the people and reach them by association, learning their problems and establishing influence through sympathy and the knowledge of problems. Priests went out from these seminaries to work as waterfront laborers, sailors, miners, truck drivers, factory hands, accepting a doubly difficult life, since they lived as priests and as laborers. Of necessity they worked slowly and it was difficult to evaluate their work, easy to see the moral dangers which the worker-priest faced. A worker-priest had little time or energy for prayer or religious discipline; even for the daily Office and the Mass.

Monsignor Montini, whose experience with communism was expanding, found what he expected to find when he was drawn into correspondence on *Mission de France*; the priests of Christ were at a great disadvantage when confronted by the priests of Marx in Marxist territory. The Marxists were not ignorant troublemakers as they were pictured: they were zealots, trained in theory and tested by exposure to injustice and brutality and exploitation. In the workers' world, the priest of Marx moved with confidence, saying and doing the right things, expressing the right attitudes. In debate under the rough, tough rules of the labor front, the priests of Christ, despite special training, were out of their element and outgunned.

Pius XI had said: "It was the scandal of the nineteenth century that the Church lost the working classes." Monsignor Montini believed that it would be the glory of the twentieth century to regain them. He was vitally interested in every movement which brought the Church into the lives of youth, of the poor, of the underprivileged and handicapped, every movement which sought to make the Church a vital factor in the daily lives of people whether the activity involved was missionary, humanitarian or political. He was viewed askance as a possibly dangerous innovator by many of his contemporaries but there were many others in the Church who felt that it had not been the way of Christ to wait in temple or tabernacle for people to come in; the first way and the apostolic way had been a going out and a seeking.

The priest-workers were exciting as men in dangerous callings are always exciting, and they were exciting for the ways they might open up for others coming after them. Monsignor Montini and Archbishop Roncalli carried on an extensive correspondence on the subject and Monsignor Montini was privately and publicly on record as in favor of developing the movement, perhaps extending it to other countries after the trial and error period provided the data which seminaries would need for training. The priest-workers, however, ran into a problem that proved too much for them.

One of the rights of the worker is to organize and to bargain for his services. The workers among whom the priests worked belonged to unions and the priest-workers joined those unions. Men of uncommon intelligence and exceptional education, they rose in the union structure and became officers. There were strikes with resulting violence. Priest-workers as officers in the unions were arrested and the resultant publicity stimulated the press to dig into the *Mission de France*. There were priests who had fallen away through moral faults and a few priests who had become converts to communism. The casualties were few considering the number of worker-priests on the firing line of the Church in its hottest sector but the Sacred Congregation of the Holy Office called for an investigation which Archbishop Roncalli, sadly but conscientiously, made. The Holy Father called the cardinals of France to Rome and the activities of the priest-workers were curtailed, their activity brought within limits of discretion.

Monsignor Montini lost some of the prestige he had gained through the Christian Democrat triumph in Italy, although such a loss is difficult to define. He had encouraged a reckless experiment which more conservative men had opposed from its inception and the experiment had failed.

In 1950, three million pilgrims journeyed to Rome for the Holy Year proclaimed by Pius XII. A greater number had been expected but the three million provided drama for the Romans and found drama in Rome.

Czechoslovakia and Poland were still imprisoning priests and bishops in unrelenting warfare on the Church. Pius XII, on November 1, proclaimed the Assumption of the Blessed Virgin Mary into heaven as dogma, the first dogmatic definition by a pope, on his own authority, since that of Pius IX in December 1854.

Monsignor Montini had carried much of the responsibility for the special events of the Holy Year and there had been many people to see. He was tired and his friend, Archbishop Amleto Cicognani, Apostolic Delegate to the United States, had been urging him for years to make a visit to America. With the reluctant permission of the Holy Father he arranged for a three-week American vacation in 1951.

In 1951, Alcide De Gasperi formed his seventh successive cabinet as Premier. Italy still had its problems but the Italian recovery had won the respect of the world.

21

THE FAVORITE FALLS

Monsignor Giovanni Battista Montini visited the United States in August 1951. The month was the least likely to offer him a contrast to the Rome summer but he did not complain of the heat. Washington in August delighted him. Much of the delight was due, of course, to his reunion with Archbishop Cicognani, under whom he had made his first timid steps into the rough and ready pastorate of FUCI. He had seen his old friend and mentor a number of times in Rome but the meeting in Washington was more like a holiday.

The visitor from Rome was honored at a reception in the National Catholic Welfare Conference building on Massachusetts Avenue. A number of civil and religious leaders gathered to meet him, including Archbishop Patrick A. O'Boyle of Washington, Attorney General J. Howard McGrath, U. S. Senator Joseph C. O'Mahoney of Wyoming, and Mauricio Nabuco, Brazilian Ambassador to the United States and formerly Brazilian Ambassador to the Holy See. Hosts at the reception were Monsignor Howard J. Carroll, N.C.W.C. General Secretary, Monsignor Paul Tanner, assistant General Secretary of N.C.W.C., and Frank Hall, News Director. Monsignor Montini revealed in conversation with the staff that he was at home in a newspaper office and sensitive to the dedicated side of Catholic journalism.

"We, in Rome, appreciate," he said, "but do not often voice our appreciation, to those who work so well, at personal sacrifice, on the journalistic front of the Church."

Monsignor Montini traveled in the United States with Monsignor Joseph McGeough of New York, one of his American friends of the war years in the Vatican and a member of the international set who had provided a measure of gaiety at a time when it was badly needed. Monsignor McGeough had been assigned then to the Oriental Congregation. Monsignor Montini had grown fond of the slow-speaking, good-natured New Yorker and when he needed a companion for the American journey, he invited him.

From Washington the two priests journeyed west. In Denver they were the guests of Archbishop Urban J. Vehr in his home adjoining that of Colorado's Knight of Malta, Oscar J. Malo. Monsignor Montini had a mountain trip by automobile and commented on the fact that the foothills of the Rocky Mountains were like those of the Brescian Alps near his Concesio home.

In Chicago, Samuel Cardinal Stritch was host and in Detroit, Edward Cardinal Mooney. There Monsignor Montini visited an automobile factory and watched an assembly line in action. In Pittsburgh, they visited the mother of Monsignor Walter S. Carroll who had been one of the three musketeers with Monsignor McGeough in Rome and a member of the Vatican's international set whom Monsignor Montini remembered with affection. Monsignor Carroll had died in 1950. He had a brother, Coleman F. Carroll, who was pastor of Sacred Heart parish whom they also visited.

After New York and a joyous reunion with the veteran Roman, Francis Cardinal Spellman, the two priests separated for a while and Monsignor Montini went to Quebec via New England with two laymen while Monsignor McGeough visited relatives. Monsignor Montini and his companions stopped on Sunday morning at St. Joseph's Church in the small town of Lincoln, New Hampshire.

"He looked just like any other priest who might come to the rectory and ask to say Mass," Father Edmund Guay recalls. "He was from Rome and he was just driving through the mountains. I happened to need a priest for the 8 o'clock Mass that Sunday morning so I was very happy about it."

The United States that Giovanni Battista Montini saw was partly tourist. He went to the top of the Empire State Building in New York and he visited Mount Vernon when he was in Washington. He was interested in the people, however, more than in scenery or shrines; in the homes of the poor, in labor unions, in schools, in recreation centers, and in politics. People who met him on his visit remember him in connection with those interests and the penetrating questions which he asked.

The United States was fighting the unfortunate Korean War against frankly labeled Communist forces, but the visitor was assured blandly, and with obvious sincerity, by Americans that there was no security problem at all in the European sense, no Communists worth mentioning, certainly none in the government. General Douglas MacArthur was appearing before Congress in a hearing on his conduct of the Korean War after his recall by President Truman and there seemed to be some question as to whether he had been given a free hand to defeat the Communists.

From the United States Monsignor Montini, reunited with Monsignor McGeough, flew to Ireland where he was welcomed by the chargé d'affaires of the nunciature in Dublin, Monsignor Benelli, and called on John Cardinal D'Alton, Archbishop of Armagh and Primate of all Ireland. The Guest Master of the Cistercian Abbey of Mount St. Joseph, Rosecrea, Father Raphael says:

"I remember that Monsignor Montini spoke excellent English and he had a magnetic personality that we all warmed to. He was a most sympathetic listener also."

It was the end of a journey. Monsignor Montini returned to Rome and to the routine which seemed as it had always been but which was subtly changed because the servant of the routine had been changed. Monsignor Montini was looking at his familiar desk with not quite the same eyes, listening to the bells with not quite the same ears. Loyalty, intense loyalty, carried him along for two years. He shared as he had shared for a long time the post which Pius XII still saw as one job divided between two men, a post which had grown enormously during the war and since, a job which required an all-important third man who wasn't there, a Secretary of State. The two half-secretaries of State were known to jocular diplomats as Monsignor Outside (Tardini) and Monsignor Inside (Montini).

Pius XII grew old gracefully but he grew old. Only those close to him, perhaps, realized his mental, spiritual, and physical involvement in the war and how selflessly he spent himself in fruitless appeals for peace, in carefully worked out peace plans, in protests against man's inhumanity to man. He was a trifle above six feet in height and at war's end he weighed 128 pounds.

He found it difficult to delegate authority and he spent much of his own energy on tasks that should not have engaged a minute of his time. He insisted, for instance, upon seeing galley proofs of his encyclicals, talks, pronouncements before they appeared in *Osservatore Romano* although proofreading had already been done by his secretaries and by the staff of the paper. He rejected letters or documents presented for his signature if there was the slightest error, an uneven impression of one key, a deviation in perfect centering. He was positive, emphatic, dogmatic in such minor matters as punctuation, the shade of differentiation in meaning between one word or another, but he disliked making decisions on matters of importance, preferring to wait, to postpone, to seek more information. He worried about decisions made by those under him when he heard of them. His timidity of decision was an old weakness, concealed in great part from the world by the fact that under pressure he had made some dazzling and daring decisions. As he grew older he found ways of evading the pressures.

He had a brilliant mind, an immense library in his brain, and he could see through an intricate diplomatic situation to the ultimate inevitable conclusion. He could interpret the mind of the Church for simple people or for scholars and he delighted in difficult moral problems arising out of new developments of science, changing world conditions. To many people he seemed facile rather than profound: certainly as he grew older he seemed content with lesser accomplishments, to be praised for versatility. He liked to surprise a visitor from a diamond-cutting area with a discussion on diamond-cutting, to astonish an American oil man with questions about depletion allowances. It delighted him to discover in a Holy Year audience two men who were circus clowns but he was chagrined that he had no prepared material on circuses.

Prepared material was essential to him. He had no "ad lib" ability, no gifts of spontaneity or improvisation. In certain oft-repeated situations, or some only rarely repeated, he could recall information he had used previously or an effective sentence or two. He had careful briefing on important visitors before they appeared for an audience. Secretaries prepared dossiers on the man, or woman, city of origin and city of residence, all manner of information. He would use this data effectively as he would use any happy combination of words from the summary. In visitor data sheets prepared by Monsignor Montini, or under his direction, such happy combinations always occurred. It was part of the service to Pius XII to put phrases that he loved in his mouth. He wrote well himself, of course, but cautiously, avoiding commitments in words and vitiating the force of papers prepared for him by the addition of qualifying phrases, the substituting of a gentle word for a strong one.

Pius XII was a gentle man. He spoke compassionately and offered consolation to people who came to his audiences with problems or grief. He could read distress in a human face as he passed in a large audience; when he did, he stopped to inquire. He prayed for people, not only for the masses of mankind but for individuals who requested his intercession. He was distressed when pain, loss, grief or disaster came to members of his staff or people whom he knew; he expressed his sympathy in thoughtful ways when he could offer no practical aid. He sought no luxury or ease for himself, eating simply and frugally, sleeping on a plain bed in a plain room, working and praying for long hours, responsive to any call for aid, any human need.

He was the Supreme Pontiff, Vicar of Christ on Earth, Bishop of Rome. He never forgot that. He had paid every last dot of respect and homage to the high and holy office when Pius XI occupied the throne: he still paid it, and demanded it from others, when he occupied it. He was reduced by his concept of the papacy to incalculable loneliness. There was a tradition that no one dines with the pope. Pius X had swept it aside, Benedict XV and Pius XI had suspended it when they willed to do so; Pius XII observed the tradition as though it were law. He ate all of his meals alone except for his pets; his canaries and a goldfinch named Gretel who were released during his mealtimes. They flew around the room or perched on his shoulders or sang to him.

He was particularly attached to Gretel and would relate anecdotes about her to his official family on relaxed occasions. Monsignor Montini, and a few others, had been invited to a performance which particularly delighted Pius XII. He had an electric razor presented to him by Cardinal Spellman and Gretel loved the sound of it. She would become alert when the Holy Father took the razor in his hands and show unmistakable excitement and delight when the humming sound began. Pius XII never ceased to be amused and entertained by her.

Such simplicities entered into the complex nature of the man who occupied the world's most ancient throne, who stood between God and man, with the fearsome responsibility of the papal office.

He was a stern, impatient, meticulous taskmaster and, seemingly, an ungrateful one; but he considered that the demands he made were in the service of God, for God; privileges granted rather than irksome tasks commanded. The respect, the dedication, the surrender of self which he exacted from others was no more than he was willing to give, and give with a beautiful serene detachment. No man personified detachment in face and bearing as Pius XII did. Arthur Symonds once described a cardinal in terms which some observers said would apply perfectly to Pius: "The air of fixed meditation, as of continual commerce with heaven, which is the Church's manner of expressing disapproval of the world." It wasn't quite that.

As he grew older, the personality of Pius XII did not change essentially but certain traits became more pronounced.

Giovanni Battista Montini was the buffer between the Holy Father and the powerful cardinals of the Curia, the heads of Congregations, Tribunals, offices, and commissions. Since the Holy Father can respond personally to only a small percentage of the demands reaching him from the Catholic and non-Catholic world, the extensions of himself must be well organized to respond for him. Audiences *a tabella* were set up to make the Curia responsive to his will and the heads of the various divisions of the Curia were required to report personally to the Holy Father at least once every fifteen days. As he grew older, Pius lost interest in the *a tabella* audiences. He either canceled them, did not grant them or restricted them to such ridiculously short time that they were meaningless. The Curia Lords so cavalierly treated were aging men, too, some of them quite old, testy, and querulous or gruff and angry, with respect for their own function in the Church and concern for its importance. Some of them would have forthrightly made decisions without consultation with Pius XII or without his approval; but power resided in him and not in them.

Giovanni Battista Montini was the target of angry Princes of the Church who could not reach the pope; the recipient of papal rebuke when he tried to obtain appointments, audiences, decisions. His associate, Domenico Tardini, had problems, too, but his department handled the larger issues which were likely to interest the Holy Father. There were suspicious men who disliked Monsignor Montini because they felt he influenced the Holy Father and other men who labeled him lukewarm and indecisive when he failed to obtain the decisions they wanted and which he, himself, could no more make than they. He had to convey bad news sometimes and take the blame for rejecting or negating because the Holy Father was opposed but did not want to be quoted or placed on the record. A man developed a professional personality that was not his own when he sat at the desk of the Substitute Secretary of State with only the rank of monsignor.

One day Monsignor Montini officiated at a wedding in St. Anne's. He liked weddings and had married a number of his Fucini. He had known the couple he married in St. Anne's for several years and was familiar with their problems. There was not much money and there had been an ill mother. When they had surmounted their problems, the wedding was a happy event in which he shared happily. A diplomat who happened to make a visit to the church, not knowing about the wedding, was astonished. He had known Monsignor Montini for many years.

"This was a man I did not know," he said later. "I would not have believed that this man existed behind the mask I have been permitted to see. This aspect of Monsignor Inside was a revelation."

The year 1953 was one of the turning point years in Giovanni Battista Montini's life. He was described in that year by Dorothy Carewe and Joseph Rosapepe who interviewed him in Rome for the *Catholic World:*

"Monsignor Montini has a compelling appearance. He looks about fifteen years younger than his age. He is tall—nearly six feet—and extremely thin. His head is impressive since his forehead is unusually high and the impression of height is emphasized by his receding hairline. Short, thin lips that are unbelievably straight make it clear that top level diplomatic secrets will not be disclosed carelessly. A large, straight nose makes his eyes seem more deepset than they are. Actually, his piercing glance strikes visitors as Monsignor Montini's most outstanding characteristic."

There were many vacancies in the College of Cardinals and Pius XII was persuaded to summon a consistory and raise new men to the purple. His own staff represented a problem and a challenge. Pius XII had grown up in diplomacy. He knew the values placed upon rank and the interpretations placed upon the lack of it. He knew how long his two assistants had served him and how well. He called them into conference.

Only one living man knows what occurred at that conference and he will never reveal the true story. There are two versions of what happened. The most widely circulated version is that Monsignor Domenico Tardini was jealous of his younger rival and certain that if they became cardinals only one of them would remain in the State Department and that he would be made Secretary; the other would be sent to an archdiocese. Certain that his associate stood higher in the regard of Pius than he did and would be retained, Tardini, it is said, declined the cardinalate which the Holy Father offered, making it impossible for the junior to accept what the senior declined.

The story casts Monsignor Tardini in the plotting villain role. He was more gruffly belligerent than crafty, more bluntly outspoken than adroit, but he was a diplomat trained to subtle moves so the story may be true. The one great interest in his life, apart from his priesthood and his work, was an orphanage for boys on the outskirts of Rome. He put all of his own money into it, all of the money he could bully out of friends and acquaintances, all of the personal time he could spare. Certainly, he would not want to leave it.

The other story says that Pius XII made a sentimental speech to his two associates in which he thanked them for the assistance they had rendered him, their willingness to share the weight of the burden he carried. He described the functioning of the department as ideal, perfectly in balance, tuned in harmony, and expressed his great regret that he must unbalance the balanced; still, they had merited cardinalates which he was certain that they, humanly, desired.

According to this version, Pius XII looked then at Monsignor Tardini, the senior, and said: "Is that not so?"

Tardini stood there, probably wanting the red hat as he had

wanted few things in his life, and said: "No. If you want me here, I stay."

Montini, then, had no alternative.

There may be still another version, and that one true. All that Pius XII said was that he had offered cardinalates to his assistants and that both had virtuously declined the honor.

At this time, the Holy Father changed the titles of his two assistants and they became Pro-Secretaries instead of Substitute Secretaries, which was a mere exercise in semantics since there was no change in their work or in their responsibilities.

The worker-priest situation came to the fore again at the Vatican. The previous year, two worker-priests had been arrested for participating in a Communist-inspired demonstration against General Matthew B. Ridgway and another investigation of the whole movement was undertaken. It was the contention of the worker-priests that they had to share even in the demonstrations of the workers if no other remedy was offered on the material level and that their spiritual influence was increased rather than lessened by so doing. They were beaten by the police when arrested and that was worth a thousand sermons but the intrusion of Rome, removing them because of the incident, devalued the value of what they had done. Pius XII, after discussion with French cardinals and cardinals of the Curia, once more limited and curtailed the activities of the priest-workers to the point where fifty, in a protest, claimed they could be of no value. Three priest-workers left the Church in protest.

Monsignor Montini, who had retained both interest in the movement and sympathy for the worker-priests, was linked in unofficial Vatican comment to this latest flareup although he had not been, in any way, directly involved.

Hubert Beuve-Mery, director of *Le Monde*, saw Monsignor Montini in Rome before this latest development and his is the best outside-of-Rome, outside-of-clergy account of the Pro-Secretary's attitude: "I am permitted to say without violating discretion that the conversation was concerned almost exclusively with the problem of the priest-workers. Monsignor Montini kept me at length, multiplying his questions and expressing a strong desire to gather news rather different, as he told me, than was most often coming to the Vatican. Without revealing any of his personal positions, Monsignor Montini left me with the impression of a rather lively spirit and, above all at that moment, an especially open one."

The difficulty of clearing through the Holy Father matters requiring decision did not ease and his public audiences came under attack. "If I were a bicycle rider or a moving picture actor I would have no trouble in obtaining an audience," one angry cardinal said.

The Holy Father particularly liked bicycle racers, watched them on television and seemingly enjoyed talking to them in audiences, in having his picture taken with them. He liked, in fact, most of the people he met in the large audiences, people of all faiths from all over the world. He spoke to them in a number of languages and he was genuinely dismayed if someone wanted to talk to him and they could find no common language. He exchanged skull caps with people and he permitted familiarities, but he blessed them, too, and he looked like a dweller in another world when he did so.

A visiting bishop said to him one day: "The audiences are extraordinary. They are an apostolate."

"I believe so," said Pius XII.

He was seen during his pontificate by an estimated fifteen to twenty million people, many of them Piazza San Pietro audiences, and he obviously felt that the time he spent on them was worthwhile, that they carried with them a favorable impression of Roman Catholicism which would be a bulwark against the violent prejudices sweeping the world. His view was not endorsed behind the scenes at the Vatican where those who considered him too rigid and too formal deplored his informality with strangers; deplored, too, the fact that bishops made their pilgrimages to Rome and could not see him.

The plain fact was that Pius XII was growing too old for the responsibility he insisted upon carrying. He took refuge from the problems with which he could no longer contend in simpler activities, seeking instinctively, perhaps, a quieter and happier apostolate after so much turbulence.

Early in 1954 he suffered a severe attack of hiccoughs and an internal disorder, probably a diaphragmic hernia. His illness brought to a series of climaxes a conflict of long duration which had been waged more or less quietly. A sick room coterie closed ranks around him, assuming the authority of papal guardians, reassuring him while arbitrarily deciding who should see him. The same people had exerted great influence before his illness. When his public appearances were curtailed over a period of forty days an issue was created.

In control of the situation were: the Holy Father's personally selected physician, Dr. Ricardo Galeazzi-Lisi; his brother, Count Pietro Enrico Galeazzi, director of the Vatican technical services; the Holy Father's nephews who held influential positions in the legal and financial world, and Mother Pasqualina. Mother Pasqualina commanded the four nuns who did the cooking and housework in the pope's apartment. She had nursed Pius XII through an illness when he was a nuncio and he placed on her the responsibility of seeing to it that he was served the proper foods, that he got any medicine he was supposed to take at the proper time and that everything was exactly where it should be in his household. She had an exacting job, was devoted to the Holy Father. She was a strong-minded, determined woman with a temper and an imperious manner.

The people around the pope were honestly motivated, no doubt. To them his health was more important than anything he was called upon to do, anything he was required to sign, anybody he was supposed to see. Granting the truth of all that, the Holy Father himself had made intrusion upon even his time of illness necessary. He had delegated no authority, not even in the all-important Secretariat of State.

Giovanni Battista Montini had to challenge the sick room coterie in order to clear matters that had to be cleared, to obtain signatures which had to be obtained. He made enemies in doing

so and even Pius XII cooled toward him. A man who is ill likes
those who see to his comfort and is antagonized by anyone who
disturbs or upsets him. Monsignor Montini was the disturber,
the upsetter, and the five people close to the ailing Pontiff were
the dispensers of comfort. A rift developed which was never
named nor acknowledged but which existed without the naming
nor the acknowledgment.

There were rumors around the Vatican which even the press
collected: that the Holy Father considered ambition a fault in
a cleric. Montini, said rumor, had proved disappointingly ambitious. Echoes of the priest-worker debate rang, too, in the halls.
Finally, Montini had interfered with the Holy Father's household.

On August 30, 1954, Alfredo Ildefonso Cardinal Schuster,
Archbishop of Milan, died. When the word reached Monsignor
Montini's desk he sat in silent prayer over the message. The
eminent Benedictine held an honored place in any story of his
life, the abbot to whom he had brought his first retreatants,
and whose retreat he had shared at St. Paul's Outside-the-Walls.
He rose and went into the Holy Father's office, carrying the
message.

He did not emerge for an hour and his face was white when
he went back to his own desk. It was said later that he received
word then that Pius XII was sending him to Milan.

The official announcement was not made until November 3,
1954, the eve of the Feast of St. Charles Borromeo.

The announcement was nicely worded, with every sign of affection and some observers said that Pius XII was giving to his
protégé the pastoral experience he needed with the hope that he
would succeed him some day on the throne of Peter. Others,
considering all the factors and looking coldly at the situation,
said that Montini had fallen from grace and that the old device was in play again: *Promoveatur ut Amoveatur* (Let him be
promoted so that he can be removed).

"Let us see if Pius gives him the red hat," the observers said.
Milan was the great city of Italy, second to Rome in ec-

clesiastical dignity and influence, and its archbishop was always a cardinal. Pius XII sent Giovanni Battista Montini to Milan and he did not elevate him to the cardinalate.

The Holy Father was a veteran diplomat. He knew how his action would be interpreted so there is no escaping the conclusion that he wanted his appointment of the Archbishop of Milan to be interpreted as it was interpreted.

Giovanni Battista Montini was not going to this new assignment as the favorite of the Holy Father: he was going on his own, responsible to himself and on trial in a post for which he had not been trained. He did not, however, move out in bitterness. His final act before he surrendered his desk was the writing of a personal letter to Pius XII from which the following is an extract:

"To say what my feelings are at the moment of my physical separation from this blessed place is not possible for me. But overcoming the mixture of memories, impressions, thoughts and plans, I feel the overwhelming need to express to Your Holiness my most lively filial gratitude for the benefits, the number of which does not permit me to enumerate or their greatness to measure, having come to me from the fatherly, generous, always new, and always affable goodness of Your Holiness."

22

MILAN

"M ILAN seemed to me an immense hostile forest,"
Giovanni Battista Montini wrote.

The quiet, scholarly strategist, the consultant on politics and
Catholic Action, the forceful, compelling writer, faced a new
array of forces in the great industrial city of the north. This
was not a campaign or an election or a rally of youth organizations; this was a command post of the Church and might well
be his career, the place and the responsibility to which God had
called him out of the years of seasoning and experience that had
been his. It did not seem, however, that his training matched
the work he would be called upon to do. In the time at his
disposal between his appointment and his consecration, he
studied and planned and drew diagrams and prayed.

He was consecrated in Rome by Eugene Cardinal Tisserant
on December 13, 1954, with Bishops Giacinto Tredici and Dominico Bernareggi as co-consecrators. A weird touch was added
to the solemn ceremony by the electronically transmitted voice
of Pius XII conveying a blessing from his sick room. Stranger
still was the spontaneous outburst of applause as the slender
monsignor appeared before the cardinal-consecrator to receive
ring, mitre, and pastoral crosier. Vatican historians could recall
no precedent for this. Applause in St. Peter's is reserved for the
pope.

It was bitter cold when Milan's new archbishop left Rome Termini on the morning of January 4, 1955. He was met by Monsignor Schiavini, Vicar General, at Lodi, south of Milan, and was driven around the periphery of the city to Rho where he spent the night at the College of the Oblates. There was ice on the road and sleet in the air. In the murky light, Milan seemed like a squatting blob of squalor, veined with tangles of streets. The car never actually entered the city but the archbishop, viewing his domain from a car window saw where and how many of the workers lived. The outskirt town in which he slept was surrounded by oil refineries and chemical works. He breathed the industrial north into his lungs and he was able to say within a week, addressing workers:

"I am certain that Heaven hears the sound of your factories as organ music and breathes the fumes of these great stacks as incense—for you are the indispensable part of God's world."

Archbishop Giovanni Battista Montini entered Milan on January 5, 1955. There was a cavalcade, each car bearing notables of the government, the municipality, or the clergy. As his car crossed the city line, the archbishop startled his fellow passengers by ordering the driver to stop. The day was as its predecessor had been, gray and wet. Archbishop Montini, in his episcopal robes, bent and kissed the earth of Lombardy, his home; of Milan, his parish.

People lined the route which he took to the Cathedral despite the chill drizzle; some of them frowning, some of them curious, some of them pleased and applauding. He was to meet them all in the weeks to come; the hostile, the indifferent, the devout. The cavalcade turned into Piazza del Duomo.

Milan's duomo reached up into the gray sky, one of the magnificent cathedrals of the world. The apostles, saints, and angels on the graceful pinnacles were lost in the swirling mist and the gargoyles had vanished from view, but the topmost spire was a slender lance which stood tall and, for at least a few moments, clear of the dark vapor. This was the spire bearing Madonnina, the patroness and protectress of Milan. This was her Cathedral, the only one ever dedicated to the infancy of Mary and so dedicated in the Middle Ages, centuries before the doctrine of the Immaculate Conception was proclaimed. The 140th Archbishop of Milan stood with his head back, looking along the line of that lofty spire. St. Charles Borromeo had dedicated this church in 1572. He, too, had been an Archbishop of Milan.

The assembled dignitaries and the spectators waited one minute more, then the archbishop entered the Cathedral. He was home. All that he possessed accompanied him, or followed him; three well-worn suitcases and ninety crates of books which were to become the wonder and the talk of the city.

On his first full day in Milan, the new archbishop visited the big prison and talked to the prisoners. "They are my people," he said, "and they cannot come to see me." The visit attracted very little attention and received no comment from the press although a similar visit by a newly elected pope years later attracted world notice. From the prison the archbishop went to the hospitals. He conferred that evening with his staff which included Don Giovanni Macchi, his secretary, and Monsignor Ernesto Basadonna, chancelor of the archdiocese.

The archdiocese contained nearly four million people. They were served by 2200 regular priests and there were a thousand young men studying for the priesthood in the seminaries. There were twelve Catholic colleges, forty-five orders of men, and 156 orders of women with twenty mother houses. Milan and the area surrounding it had been brutally bombed during the war and in the rebuilding, church construction had not kept pace. Communism had made converts and Catholicism had supplied those converts out of its lost sheep. Catholic morale was low and the priests lacked zeal. The Church moved sluggishly when it moved.

Alfredo Iledefonso Cardinal Schuster had been loved and esteemed in Milan where he was referred to as "the Cardinal of Prayer." He was considered a saint by many people. No one had loved or esteemed him more than his successor but the archdiocese had gone slack. It was not meeting the necessities of the people, the bare necessities, and there was no plan, no provision for growth. Cardinal Schuster had been another man grown old in responsibility who had fallen out of step with his time. He had been a man of intense patriotism and love of country who had blessed troops and hailed as crusades the adventures of Italian arms, so he had been labeled a Fascist. At the war's end his influence was negligible and he closed himself up in the episcopal palace, rarely making a public appearance. The archdiocese had run on momentum. That period was over, very definitely over.

Archbishop Montini had many assets with which to work, the most vital of which were priests. He gathered the clergy together for a retreat.

"A true, a good, a saintly priesthood would save the world," he told them. Later in his address, he added: "Do not seek immediate successes. Do not look for thanks. Leave results in the hands of God. You are only sowers and have only one preoccupation; to cast live and true seed."

Later, speaking to a class of newly ordained priests, he said: "I send you into the world. Go into that world, but take care! You must share its hopes and sorrows, not its baseness and its vulgarity. You must live spiritually, aware, but apart from, gross errors and decadent habits. You must know the diseases and cure them without catching them."

There were changes made in pastoral assignments and changes in the chain of command. Archbishop Montini stated that he wanted to know each priest personally. He knew that this would take time, and his priests knew that it would. The announced intention improved morale.

On January 9, his third day, the archbishop went to the Sesto San Giovanni section to dedicate a children's home. This was a notorious Communist stronghold, known for its practically solid party vote in elections. An archbishop alone could not have attracted an audience but a house for children was needed and considered proper to support. There was an audience, quiet but sullenly hostile.

"Everyone is asking," he said, "who is this new Archbishop of Milan? How will he act? I will say to you now; I am the Archbishop of the Workers."

His audience was politely skeptical. So were other audiences. He went into a factory and was permitted to address the workers on their lunch hour. He stood facing men who chewed sandwiches and scraped food from the lids of lunch buckets, men who had little interest in him.

"The first ones to separate themselves from religion were not the workers but the moguls and the powerful economists of the last century who dreamed of establishing a progress, a peace, a civilization without God and without Christ," he said. "We do not say any more that religion is the opium of the people. Religion is man's light and his glory and his strength."

He visited many factories and he walked among the workers and he introduced himself. Sometimes, after an instant of hesitation, a worker would drop to one knee and kiss his ring. He shook hands with those who did not and his handgrip was firm. He spoke with force and simplicity and his eyes met even savagely hostile eyes without turning away.

"The working classes are those chosen for the evangelical message announced by the Church," he said. "You, precisely because you have a great experience of human weariness are close to Christ, and His gospel has meaning for you. You, who have experienced injustice among men, must know the Church as your friend, your spokesman, understanding the value of your weariness."

He spoke in those terms to small groups and his visits were often unannounced, a dropping in, which was an ecclesiastical novelty. He asked questions where he was shown any friendliness. He never seemed astonished that men were Communist; nor reproachful, nor hostile, even when they proclaimed the fact belligerently.

"It is a sad thing to be a Communist," he would say sometimes. "You must have suffered greatly or you would not embrace a creed which offers so little hope, which grants you no dignity."

A young monsignor who traveled with him said delightedly: "He baffles them, especially with the handshaking. He acts like someone who is running for office but he does not ask them for anything."

The workers were baffled more by the humility of this high-ranking prelate than by his handshaking. He was so obviously interested in the men who labored and in the work that they did, often awed by them and not ashamed to admit it. He visited one large foundry and, after a trip of inspection, he addressed the workers.

"There was insufficient time," he said. "I wished to stop and to observe more closely, to understand if I could the various stages of a casting operation. In witnessing this Herculean effort, the difficulty and the danger of the work, I felt my heart full of admiration for you, for this gigantic human enterprise exerted to so useful an end. How could we live in our world without you: your arms, your ability, your capacity for dominating matter, for taking it from the infernal jaws of flame and putting it beneath tremendous drop hammers? Your effort not only commands my admiration, but astonishes me. It leaves me, too, with a psychological problem. Can we, you and I, understand each other?"

He reached men with such simple talks and he broke down many barriers of hostility but the worker campaign was only a small part of the archbishop's activity and not very productive on the surface. He was reaching a comparatively small number of people and seemingly not more than casually, along the surface. He was taking his own advice, however, sowing seeds, not seeking immediate success. There were other lines of action. There were 247 mayors in the province, many of them obviously in very small towns but each of them a man of importance in his own community, a man who worked for the community and understood the needs of people. Giovanni Battista Montini had grown up in the household of such a man, a man who worked in large arenas but who never met another whom he considered small.

"I want to meet every one of the mayors," he said.

He started meeting mayors. He started a program of parish visitations. He had 822 parishes and planned to establish more. He promised that he would visit every parish and meet every priest and every parishioner if God gave him the time and if the archdiocese was patient. He met with architects and builders and planners of subdivisions. His day had sixteen working hours in it. When possible he made himself available for those who wanted to call on him. He had a call from one committee of wealthy men who had been cajoled by Cardinal Schuster into financing scholarships and supporting a school for retarded children.

The callers explained that they had backed Cardinal Schuster whenever they could and would do the same for him, of course, but since they had started this worthy effort, they felt they had done enough and would have to withdraw their support. The new archbishop leaned back in his chair.

"You can't afford it?" he asked bluntly.

Two of the committee hesitated, but the third said: "Frankly, Your Excellency, we cannot. There are many demands on us."

Archbishop Montini lifted a sheet of paper from the top of his desk, the report of the scholarship fund. He read the names of the three men slowly aloud, as though memorizing them, then nodded his head.

"I regret that you have suffered reverses," he said. "I shall undertake immediately the task of finding three men who can afford to carry on this worthy enterprise."

He rose, terminating the interview, and the three men were disconcerted. They were obviously thinking that if the archbishop was not discreet in handling this the impression would spread that they were not doing well, could not afford any longer what they could afford once.

"Excellency," one of them said. "Give us time to talk this over. We may find a means of continuing our support."

They found the means and the archbishop heard no more about withdrawing from the scholarship fund. Anecdotes such as this were told of him and the impression spread that this was a hard, direct sort of man. "He never drives anyone and never insists that a person agree with him," one of his staff said, "but he knows how to make it impossible to refuse him anything he wants."

He wanted churches and he couldn't afford them. Out of his many conferences he obtained a standard-design, pre-fabricated church which could be erected reasonably. He erected this church in multiples, many multiples, the identical church in appearance, located in many areas of the province; where bombed churches had not been rebuilt, where worker neighborhoods had become too heavily populated for the existing churches, where a new settlement had been started. He startled the residents of heavily Communist areas by appearing at the office of the mayor, or the head of a union, and stating that he wanted advice on the best location for a new church in their area.

He erected his churches, in and out of Communist neighborhoods, and he added other buildings which he deemed necessary. "A church," he said, "is a house of prayer, certainly, but let us think of it as God's house where neighbors and friends come to visit, to enjoy themselves, to feel welcome. There should be a playground for the children and a place where adults can have discussions and entertainment. It would be good to have a library. Let us not limit our concept of God's house. We can share all things with Him."

It worried him that priests were difficult to reach in many parts of his archdiocese, that people were left without a priest in a time of trouble, unable to locate a priest when death entered a house. He raised money through a drive on the pocketbooks of wealthy industrialists and he supplied a telephone for every parish house. He bought automobiles for priests with large parishes and marked as a goal the ultimate purchase of an automobile for each of the priests who received telephones. He wanted the Church in communication with the people and on wheels to reach them rapidly when they asked for help.

He considered pastoral visits his most important duty and he tried to make a minimum of four a week. He went to the most backward and least accessible first, some of them in mountain country where he had to ride a donkey to reach the village he sought. He said evening Masses in the churches. Usually the people of the parish met him in front of the church. He spoke to the pastor and went into the church for the Mass, then preached a short sermon and visited with the parishioners. He paid particular attention to the children.

"We trust them with our future," he said. "We must create for them happy memories of their childhood church."

He did not have his dinner until 9:30 or 10 on these visit nights and he usually dined with the pastor, discussing his problems with him. He carried a notebook with him wherever he went and jotted down observations, notes, items to remember. He filled many needs which he entered in the book and surprised many men and women with a practical answer to some wish he heard expressed and which to him seemed reasonable.

In one particularly gloomy and remote mining community he talked with the parishioners as he did everywhere, then encouraged questions. It was difficult to inspire questions or any show of interest from the obviously tired, discouraged, and hopeless people before him. One man, bolder than the rest, said:

"This is an unhappy place. It is poor and nobody comes here and there is nothing to do but work."

The archbishop said: "Does anyone have a musical instrument?"

Blank stares met him, so evidently no one had. He asked if anyone could play an instrument. That was better. Several of them had played or knew a little music. The following day he purchased an accordion with his own money and sent it to the priest of the sad village.

His visitation program abounded in incident, but all of his

activities had drama in them. He seemed possessed of an in-exhaustible vitality and when he was cautioned to slow down, he said: "There is so much to do. All of these people!"

He had been devout, dedicated, concerned with souls in Rome, of course: a fine priest who performed essential work brilliantly and who sought pastoral opportunities where he could find them. The actual people of any pastorate of his had been small, however, at any given time and people en masse tend to become abstractions. In Milan the sheer numbers overwhelmed him but individuals emerged from the mass every day, people differentiated from their contemporaries, separate and distinct personalities, immortal souls. He talked of them with tenderness and he tried to serve them.

No archbishop ever spent his time, thought, and energy more generously on the effort to communicate with his people. His "Discorsi," pastoral letters to all of the Milan archdiocese, to those within and without the Church, are brilliant discussions on a wide range of subjects; offering counsel and guidance in terms of unmistakable concern for the spiritual and temporal welfare of those under his care. He did not hold himself aloof from the practical problems of daily living or evade controversy by taking refuge in clouds of rhetoric.

Of business he wrote: "Using sophisticated formulae, one says: the economy is autonomous; it is queen; it should not be subject to moral scruples; we have to develop a free economy. That economy is considered free which is controlled only by the built-in laws of opportunism and the play of the market. One does not consider that the economy is actually a human fact which should obey human law. Man is superior to the economy and the economy should be subordinated to man's use; not merely subjectively understood, because that would be egoism, but to the utility of the entire social world. In fact, the goods of this earth have to serve society, mankind *in toto*."

Of politics he wrote: "Politics which separates itself from the moral order has laws only to itself and for itself; it becomes the art of succeeding, the science of techniques, the science of proximate ends."

Nor did he ignore the arts. "Art," he wrote, "is a most beautiful expression of the human mind, the human soul, of man's aspiring. Art has its own laws, its own needs, its own interior purity. Art can, but may not, harm life, moral life, childhood and youth. Art must be obedient to that which is of greater importance than itself, to that which arranges the whole order of human life. It is not permitted in the name of art to smuggle evil to the youngest human generation or to those who may experience scandal. Art is accountable to that superior harmony which respects the ultimate ends of man."

Giuseppe Lazzati, editor of *L'Italia* the diocesan newspaper of Milan, read all of the Montini discourses and the reports of talks and sermons, formal and informal. He was the contemporary historian of the archbishop's tenure in the north and he summed up the ends and the aims thus:

"First, to revive the spirit of religiosity. Second, to establish unity among Catholics, the unity of understanding. Third, to meet and to embrace the separated brothers of the Church."

A quotation from the archbishop himself forms a fitting postscript. "The modern world, bringing us new things, must be understood, approached and welcomed," he said. "Certainly that. But above all, it must be renewed, spiritually instructed and redeemed."

23

IN NOMINE DOMINI

MILAN needed churches. The new archbishop built forty-five in his first two years and felt that this was a mere beginning. He was falling short, however, of the necessary money and the edge was off the public enthusiasm for his program. He needed a new appeal, a means of dramatizing the need.

He was driving one day to a visitation and his route took him past a section of new apartment houses where a great many families would be housed and where there was no provision for a church. The sight of these multiple dwellings depressed him. They symbolized so perfectly the problem which he faced. When he returned to his room late that night he composed a letter to the priests of his archdiocese.

It was common knowledge, he wrote, that priests are among the poorest of people, measured in terms of worldly possessions, but he was forced to address an appeal to them for funds because other sources, seemingly, were exhausted. He wanted from the priests of the archdiocese any amount, small or large, which they could give him and he promised that he would extend his appeal to his personal friends in the priesthood elsewhere. He wanted for his archdiocese, built entirely from the personal contributions of priests, *one church*.

The money for that church came in slowly, in agonizing

amounts, and the archbishop kept the city informed on the progress of the fund. Laymen, touched by the gallant effort, tried to help and the archbishop declined graciously but firmly. This was going to be a priest's church, every lira of it.

There had never been, perhaps, a more dramatic presentation of the need for churches. Laymen rallied to the cause again and money flowed in. Many churches were completed with secular funds while the priests, slowly but doggedly, built their fund. It took them several years but that *one church* was built without one penny spent on it that did not come from the thin wallet of a priest. Appropriately, the church was named for a great pastor of souls, the Cure d'Ars.

An old friend of FUCI days, Don Carlo Gnocchi, was chaplain of Collegio Dei Mutilatini (School for Mutilated Boys). Archbishop Montini was greatly interested in the work of this school which was little publicized because people found the fact of its existence disturbing. The victims of bombs and war and of industrial accidents reproached the fortunate. The archbishop asked his old friend if he could say one of his Christmas Masses at the school.

On Christmas Eve, the Archbishop visited the school. Don Carlo Gnocchi was going through his holiday mail. A journalist friend, Flora Antonioni, had come in to help him. Don Carlo, talking to the archbishop, tore one letter into small pieces thinking it a piece of advertising. Miss Antonioni cried out as the pieces fluttered to the ground. There had been a check inside the envelope, one for a sizable amount.

The priest, the girl reporter, and the Archbishop of Milan went down on their knees, picking up the pieces—which they pasted together on the tabletop.

In the morning, Archbishop Montini said Mass for the blind, the armless, the legless, the deformed. He spoke to them gently, but distributing Communion to them was one of the ordeals of his life. He faced them at the rail with the golden ciborium in his hands and his face was described by one of those in attendance as "drawn and pallid to the point of transparency."

249

Another visit of the archbishop's Christmas was to his old tutor, Padre Giuseppe Persico, S.J., who had been transferred to the Instituto Leone in Milan when Collegio Arici in Brescia passed from Jesuit hands. Padre Persico was growing old and he did not expect to be remembered, particularly by an archbishop, but Battista Montini had brought him gifts.

"Everyone kissed the archbishop's ring," the elderly teacher said, "but me he embraced."

As long as he remained in Milan, Giovanni Battista Montini visited his boyhood teacher every Christmas but one, every Easter, bringing him gifts. He called on the phone when he had to miss one Christmas and he made his visit on the following day.

During Lent the archbishop visited orphanages and institutions for the aged, the poor, and the sick. He preached to the people in these institutions while kneeling before them. Asked why it was that Archbishop Montini assumed this kneeling position, Monsignor Basadonna said simply:

"Because the poor are Christ."

Archbishop Montini avoided politics in Milan. The voters had parties now through which they could express their will and a principle had been established. Beyond that point he did not believe that the Church should go. He was still opposed to communism uncompromisingly but he sympathized with people who were Communists. They wasted in their lives, and in their dark apostolate, qualities which belonged to God.

The Communist Party had taken note of him. Palmiro Togliatti remembered him well from the campaign of 1948 and the Christian-Democrat victory. Togliatti sent his number-three man, Pietro Secchia, to Milan to tighten Communist defenses. Secchia, known as "The Cask," was a former bricklayer who had spent a decade in Fascist jails and who had fought in the underground movement. He was a remarkably ugly man in appearance, language, and disposition. He immediately made a speech deriding the new archbishop.

"He tells you that he is the Archbishop of the Workers," he said, "but he is the Cardinal of the Bosses."

Archbishop Montini left to others the logical retort that Milan's archbishop was not a cardinal; to his own intimates he confided the fact that he was complimented. "I did not believe that I was making any impress on them," he said.

The matter of their archbishop's rank was a sore point with the Milanese. Theirs, they claimed, was the largest diocese in Europe and one which had always had the distinction of a cardinal in residence. Archbishop Montini had an international reputation and, at the time of his consecration, had been described in an American newspaper as "one of the ablest churchmen of his generation." Yet, the red hat was, inexplicably, withheld from him. By their own will the Milanese elevated him, addressing him as "Your Eminence" and referring to him in the same terms.

In 1956, a homemade bomb was hurled through the window of the archbishop's room. He had left the light burning but fortunately was not in the room at the time. Although the bomb was small and crudely made it did considerable damage to books and furniture. It could have killed a person within its range when it exploded.

Archbishop Montini issued no statement on the bombing and he emphatically refused to blame communism or Communists when newspaper correspondents interviewed him. He did not know who had tried to kill him or why, but he had no intention of changing his way of life. He forbade his staff to mention Communists in connection with the attack. After the room had been redecorated the light burned again late into the night. Usually the archbishop was in the room working, particularly in the hours after midnight. He still played music when he wrote.

His advisers told him that the real Communist problem was related to defeats in national elections. Milan was the Communist stronghold as it had been the Fascist stronghold. Fascism had been born in Milan and Mussolini's body had been lynched there. The industrial north was violent and the suffering of the war had prepared the ground for the Communists. Of late, however, since political alternatives had appeared there were anti-Communist forces at work in the big labor unions. Togliatti had actually lost control of some unions, was threatened with loss of control in others. He was sensitive to any challenge, even if it threatened only a slight diminution of his strength.

The archbishop planned more than a slight diminution. He had made swift trips out of town to visit his neighbors: Giacomo Cardinal Lercaro, Archbishop of Bologna; Giuseppe Cardinal Siri, Archbishop of Genoa; Angelo Cardinal Roncalli, Archbishop of Venice. They were all his friends but he had worked in closer intimacy with the former Nuncio to France, Cardinal Roncalli, who was a fellow diplomat converted, like himself, to the service of the Church Militant. Archbishop Montini discussed his idea for Milan with these men, blended their ideas with his own, and organized the clergy of his province. He started writing then to other friends in other dioceses to borrow priests.

In 1957 Archbishop Montini launched the Mission of Milan. For three weeks every church blazed with light. There were processions in the streets and one thousand borrowed priests spoke on street corners, in halls and parks, anywhere and everywhere. The diocesan priests were stirred and each made special plans for his own parish, calling on his people for aid. Youth groups and all of the various organizations, charitable, educational, social, which compose Catholic Action marched and held meetings.

The city of Milan, taking for granted the fact that it was "a Communist stronghold" as the press declared, was astonished to discover that it contained so many Catholics. The whirlwind campaign was designed to dramatize the Catholicism of Madonnina's city and she stood in glory above the floodlighted grandeur of *il duomo*, but, specifically, the campaign was aimed at the *lontani*, the fallen away, the sheep that had strayed, the lamb that was lost. The archbishop called to them and set a keynote for his priests.

"Return again!" he said. "The arms of God are open to you. Do not delay. Whatever your problem, whatever ill or care or grave disorder of the soul you bring to the ministry of Christ, only one spirit will control our relationship, the spirit of paternal love."

Cardinal Lercaro came to Milan from Bologna and gave six sermons and with him came the "Flying Friars" who were shock troops of his archdiocese in the combat against the aggressive godlessness of Bologna's Communists. The Flying Friars, twenty of them, rode motorcycles and preached anywhere, in the slums, at the gates of factories. If word came that a Communist speaker was attacking the church, one of the friars leaped on his motorcycle and roared off to debate with him; in a hall, a public square, a city street. They were spectacular and dear to the Italian heart for that reason, but they were intellectually equipped to debate, to attack or to defend, to explain or to explode weak explanations. Communist speakers, with the exception of the very best of them, dreaded the roar of a motorcycle and the appearance of a friar. As they had done in Bologna so they did in Milan.

Cardinal Siri came from Genoa and gave seven addresses. He was not the showman that Cardinal Lercaro was but he was one of the brilliant Princes of the Church and he took the position that the business community, the industrial complex, which suffered most from communism was the creator of communism. He appealed for a Christian approach to problems of capital and labor, an honest Christian effort to improve the living conditions of workers.

Twenty-two bishops and archbishops from other sections of Italy supported the two cardinals, speaking to organized business, professional, and labor groups, to congregations in the churches. The might of the Church was on display in this Mission but it was not frightening: it was cheerful, confident, inviting. Catholics were enjoying themselves, excited as by a carnival, and priests developed new confidence, new zeal, a sense of importance, a sense of association with greatness.

Portable confessionals were set up in parks and piazzas and people flocked to them. Men and women who had not made their Easter duty in years came back to the Church and some of them left the confessionals with tears of joy. They were home again. In the churches, Masses were said at all hours and there were people to attend, to worship, to share the sacrifice.

In the center of the campaign was Archbishop Giovanni Battista Montini. He visited every section of the archdiocese, participated in every type of activity and spoke on the radio every night. It was the year of Sputnik, the Soviet satellite which circled the earth and began a new era in man's exploration of his environment. The archbishop praised the Russian achievement, then he said:

"Behind scientific reality, there is Divine reality."

Osservatore Romano carried the story of the Milan Mission every day and newspaper correspondents who had never visited Milan came to it now. They were impressed by what they saw. Milan was a virile city, more like an American city than any other in Italy. It admitted, almost boasted, that it had the worst climate in Italy but the weather in the streets was like the weather in anyone's streets, good or bad and that mainly in terms of individual preference. In Milan few people took siestas. There was the world's most famous opera house, La Scala, and fine shops and high fashion and a rich intellectual life. The Italian publishing industry centered in Milan and Italy's books were edited and published there.

"We tried to define the Archdiocese of Milan," one of the priests of the chancery said when the big three-week campaign ended. He did not spell the definition out but the most popular feature of the three weeks with the people had been the simplest: the retelling of the story of Christ as though no one had ever heard it before, the discussions of His words, His ideas, His promises, the explanation of the Church and how it had come to be. In plain terms, the Archdiocese of Milan was mission territory in which it was better to assume ignorance of God than to take knowledge for granted. As Africa called and Asia called, and the undeveloped lands of the earth, so did one's home city call. The priest who walked to his own pulpit was obeying the command to "go, teach all nations!"

"It is not enough for a priest to ring his bell and wait," Archbishop Montini said. "He must go forth and seek the strayed and the bewildered, the lost and the lonely."

24

THE DAYS OF JOHN

Pope Pius XII died at 4 a.m. on October 9, 1958.

The cardinals assembled for another conclave. Archbishop Montini prayed at the bier of the man who had been, in a special way, both father and Holy Father to him, rose with tears in his eyes and returned to Milan. Whatever he may have felt about his fall from favor, he had maintained silence. He had neither criticized Pius XII nor tolerated criticism of him. During the illness of the Holy Father he had been moved to reminiscence one night while conversing informally, as he often did, with members of his Milan curia.

"I remember a small but significant episode on Christmas night in 1944," he said. "Pius XII entered St. Peter's to say Mass in the presence of the soldiers of various nations who were then in Rome. It was an unforgettable night. A diplomat of a great nation was seated close to me. He was a Protestant. I tried to see and experience, as he would, the majestic solemnity, the splendor of ritual, the almost tumultuous simplicity of the hymns in various languages. At the Communion, when the Holy Father came down the steps of the monumental Altar of the Confessione to distribute the Sacred Host to the faithful like any other pastor, the scene took on the quality of a vision. The serious diplomat, the avowed Protestant, bent himself toward me and asked hesitantly: 'Could I also go to Communion?'"

The world was discussing Pius XII during the mid-October of 1958. Archbishop Montini, too, was discussed. He was one of the papabili, a possible pope. Although a cardinal was usually selected there was nothing save tradition which said that a pope must be chosen from the College of Cardinals. Cardinals Lercaro and Siri were favorites in pre-conclave speculation, with Cardinal Agagianian and several others mentioned, but there was genuine press interest in the exile of Milan who was a romantic figure.

Out of the Conclave came the affable, astonishing Angelo Cardinal Roncalli, Archbishop of Venice, Pope John XXIII. He had been mentioned seldom in pre-conclave speculation but he caught the imagination of the world immediately. He had great dignity but did not stand on it; he had great learning and made no display of it; he was a cosmopolite, a diplomat, and he had the simple, friendly manner of a neighbor. One had a sense of familiarity with him as though one had known him always. He expressed himself in homely terms but he had an odd eloquence: one understood what he meant and believed in him. He seemed to have no prejudices, to hope sincerely that non-Catholics would accept him and he talked in terms of the reunion of divided Christians rather than of return to the Church.

"Pope John is what you might call a non-sectarian pope," wrote George W. Cornell of the Rome *Daily American.*

In his first consistory, in December 1958, the new pope raised the Archbishop of Milan to the cardinalate. He was his first cardinal, the head of his list, and the two old friends embraced warmly. Later, the Holy Father was quoted as saying:

"If Montini had received his red hat when he should have received it, I would never have been pope."

Giovanni Battista Cardinal Montini went back to Milan and the cardinal worked no less hard or long than had the archbishop. He continued to build churches and he built a new seminary and he continued his visitations. As a result of the Milan

Mission and all that it had revealed about the needs of the people, he established a research office for the archdiocese to seek modern and efficient ways for evangelization, liturgy, and catechetics; an office for pastoral sociology dealing especially with the problems of immigration, and a modern office for social assistance. He also founded an association for the immediate assistance of those committed to prison; "before imprisonment has hardened and embittered them." He diverted new funds into the diocesan newspaper and added a new magazine, *Diocesi di Milano.*

The Mission of Milan had demonstrated one fact about priests, an obvious fact but one to be underlined. The spectacular rally, the driving mission, the street-corner evangelism, all belonged to a single pattern, a pattern within which certain priestly types worked with zeal and enthusiasm, within which other types could not work at all. There was a tendency on the part of some priests, particularly young ones who had discovered that the successful mission method matched their temperaments, to assume superior attitudes toward those who had participated badly.

Archbishop Montini knew and understood priests and he knew how important it was to a dedicated man that he be used where he had an opportunity to be useful. Some of Milan's parishes required fervent evangelists, others called for quiet caretakers of the Faith. There were many transfers of priests after the Mission.

On his trip to the United States the archbishop had been impressed with the street garb of priests, so like the civilian yet possessed of its own dignity. In Italy all priests were required to wear the cassock, or soutane, in public, another heritage from Pius IX who established clerical attire by edict. Archbishop Montini eased the restriction in his archdiocese, following the American pattern.

On pastoral visits, the cardinal archbishop ran his total to 124 out of the city's 146 parishes, 694 of the 822 parishes in the archdiocese. He found time, as he always had, for simple, human adventures.

Monsignor Francisco Olgiati reports one incident at a confirmation ceremony. There was a small party for the children who had been confirmed and the cardinal archbishop attended. There was noise outside the parish hall and Cardinal Montini went to the window where a number of children were poised, peering in. He turned to the children he had confirmed.

"Why aren't these children at our party?" he said.

"They are not Catholics."

"They are Communists."

The childish voices answered him. Cardinal Montini nodded his head. "Don't you believe that they would like some candy?"

There was silence, then hesitant agreement. The cardinal lifted a dish of candy from the table and handed it to one of the boys. "Tell them that we want to share with them."

He noticed then the expression of disapproval on the face of the elderly pastor. "You do not approve?" he asked.

"Eminence," the pastor said, "I am afraid that these children will not understand. It is their special day. These others are not entitled to share in it."

"Perhaps not," the cardinal said. "Yet, wouldn't it be wonderful if our children learned that they should share their faith, too, with these others?"

Adrio Casati, president of the Province of Milan says: "The cardinal was unfailingly present in every civic affair, both in joy or sadness. When there was a railroad disaster, he was one of the first on the scene. He was the only prominent figure in Milan who never missed being present for the annual civic awards presentation on Christmas Eve."

One glimpses the man in such statements but it is only a glimpse. The informal snapshots round out the picture of the human being. Shortly after he was raised to the purple, Cardinal Montini encountered his old friend Padre Giulio Bevilacqua at the reception. The priest kissed his ring and addressed him as "Eminence." The cardinal laughed gently.

"Padre Giulio, let us not make jokes," he said. "You have always used 'tu' with me. Do not permit yourself to be intimidated."

His memory for people was remarkable and his affection for old friends enduring. He visited Brescia in 1959 on his way to Concesio for the thirtieth anniversary of the Church of St. Rocco. There were many civil and ecclesiastical dignitaries at the reception which was held for him. Don Luigi Benassi, a country priest from Farfengo, stood on the edge of the crowd remembering when this man and he had been boys together, boys who decided on their vocations at the same time.

"I told myself that he had forgotten me and that it would be foolish to approach him," Don Luigi says. "Suddenly I heard his voice. It came from the night of times gone by. 'Don Benassi,' the voice said, 'where is our grandmother Maddalena?' He was approaching me, his arms open to me, and I could not answer him. He patted my shoulder. 'I understand,' he said, 'She has gone ahead to await us in paradise.' He wished then to know of other things and for a few minutes I seemed to find myself still seated at the table under the portico of my poor old farmhouse home. Instead, here I was, conversing with the Cardinal of Milan."

At Concesio, the cardinal was greeted by St. Rocco's pastor, Don Luigi Bosio, and his assistant, Don Renato Zucchini. He met, too, another old friend, Primo Savoldi. As they were entering the church, someone in the crowd called out: *"Enviva il prete di Sinistra!"* ("Hurray for the priest of the Left!") The cardinal turned, startled, to Don Luigi Bosio.

"What do they mean, priest of the Left?" he said. "Of the workers, yes! Of the Left, decidedly not!"

Rome called him often now. Pope John XXIII leaned heavily on the cardinal archbishop of Milan, as consultant and friend, as retoucher of phrases, as an expert in the strange ways of the Curia, existent as an extension of the Holy Father himself but possessed of an often-perverse life and will of its own. Of this close attachment between the pope of the unexpected and his first cardinal, the voluble Padre Giulio Bevilacqua says:

"Roncalli and Montini? Yes. They were great friends. Roncalli, to tell the truth, was always in awe of Montini. Montini had been his commander when Roncalli was in the diplomatic service and Roncalli never got over the habit of looking up to him. Afterward? Ah, afterward Roncalli said to him: 'Now that I have made you a cardinal, you before all the others, you know well what is the duty of the first cardinal. You must come down to Rome every anniversary of my coronation and you must sing a Mass for me. It is an obligation. I know. Who knows better? I know that coronation day is the fourth of November, the feast day of St. Charles Borromeo, patron of Milan. Still, I expect my Mass.' That is how Roncalli talked to him."

On his frequent visits to Rome, Cardinal Montini saw his old collaborator, Domenico Tardini, who had found a virtual rejuvenation in his red hat and in his exalted rank as Secretary of State. A querulous, pessimistic, semi-invalid in the last years of Pius XII, carrying high responsibility and low rank, Tardini was almost cheerful now, vigorous in manner and in gesture, telling an occasional joke or relating a droll anecdote.

Amleto Cicognani, too, was in Rome, one of Giovanni Battista Montini's friends of longest standing, his superior and guide in FUCI days, his counselor in many a troubled spot since. John XXIII had recalled Archbishop Cicognani from the United States after his long tenure there to be raised to the cardinalate and to help in the complicated task of untangling the confused Vatican finances.

In connection with the finances, several bankers from Milan spent considerable time with Cardinal Cicognani who presented them to the Holy Father before they left for home. One remark, or alleged remark, at that audience inspired an astonishing sequence of speculation, conjecture, and rhetorical nonsense. According to a press account carried in the papers of the world, Pope John XXIII greeted his Milanese visitors with the query: "And how is your Hamlet cardinal?"

Leapers to conclusions are often leapers into print and solemn theories were enunciated to the effect that Pope John obviously considered Cardinal Montini indecisive, unable to chart a course of action, Hamlet-like. Some heavily profound analyses of Cardinal Montini were prepared, psychoanalyzing him, relating him to the Hamlet image. If the quote from the Holy Father was accurate, it could, of course, have meant merely that he considered Montini, like Hamlet, a man called upon to perform as a duty a task for which he was temperamentally unfitted. There is, however, a more likely explanation.

Another account of that audience states that the Holy Father greeted the visitors from Milan and inquired about their cardinal archbishop. When the replies were warmly enthusiastic and complimentary to Cardinal Montini, Pope John chuckled and placed his hand affectionately on the shoulder of Cardinal Cicognani.

"You know," he said, "he has much of Hamlet in him."

Hamlet (Amleto) is Cardinal Cicognani's first name.

The world was opening wide for the Cardinal Archbishop of Milan. He made a hurried trip to the United States in 1960 and received an honorary degree from Notre Dame University in company with President Dwight D. Eisenhower. There was a presidential campaign in the offing with a Catholic entering the lists as a candidate for President, so Cardinal Montini avoided any association with politics. He did explain to the press the special features of the Italian election campaign of 1948 which had justified Church involvement.

In 1962 he made an extensive visit to Africa, visiting the missions. He had the missions in his mind now as the true symbols of the Church. Africa, more than any other continent, represented the rising tide of color which was changing the thinking of the world. He visited another old friend, Archbishop Sergio Pignedoli, and he added new terminology to his vocabulary. He had spoken of America as "the second world" and he referred to Africa now as "the third world." The terms became his in standard usage. In Africa, too, he saw a sign, one of many

held in the hands of Nigerians who greeted him. He was delighted with the slogan and had his secretary, Don Giovanni
Macchi, copy the text in a notebook. It read:

"God is a majority of One."

The Holy Father had been working while Cardinal Montini
was away on a project which they had discussed and planned
together and which had been announced on January 25, 1959.
Pope John XXIII, who had been expected to make himself comfortable in the Vatican as an interim pope, believed that he
had more to offer than interim service to the Church which had
honored him and to the world which had granted him respect.
He sounded a call for an Ecumenical Council.

Millions of words have been written about the Council of
Pope John XXIII and millions more will be written. There are
long books dealing with certain technical aspects of it. It is a
subject which can only be treated elaborately or treated with
utmost simplicity. The latter alternative calls for oversimplifica-
tion, of course, but there is no middle ground.

The Church had become unwieldy in organization, its power
to move slowed by an outmoded bureaucracy, its power of decision centered. The failure of Pius XII to appoint and to replace had emphasized the dangers inherent in too great a cen-
tralization of power. The speeding up of transportation, of all
forms of communication had made it evident that speed of decision must be part of the new equation. The dynamics of communism, of a new world religion, had made it apparent that a
mere holding operation on the part of Christianity would not
do and had called attention dramatically to the fact that Christianity, warning against a house divided, was precisely such a
house.

John XXIII, because he was a personality who could project
an involved subject simply, accepted the role of Peter and
turned back to the dawn of the Church. There were problems
to be discussed so he called the other apostles and presented the
problems and said: What would you suggest?

The Church had grown in obedience to the command of its

Founder, and there were a great many bishops instead of twelve. It made no difference essentially. They came and they conferred and if one of the problems was that the head of the apostles was taking too much authority in his own hands, that was a legitimate subject for discussion. The bishops had had equal authority once, with the chief of the apostles acting as presiding officer and breaking deadlocks, clarifying differences. Certainly in a complicated world, bishops could be closer to the complications of their own areas than any distant member of a Curia who acted for the chief of the apostles. Missions, too, demanded more power invested in bishops.

The press looked frowningly upon the Curia and presented it darkly. On the lines, or between the lines, the impression was conveyed that this semi-sinister Vatican society held reins of power, schemed to retain those reins, obstructed progress, scorned all liberal ideas and sought to anchor the Church to the Middle Ages. The terms "conservative" and "right wing" were applied to it. Actually, the Curia had been shaped by the demands made upon it and the men of the Curia who opposed change could say honestly that they knew and understood the areas of proposed change better than did the innovators who proposed changes.

The Curia had grown out of the need of the pope for many arms, many minds, many languages. It was the extension of himself. The ill-starred Pius IX had established the papal image as he had established so many ideas which were to plague the Church for generations. Pius IX had summoned a Council which had not completed its work but which did proclaim the doctrine of papal infallibility, alienating the rest of the Christian world when it did so. In vain did Catholics contend that there is no papal infallibility save when the pope speaks ex-cathedra, speaking for the Church rather than for himself. Pius IX had destroyed that argument, too. He had proclaimed the doctrine of the Immaculate Conception on his own authority, without a Council. It was logical then, and inevitable, that the Curia should be authoritarian, dogmatic, and conservative as the instrument of an infallible pope, the extension of his own person, the living organism through which he maintained contact with the Church of clergy and laity; it could be nothing else. The pope, since the reign of Pius IX, was supreme, not answerable to the bishops—and the Curia was the pope.

The new concept of the bishops as rulers of the Church, guided by a pope, came closer to the Catholic layman's interpretation of the papal infallibility since it claimed freedom from error in matters of faith and morals for the Church itself rather than for the head of the Church. A Curia working under such a concept would be shaped by it and the shape would differ from that of the present Curia; not necessarily of greater virtue but different. There would still be the human element, the inevitable clashes between introverts and extroverts, of deskmen and field men, the difficult problem of old men in posts of major or minor authority, wise in the ways of preserving themselves in power.

"It is wrong to think," the Cardinal Archbishop of Milan told his people, "that the Council will decree radical and bewildering reforms in the present rules of the Church to the extent of changing its centuries-old features and turning it into a completely new institution. The Council will help the Church come into contact with the world, but not by radical steps."

Giovanni Battista Cardinal Montini could speak with authority. He had worked closely with the Holy Father and knew his mind. Between them they knew the Church very well; on the diocese firing line and in the offices of the Curia. It was remarked by correspondents that Pope John's arresting address which opened the Council sounded much like the Montini "Discorsi." Correspondents had commented, too, on the sound of Montini in the famous John XXIII encyclical, *Pacem in Terris*, without casting any doubt on the fact that this was the thinking of John. There were people who actually *blamed* Cardinal Montini for that encyclical which, they claimed, was soft on communism and an encouragement to people who wanted to be both Communists and Catholics.

Whether he wrote the disputed encyclical or did not, the Cardinal did write and speak one line at the opening of the Council which is more eloquent, and says more, than many long dissertations:

"There begins a solemn dialogue, noble and new, between the Church and modern society."

Cardinal Montini was the only out-of-Rome Cardinal who lived at the Vatican during the Council. He said Mass for the Holy Father when John XXIII was ill. He did not have much to say in the deliberations. That was not his role. The first Council could only be exploratory, as John said: "an open window to let fresh air into the Church."

The fresh air was good. It blew in opinion. Vitality surged and swelled in the hierarchy when realization came that this was truly an invitation to speak openly, to suggest, to criticize if one must, to propose and envision. There were barriers between people who wanted to be Catholics and the Church which wanted them. Such were barriers between God and men, a grievous matter. There were rebellions among Catholics against certain regulations and certain interpretations. There was a growing problem of broken homes, an increase in divorce, a crisis on the subject of birth control.

Fresh air could not solve or soften another problem which was one of the reasons for the Council. The cement of tradition had hardened around procedures which were merely good in, and for, their own time. It would not be easy to strike and chisel away that cement but it was going to be necessary.

It was heartening to see the response of the Protestant Faiths to Rome's willingness to discuss and to explain. Reunion became more than a word and a slogan; it became a great hope.

Pope John XXIII launched the Ecumenical Council. He opened his window to the world. He convinced an incredulous world that in a time of fierce ideological warfare, man could truly love his neighbor. Having done that, he lifted a heavy cross of pain and walked with it into eternity.

25

THE HIGHEST KEYS

THERE is terror in the heights, as well as glory and exalta-
tion and the sense of triumph which belongs integrally
to attaining, whether the high places be physical or spiritual.
Men chosen for the throne of Peter, the most highly placed
throne on earth, have lost courage and prayed for rescue, prayed
that they might return to the level places where men rub elbows
and climb, if climb they must, in companionship. Other men
have accepted, as they would accept martyrdom, the returning of
their personal lives to God in the lonely isolation of His earthly
vicariate.

Giovanni Battista Montini was, probably, one of the few
who aspired to the high office, who was unafraid in the con-
templation of it, who knew with certainty of soul that his life
had been shaped to so logical an end. He was neither proud
nor arrogant but he was a man of intelligence and of sensitive
conscience. He had drawn back from the throne of the Archbishop of Milan because it was not inevitable, not a responsibility for which he had been trained, shaped, or fashioned. He was
a diplomat and Milan was a stormy pastorate. He acknowledged
in humility that God would be badly served in Milan by the
failure of a man trained to serve elsewhere when he questioned
the decision of Pius XII to send him there. He bowed in
obedience and he faced Milan.

In the period which followed the death of John XXIII, the gathering of the cardinals, the novendiali, he was obviously at peace with himself, resigned to what must be. After his pastorate in Milan he must have known that there was no man in the Church trained as he was trained for the highest responsibility, no man to match the breadth and depth of his experience. He had always believed that a man owed to God the service for which he had been prepared through the opportunity which came to him. Because his was not a passive nature, content with accepting, he moved in the direction of his destiny, wanting that which promised the greatest scope for his gifts of knowledge, of understanding and of command. Whatever doubts he entertained must have been resolved during conversations with Pope John who predicted many times that Montini would be the next pope. He moved through the week preceding the conclave in the manner of a man winding up his affairs. He visited his brothers and their families and he talked with old friends in Brescia. The demands of the conclave did not permit him much personal time.

On the eve of leaving for Rome, his secretary, Don Giovanni Macchi, called his attention to a play entitled *The Vicar* by a German playwright named Rolf Hochhut in which Pope Pius XII was portrayed as a cowardly pragmatist who acquiesced through silence in the Nazi slaughter of the Jewish people. Cardinal Montini retired to his study and wrote a letter to the editor of the *London Tablet* which had published a summary of the play, with a copy to Raimondo Manzini, director of *Osservatore Romano*. The letter stated that the writer had worked in close contact with the late Pius XII from 1937 till 1954 when Pius, as Cardinal Pacelli, was Vatican Secretary of State and during most of his later pontificate; that the characterization of Pius XII was false. The late pope, he wrote, was noble, virile, compassionate rather than cowardly and opportunistic.

"The thesis of *Die Stellvertreter* lacks psychological, political and historical insight into reality," he wrote, "and theatrical charm is a poor substitute for reality. If Pius XII had acted as

Hochhut would have had him act, there would have been such reprisals and such devastation that, after the war, Hochhut himself, with better historical, political and moral insight could have written a more realistic and more interesting drama than the one he has so unfortunately staged. If Pope Pius XII had carelessly or recklessly let loose further ruin upon a tormented world in a spirit of bravado or political exhibitionism then, indeed, might Hochhut have held him guilty for the fate of countless innocent victims."

"One should not play with such subjects nor accept the distorted images of historical personages which have been twisted and torn within the imagination of theatrical artists insufficiently endowed with historical judgment or, God judging them, honest intent. . . . Pius XII was sensitively aware of his duty to mankind and of historical reality. He did not condone the horrible crimes of German Nazism. . . . An attitude of condemnation and of protest which Hochhut blames the pope for avoiding would have been not only useless but harmful in ways beyond his power of imagining."

Cardinal Montini wrote this defense on the famous white typewriter of Pius XII which had come to John XXIII and which John had given to him. It was the last document which he was to write in his Milan study where so many had been written. The room was lined with bookcases. His parents looked down upon him from their framed portraits on the wall. The only other portrait, significantly, was one of John XXIII. There were two small icons on a bookcase top, the gift of Don Carlo Gnocchi. On his desk, pushed to one side when he began his letter protesting the Hochhut play, was a copy of a Bolognese cultural magazine and a sheet of paper on which he had written: *Pensions for the clergy.* This was a project on which he had been working. There were two modern novels, which he hadn't read, on his desk and a book titled *Dinamismo Sociali* by Ban Gestel which he had been reading. On the stand beside his bed was a copy of the Divine Comedy.

He walked out of the room and left it as it was. He entered

the Cathedral and he prayed for a half hour at the tomb of St. Charles Borromeo; then he went to Rome.

The newspapers of Rome were filled with speculation on the identity of the next pope. There were prophecies and inspired guesses and guesses that were less than inspired. Inevitably, the cardinals were classified in political terms. Of the papabili (the possible popes) Siri was identified as right, Lercaro as left, Montini as moderate but leaning to the left. These were the three leading candidates. The differences which the news writers found and labeled had not been apparent during the Mission of Milan when they were confronted with the issue of evil, of communism, of problems in the area of faith and morals. In that area they were, and always would be, priests and allies.

Cardinal Montini was regarded by the press as the favorite, the man most likely to come out of the conclave as pope. All agreed, however, that he would be elected early or not at all. The conservatives, allegedly, were afraid of him and the Spanish cardinals were expected to oppose him, swinging many of the non-Italians with them. The Spanish situation was interesting.

In 1962 the Cardinal Archbishop of Milan had received a garbled account of the arrest and trial of youths in Spain who were, he was told, devoted Catholic Action young people in trouble through a clash with youths of another type. The situation as described was reminiscent of Cardinal Montini's FUCI period and his sympathies were touched when he was told that the youths had been sentenced to death. As a veteran diplomat he knew that a private citizen does not address a chief of state except through channels, not even if the citizen is Cardinal Archbishop of Milan. He knew, too, that an Italian prelate had no right to interfere in the internal affairs of another country. He knew that he could lift the receiver of his phone and ask a Spanish cardinal for the facts in the case which had been reported to him. Inexplicably, he went against everything that he knew to be right and proper; he wired an appeal to Francisco Franco, Chief of State of Spain, in behalf of the youths.

The reply from Franco was cold. The Cardinal Archbishop of

Milan was misinformed on the facts, the matter had been handled properly by the courts of Spain and no death sentence had been passed. Franco's answering telegram ended with the formal phrase which, in this case, had great irony: I KISS THE ROYAL PURPLE.

The Spanish blunder was one of the outstanding mistakes of Giovanni Battista Montini's career and it caused many people to doubt the stability and the judgment of a man who could have made it. Others were surprised that the supposedly cautious and calculating ex-diplomat could be impulsive. Those who knew him well wondered who had imposed upon his sympathy for youth to betray him into an indiscretion. The Spanish cardinals and their friends were, according to rumor, incensed at the cardinal from Milan and willing to accept anyone else as pope in preference to him.

Cardinal Montini spent a night at Castel Gandolfo and, as Achille Ratti, another Archbishop of Milan, had done in the days of his youth, he moved into the Lombard House. He asked for and received the room which he had occupied as a student. The students came through as he stood in a reception line, solemnly respectful, and any one of them could well be another Don Battista. He accepted them as students, as young clerics, and they accepted him as a cardinal, and nothing had changed in the essentials since Ratti came from Milan to become Pius XI.

No one presented flowers to the Cardinal Archbishop of Milan in 1963 so he ordered flowers himself and, as Cardinal Ratti had done, he laid them on the altar of the Blessed Virgin. He went then to the conclave and he came out of the symbolical white smoke of the Sistine Chapel as Paul VI, Bishop of Rome, Vicar of Jesus Christ, Supreme Pontiff of the Universal Church.

"The Pope always dines alone."

Pius XII had believed that and no one ever dined with him. John XXIII ignored the tradition as it pleased him. Paul VI did not acknowledge the tradition as binding. His first meal after

271

his election was taken at the table with the cardinals who had elected him, seated in the place which he had occupied as cardinal. There was a forecast in that of meals which he would share with his secretaries or with anyone who interested him, snacks when the work was heavy, as he had done in Milan.

He made phone calls to his brothers and to his chancery in Milan and he visited the basilica to lay a bouquet of gladioli on the tomb of John XXIII. He laid lilies on the tomb of Pius XI and carnations on the tomb of Pius XII. From the basilica he went to the hospital of Santa Marta where he visited ninety-year-old Monsignor Angelo Rotta, the former Apostolic Nuncio to Hungary. His second visit was to the little palace of the Vatican, to Monsignor Slypij, the Ukrainian Metropolitan, who was ill, imparting a special blessing upon him and upon all Ukrainians. Gustavo Cardinal Testa was ill and confined to his room on another floor. The newly elected Holy Father visited him and, as he was leaving the little palace, he met the aged doorkeeper whom he had known since the long ago when he was Don Battista. His voice broke slightly when he said: "Greetings, Pierino."

The old man stood rigid, staring at him with tears in his eyes, forgetting the obeisance. "Greetings to you, Holiness," he said.

At 5:45 P.M., Friday, June 21, the day of his election, Pope Paul VI made his first visit outside of the Vatican, to the Spanish College in Via San Apollinare where he visited the Archbishop of Toledo, Pla y Deniel, who had been ill with influenza. He was officially greeted here by the three Spanish cardinals; Benjamin de Arriba y Castro, Jose Maria Bueno y Monreal, and Fernando Quiroga y Palacios. As he left the college, the young clerics in their black-and-sky-blue cassocks cheered him.

The route of Paul VI on his return from his first trip as Pope was, by accident or design, along Via Zanardelli, named for his father's rival and foe, anticlerical journalist and politician; then across Ponte Cavour, named in honor of the great statesman of the Risorgimento and an enemy of the Church in his time. Paul VI had to be aware, reminded by these names, that in 1970 he would be confronted, if he lived, with Italy's centennial as a nation in which the revolution would be celebrated and its heroes glorified. His would be the decision on the attitude of the Church; either to participate in celebrating the event which Pius IX had marked with the excommunication of a King or to stand aside, taking the Church again into withdrawal from contact with its people.

There were cables and telegrams awaiting him at the Vatican, congratulations and good wishes from the heads of virtually every government, from celebrities, statesmen, the great of earth. There were intimate messages, too, and one from Brescia that was perfect in its understanding of the man and his interests, his deep concerns:

"To His Holiness Pope Paul VI—Vatican City—Exulting Brescia bows reverently to the new Pope. Your Holiness, after the first blessing to the Universal Church, may the second blessing be for the beloved diocese which gave your Holiness your place of birth and for all of Brescia. Bless, Most Holy Father, your old Archbishop, the auxiliary, clergy, all the authorities, the people, and the institutions. Receive the homage of the entire diocese, especially of the children, of the sick and of the poor. Abp Giacinto Predici, Brescia."

On the warm summer evening of June 30, under a crimson sky, Paul VI celebrated Mass in St. Peter's Square and under artificial light as the evening deepened, he accepted the triple tiara. He faced the throngs in the Square and, through the magic of television, the people of the world. He spoke to them in nine different languages from the throne, varying his message as he changed from one tongue to another.

"The vastness of the task that awaits our poor energies," he said, "is such as to bewilder the humble priest called to the heights of the supreme keys."

He had moved up the many steps to that high throne. He had stumbled and he had made mistakes, and he had not always seen clearly, but he had climbed. The events of his pontificate were of the future and a mystery in the knowledge of God, but the man who had faced the city from the balcony on the day of his election and who faced the world from his throne on the day of his coronation had written his own prophecy. One knew the pope that he would be because a man is forever all that he has been.

He would keep Pope John's window open, letting the fresh air of the world flow into the Church. He would speak of union and of a reunion to men who yearned to the same ends, differing only in their concepts of means. He would oppose with all of his eloquence and all of his being the State which sought to become God, the priesthood of that State and the religion which it dogmatized. He would walk humbly but the power of intellect was in him and the magic of words. He would love youth and spend himself for the aged, the ill, and the lonely. He would kneel before the poor because they are Christ. There would be an Ecumenical Council, and a third and a fourth if necessary, that many men might be heard, many ideas expressed, new means discovered for presenting the old, the eternal, truth. There would be more missionaries facing out and fewer priests waiting, solitary, beneath a summoning bell. There would be a sincere attempt to heal wounds, to clarify misunderstandings. Of the tragic separation of Christians, he was to say:

"If we are in any way to blame, we humbly ask God's pardon and beg forgiveness of our brethren who feel that they have received injury from us."

Another story, perhaps one of the most dramatic in all history, begins with these words.

INDEX

Filastio, St., 61
Finland, 169, 207
Fionda, La (magazine), 61
Fiorini, Don Gio., 45
First Communion, 60
Flanders, 67
Florence, 171
Flying Friars, 253
Foppa, Cristoforo, 59
Fordham University, 147
France, 60, 86, 110, 165, 168, 218; and Risorgimento, 28, 30, 33, 34; Socialists in, 148; worker-priests in, 219–21, 232; during World War I, 67; during World War II, 169, 172, 178, 188, 200–2
Francis of Assisi, St., 111
Franciscans, 74, 193
Franco, Francisco, 146, 148, 149, 157, 165; Montini's telegram to, 270–71
Frascati, 29
Frederick Barbarossa, 36
Freschi, Cardinal, tomb of, 196
Fronti Democratici Populari (People's Democratic Front), 216, 218
FUCI, 97, 99–106, 111, 117–21, 143, 157, 201, 203–4, 212 (*see also* C.U.C.R.); alumni society, 153–54; Montini leaves, 124–25; Montini's correspondence with former members, 146; Montini's marriages of couples from, 230
FUCINA, 104–5

Gaeta, 32
Gaggia, Giocinto, 73, 74
Galeazzi, Count Pietro Enrico, 234
Galeazzi-Lisi, Ricardo, 234
Galen, Bishop von, 138
Galli, Ugo, 103
Galvin, Father Edward J., 79
Garda, Lake, 36, 61
Garibaldi, Giuseppe, 28, 33, 109; statue of, 47
Gasparri, Pietro Cardinal, 83, 112, 117

Gasperi, Alcide de. *See* De Gasperi, Alcide
Gasquet, Francis Cardinal, 113
Gauls, 36
Genoa, Duke of, 62
Genoa, 188
Georgetown University, 147
Germany and Germans, 96, 129, 132–34, 136–38, 147–48, 151–54 (*see also* Hitler, Adolf; Nazis); anti-Semitism in (*see* Anti-Semitism); Gestapo in Rome, 188–89; and Italy's anti-Semitic law, 160; march into Rhineland, 142; and Munich, 161–62; Pacelli as Nuncio to, 72, 80, 116, 133; report on Montini, 144; seminarians, 77; and Versailles Treaty, 86; in World War I, 67, 72; in World War II, 167–69, 172, 174, 178ff., 184, 188–89, 193, 198ff., 205
Gestapo, 188–89
Gestel, Ban, 269
Girls, in FUCINA, 104–5
Gnocchi, Don Carlo, 249, 269
Goebbels, Joseph, 153
Great Britain (or England), 33, 144–45, 161, 165, 168; English College, seminarians, 74, 77, 175; minister to Vatican, 137, 180–81; and post-World War II Italy, 214; Roman Church in, 35; Sturzo's exile to, 97; in World War I, 67; in World War II, 169, 172, 177, 178, 188
Greece, 144, 178. *See also* Greek College and seminarians
Greek College and seminarians, 74, 77
Gregorian University, 74, 75, 76, 77
Gregory XVI, 28
Guarantees, Law of, 34
Guay, Father Edmund, 225

Hall, Frank, 223
Hannibal, 36
Haynau, Julius von, 37, 39
Helena, Queen of Italy, 62, 172

Himmler, Heinrich, 188
Hiroshima, 205–6
Hitler, Adolf, 129, 132–33, 137, 157, 165, 184, 199; death, 205; liquidates S.A., disbands Catholic youth, 138; Mussolini and, 145, 157, 172, 178; United States and, 148
Hitler Youth, 136
Hochhut, Rolf, 268–69
Holland (Netherlands), 172, 218
Holy Office, Congregation of the, 221
Holy Year of 1925, 96
Holy Year of 1950, 218–19, 221–22, 227
Hoover, Herbert, 110, 111
Horthy, Miklós, 158
Hotel Eden (Rome), 133
Humbert I, 43
Humbert II, 216
Hungary, 157–60
Hutton, Edward, 37

Immaculate Conception, 35, 264
Imola, 28
Incarnation, Church of the (Budapest), 158
Infallibility, papal, 35, 37, 41, 264–65
Information Bureau, Vatican, 174–76, 185, 193
Instituto Leona, 250
Intelligence, Vatican, 173, 218
Ireland, 225. See also Irish College; etc.
Irish College, 74
Irish Free State, 129
Irish missionaries, 79
Italia, L' (newspaper), 247
Italian Federation of Catholic Students. See FUCI
Italian seminarians, 77
Italian Workers' Socialist Party, 216
Italy and Italian government. See Politics; Risorgimento; World War I; World War II; etc.; specific heads of state, political parties

Japan, 179, 184, 186; and atomic bombs, 205–6
Jesuits, 56, 57, 74; in Spain, 129
Jews, 169, 200 (see also Anti-Semitism); in Italian government, 38; refugee, 174, 178, 179, 188
John XXIII, 80, 260–62, 268, 269, 272 (for earlier life, see Roncalli, Angelo Cardinal); birthplace, 37, 50; death observances, 15–19; and Ecumenical Council, 21, 263, 265–66, 274; election, 252; and tradition that pope dines alone, 271
John the Evangelist, St., 194
Journalism. See Newspapers
Julius II, 194

Kennedy, Joseph P., 169
Kesselring, Albert, 198
Knights of Columbus, 110, 119
Korean War, 225
Kramer, Rev. Karl, 153
Kun, Béla, 159
Kurile Island, 207

Labor. See Workers
Ladrone, Bishop Francesco, 46, 64
Ladrone, Bishop Sebastiano, 46
La Fontaine, Peter Cardinal, 83
Landon, Alfred M., 147
Languages, 144, 183 (see also specific languages); seminarians' vocabulary, 77
Lateran Palace, 112
Lateran Treaty, 107–14, 117, 143
Latin, use of, 18, 19, 76, 77
Latvia, 207
Lauri, Lorenzo Cardinal, 85, 86
Lavitrano, Archbishop Luigi, 116
Law, Code of Canon, 67
Law of Guarantees, 34
Lazzati, Giuseppe, 247
League of Nations, 136–37, 169
Leo I, St. (the Great), 36, 61
Leo XIII, 41–43, 53–55, 60, 68
Lercaro, Giacomo Cardinal, 252, 257, 270
Libya, 178
Licio Arnaldo (Brescia), 69